D0330734

JFK

WANTS TO KNOW

JFK

WANTS TO KNOW

Memos from the President's Office
1961–1963

SELECTED AND EDITED BY
EDWARD B. CLAFLIN
Preface by Pierre Salinger

WILLIAM MORROW AND COMPANY, INC.
New York

Library of Congress Cataloging-in-Publication Data

Kennedy, John F. (John Fitzgerald), 1917–1963.
    JFK wants to know : memos from the President's office, 1961–1963 /
selected and edited by Edward B. Claflin.
        p.   cm.
    ISBN 0-688-08846-5
        1. United States—Politics and government—1961–1963—Sources.
    2. Kennedy, John F. (John Fitzgerald), 1917–1963—Archives.
    I. Claflin, Edward.   II. Title.   III. Title: J.F.K. wants to know.
E838.5.K42   1991
973.922—dc20   90-47224
                                                                                CIP

Printed in the United States of America

First Edition

1 2 3 4 5 6 7 8 9 10

BOOK DESIGN BY KATHRYN PARISE

Preface

There have been many books written about John F. Kennedy, but this one is rare in its insight of his presidency and how he dealt with national and worldwide problems. Instead of personal assessment of Kennedy, either by friends or foes, this book is his voice, what he thought, what he wrote. It is particularly enlightening twenty-seven years after his tragic death.

For example, after having lived through Kennedy's most dramatic mistake while he was President, the Bay of Pigs attack on Cuba in 1961, I find it interesting to compare his public and internal reactions. Publicly, Kennedy took full responsibility for the error. He did not attempt to pass over the responsibility to others. But in reading his private memorandums, one understands his feeling that he was misguided in the operation by U.S. military leaders of that time.

As I look back in history, backed by many of the documents in this book, it reinforces my belief that John Kennedy's death was a tragic loss for the United States and the whole world. I am convinced, for example, that at a time when we still lived in the cold war, relations between the Soviet Union and the United States would have moved forward much more rapidly had he lived. The Cuban missile crisis of 1962 had been an important factor to this step toward new relations. It is clear that both Kennedy and Soviet leader

Nikita Khrushchev realized that nuclear war was not a viable option. After the crisis, relations between the two countries moved forward with amazing speed, partly based on the exchange of forty-three private letters between Kennedy and Khrushchev that have not yet been published. But the letters that are in this book show Kennedy's desire to move the two superpowers away from confrontation. At the same time they also show that Kennedy understood that when you are in a confrontational situation with another power, there must be direct dialogue for the problem to be solved.

This book also demonstrates another quality that Kennedy had—and which has not been duplicated by most of his successors. He believed the United States had a responsibility to help the third world. He organized a very positive program with Latin America that brought relations in our hemisphere to the closest point we had seen in this century.

What I admired most about Kennedy was that he was not a President who believed his responsibility was dealing with problems simply on a day-to-day basis. As these documents show, he was looking far ahead, looking at the United States and the world of the future.

The contributions of this book are, for me, extraordinary. That someone who worked in the Kennedy administration would think that shows this book should make an immense contribution to those who want to know more about JFK.

—PIERRE SALINGER

Acknowledgments

It all began with a news clipping concerning the as-yet-untapped wealth of information hidden among the papers at the John Fitzgerald Kennedy Library in Boston. From that came the exploration, the winnowing, the usual frustrations endemic to research—and, at last, the glee of discovering a narrative thread among the JFK documents. My thanks to Jay Acton for clipping the clip and to Jane Dystel for her support, encouragement, and confidence throughout the long (and sometimes frustrating) research, editing, and writing process.

Many at the John F. Kennedy Library were helpful. I would especially like to thank William Johnson, Suzanne Forbes, Darcy Hope Lee, Maura Porter, and Michael Desmond.

My thanks to Richard Neustadt at the John F. Kennedy School of Government at Harvard for an interview that gave me some insight into the "Kennedy style" of day-to-day operations. Henri Barkey at Lehigh University's department of international relations provided me with valuable information related to the Cuban missile crisis.

Josh Rubenstein in Cambridge gave me a number of helpful suggestions at the outset of the research. I am also grateful to those who gave me shelter in the Boston area during my forays—Dick and Eve Goodman, Elizabeth Bernhard, and Bruce Figueroa. In Philadelphia Holly LaMon and Kathy Heinsohn provided valuable assistance in organizing materials and helping with research. My thanks to Glenn Russell for his editorial work.

On the home front my wife, Diana, and my daughters, Jessica and Abigail, kept my heart in the present when my head was locked in the past. As every slave of the word processor knows, such support is much needed when the computer's green screen becomes an obnoxious intruder and the days till deadline are numbered.

On projects great and small, my parents have been a source of constant encouragement: I'm glad, at last, to be able to thank them in print.

From the outset of this project, I have been fortunate to have the best combination a scrivener can hope for—the right editor for the right book. That editor is Lisa Drew, whose clearsighted views and much-needed suggestions helped to separate wheat from chaff and find order amid what threatened to become chaos. My thanks, also, to editorial assistant Bob Shuman and copy editor Pearl Hanig at Morrow. It's been said many times before, but just to make it official: The errors herein are mine, not theirs, but for all our sakes I hope those errors are few.

Contents

Introduction

Far more has been written about John Fitzgerald Kennedy than was ever written by him; as a result, it is sometimes difficult to find the man among the mirrors. Images abound. We have Kennedy the consummate politician, Kennedy the bon vivant, Kennedy the PT boat commander and hero, Kennedy the author, Kennedy the friend of the press, and, among other portraits flattering and unflattering, Kennedy the man of ideals, the wavering decision maker, the hero of liberalism, the cold warrior, the flag waver, the diplomat, and the implacable defender of democracy.

In most accounts of Kennedy's presidential years, some of these qualities are exaggerated at the expense of others, precisely because Kennedy reflected the ideals, causes, and ambitions of so many of those around him. He was young. He was charismatic. His energy seemed limitless. During his campaign and his years in office, he became a magnet for the contradictory wish fulfillments of a nation wrestling with its own power. He offered the hope that a postwar America could be both strong and considerate, pragmatic and visionary, that the United States could provide leadership for the world and the highest quality of life for its own people.

The memos from the presidential office, dated from January 1961 to November 1963, focus on the pragmatic issues, though not entirely to the exclusion of the vision, principles, or politics of John

Kennedy in office. In some memos the President was simply asking for information; in others, issuing directives. Often he was concerned with communication among departments, agencies, or advisers. Were matters being handled as effectively as possible? Were programs being carried out? Was information correct—and had it been verified?

The memos included in this book are of various kinds. Many are relatively brief memos dictated directly to the President's secretary, Evelyn Lincoln, to pass on to Cabinet members, aides, heads of departments and agencies, members of the White House staff, and other administrative personnel. Secondly, there are a number of memos from those who had met with Kennedy or attended meetings with him, in which they relayed the words of the President, passed along his instructions, or conveyed questions to other departments or staff. Memos "for the record" or "of actions taken" frequently specified further assignments to staff members.

Thirdly, there are numerous National Security Action Memorandums. Usually they were marked "sensitive," "secret," or "top secret," and they include a number that have only recently been declassified. Though often drafted and signed by a staff member (most frequently, National Security Adviser McGeorge Bundy), the NSAMs are significant as precise statements of the presidential decisions on specific matters of security and intelligence as well as military and foreign policy. Among all these memos, from the most informal to the highly classified Security Action Memorandums, are a number that provide broad policy statements addressed to individuals in the administration or to departments and agencies.

In addition to the memos, this selection includes a limited number of letters from the President. Among these items are notes to staff members and letters to leaders of labor and industry. Also included in the correspondence category are several of John F. Kennedy's letters to Soviet Premier Nikita S. Khrushchev. The memos, correspondence, and selected excerpts from related documents are presented here in chronological order.

Wherever relevant, some background material has been provided to introduce individuals or to explain events and policy concerns that are part of the record. In some instances, memos refer to interoffice, intragovernmental, or interdepartmental controversies that have convoluted histories. In most instances, however, the memos are directly related to current events or to government matters that eventually were made public.

By necessity this is a selection rather than a collection. In the John Fitzgerald Kennedy Library at Columbia Point in Boston, Massachusetts, are stored thousands of linear feet of memos and correspondence related to the presidential years. Though many of those papers are records of staff work, there is much that might be considered relevant to the selection included here. Relatively few of these papers, however, were dictated, signed, or directly initiated by John F. Kennedy. In making the present selection, I have looked for those few that most closely bear his imprint.

The goal should be clear, though perhaps it can best be stated in the form of Kennedy-style questions: Can we see the man in office apart from the man who was mirrored by chroniclers, critics, and policy makers? What did Kennedy sound like when he was not tuned to the vast audience of the American electorate? What voice do we hear when Kennedy addressed the closest associates in his administration? In the paper work that flowed directly from his office, is it possible to see the imprint of his will and his personality?

The hope is that by bringing together the memos, notes, and letters in chronological order, we come one step closer to answering the question at the core of biography itself: Who was this man?

To a great degree Kennedy left his personal imprint on everything he did. Yes, the clues to the person as well as the politician can be easily found in the paper work. The White House was definitely run in the "Kennedy style."

John Kenneth Galbraith, Kennedy's ambassador to India, described that style in an article that appeared in *The Washington Post* on November 25, 1963, three days after the President was assassinated. "The Kennedy style, though it involved detachment from self, involved no self-deprecation. . . . His style called for unremitting good taste and good manners. It called also for a profound commitment to information and reason."

On these pages there is ample evidence of all these elements. Among the notes, memos, and queries that John Kennedy addressed to those who surrounded the presidential office, there are certainly signs of impatience, of frustration, occasionally of anger, but the detachment from self, the good manners, the commitment to information and reason are omnipresent.

Yet another aspect of the Kennedy style was simply the way he ran the office. In a panel discussion conducted on January 5, 1990, by news commentator John Chancellor with former White House chiefs of staff, Kennedy's speech writer and special counsel Theodore Sorensen described how Kennedy's administrative style differed from Eisenhower's. After Kennedy's election, Sorensen talked to President Dwight D. Eisenhower's chief of staff, Wilton B. Persons, to find out how the White House worked under the general's leadership.

"Not a piece of paper goes into Eisenhower's desk unless I've initialed it," Persons told Sorensen. "Other than the press secretary and secretary of state, no one goes in unless they come through me first."

"John F. Kennedy would have never accepted that system," Sorensen told Chancellor. "He would not have been comfortable with me or anyone else operating that way. So we had a modified system under which [there was] one person on policy program, one person on national security operations, one person on press, and one person on congressional relations. Each person had equal access to the President."

As is apparent from the memos, in the Kennedy administration "equal access" went both ways. Many of the President's memos were addressed to National Security Adviser McGeorge Bundy and Secretary of Defense Robert McNamara. Others went to White House advisers, the secretary of state and selected officials in the State Department, heads of agencies, military advisers, and occasionally specific personnel within departments. In addition, Kennedy frequently asked advisers or heads of departments to consult with others before making decisions, taking actions, or responding to his inquiries.

This was more than an administrative style. It reflected a personality trait. It was the way he had operated on the campaign trail and during his years in Congress. There was a distinctive Kennedy way of doing things—an impatience with bureaucratic procedures, a call for information and opinions from many sources, an urgency to get things done. Those who got the knack of writing reports and memos to this President quickly learned that they did not gain stature by filling up reams of paper.

Kennedy asked for clearly stated opinions, based on evidence and expert judgment, and he fought an ongoing war with State Department jargon and Defense Department posturing. On June 28, six months into his administration and some two months after the Bay of Pigs disaster, Kennedy stated in precise terms what he expected of those who surrounded him. The President's crisply worded National Security Action Memorandum, addressed to General Lyman L. Lemnitzer, was titled "Relations of the Joint Chiefs of Staff to the President in cold war operations." It began: "I regard the Joint Chiefs of Staff as my principal military adviser responsible both for initiating advice to me and for responding to requests for advice. I expect their advice to come to me direct and unfiltered." Beyond that, he looked to the Joint Chiefs to keep the broader objectives in mind: "While I look to the Chiefs to present the military factor without reserve or hesitation, I regard them to be more than military men and expect their help in fitting military requirements into the overall context of any situation, recognizing that the most difficult problem in government is to combine all assets in a unified, effective pattern."

Clearly, this was the assistance that he expected to receive from other advisers as well—"direct and unfiltered advice" that fitted "into the overall context of any situation." Of course, presidential wishes were not instantaneously fulfilled. In reality, as Kennedy discovered time and again, the President himself had to do much of the filtering. And it was largely up to him to determine how the advice and opinions of his chief advisers fitted into "the overall context of any situation."

Yet another clue to the Kennedy style of administration is contained in a four-point memo from McGeorge Bundy to Special Adviser Kenneth O'Donnell, written in early January 1962, in which Bundy pleaded for more space and staff for his national security operations. Bundy told O'Donnell he urgently needed a "communications receiving room" to handle all the White House traffic and national security information that was received in the office and sent on by cable and pouch when the President was traveling. "I need about two more people," Bundy asked, "to handle my own immediate paper-work for the President. An appalling percentage of what comes over for him from State, Defense, CIA [Central Intelligence Agency] and AEC [Atomic Energy Commission] is raw and unsatisfactory paper-work, and we are not doing a tight job of turning it into 'completed staff work.' " Bundy concluded: "It all comes from having a President who has taken charge of foreign affairs."

As Bundy's memo indicates, the administrative demands of the President were inseparable from Kennedy's most fundamental policy decision: to "take charge of foreign affairs." If he was not only to take charge but also to administrate the conduct of foreign affairs, he needed an extensive, reliable communications network. He required effective ways of distilling information before implementing actions that would have international consequences. And he needed clearly stated opinions from trusted advisers.

In the memos the multitude of references to foreign leaders and nations indicates just how demanding was the task the President had taken upon himself. The memos refer to events in the Dominican Republic, Honduras, Mexico, British Guiana, Panama, Brazil, Argentina, Peru, and other Latin American nations. On the African continent Kennedy closely followed occurrences in the Congo, Guinea, Ghana, Angola. The Portuguese Azores (site of a U.S. air base) became the focus of an ongoing controversy with Portugal. In the Middle East the President kept up with developments in Israel as well as the United Arab Republic, Saudi Arabia, and Yemen. The memos reflect his deep involvement with NATO, developments in the European Economic Community, and Western European affairs. Militarily and politically Kennedy was extending U.S. involvement in India, Pakistan, Nationalist China, Indonesia, and nations throughout Southeast Asia. Above all, Kennedy was critically concerned with the mood, posture, political stance, foreign interventions, and military incursions of the USSR.

In sum, the memos confirm Bundy's observation that this was a President who had "taken charge of foreign affairs." The range of Kennedy's worldwide concerns appeared unlimited, and the demands on his advisers, as well as the President himself, were great. He had high ambitions—to understand and evaluate an exceedingly complex landscape of world events—yet in most of his dealings with those nations, many of the complexities are reduced to a simpler equation. Repeatedly the memos return to the theme of anticommunism.

If the strength and stridency of Kennedy's anticommunism have ever been in doubt, they should be dispelled by this chronicle of his decisions and actions. The theme of anticommunism is recurrent. However altruistic the purposes of the Alliance for Progress or Food for Peace programs, they were consistently justified in terms of stemming the tide of communist influence. In Africa and Southeast Asia, American aid was clearly linked to the willingness of the recipient nation to fight communist influence, incursions, or infiltration. In Kennedy's view, unstable regimes such as those in the Dominican Republic, the Congo, Pakistan, Laos, South Vietnam, and Indonesia would eventually have to choose sides. It was imperative, in his estimation, to watch them closely at all times for the signs that betrayed which way they were leaning.

Unquestionably Kennedy's cold war views were supported by the electorate. America was in the throes of cold war fervor, Khrushchev repeatedly announced and acted on his intentions to expand Soviet global influence, and a "hard line" on communism was a political necessity. As the memos reveal, however, viewing the world as a dichotomy sometimes left the administration groping for a position. Political and economic instability in Latin America made it difficult to decide whom should be supported—and to what degree—whenever there was a change of regime. In northern Africa, where the French and Portuguese still had colonialist power, the dilemma was how to support independence movements without either alienating European allies or supporting leftward-leaning leaders. In Laos and South Vietnam the policy and practice of supporting any leader who was sufficiently anti-communist led the United States to back regimes that proved unpopular, unstable, and ultimately indefensible.

In direct dealings with the Soviet Union, Kennedy was deeply and unalterably committed to showing American strength. During the Berlin crisis in August 1961 and the Cuban missile crisis in October 1962, the President took the case for democracy to the court of world opinion. In both instances he made it clear that the United States would take any measures to halt Soviet aggression. The internal memos from that time are consistent with his public position.

Yet the memos also show clearly that Kennedy was fighting a multipronged cold war that involved postures and propaganda as well as men and weapons. Maintaining and increasing nuclear "superiority" was only one element of defense. Another part of the battle was improving relationships with nonaligned, underdeveloped, or emerging nations through diplomacy and direct aid. Yet a third prong of the Kennedy offensive—repeatedly emphasized in the memos—was counterinsurgency.

Among the President's first actions after taking office was his organization of a special group (counterinsurgency) to study guerrilla warfare and unconventional military tactics. At first the President's counterinsurgency plan focused on military training of special forces to prepare for guerrilla combat. Ultimately the program was to include police training of foreign nationals. In September 5, 1961, in a memo titled "Training for Latin American Armed Forces" (NSAM 88) to Secretary of Defense Robert S. McNamara, the President said:

I would appreciate hearing what steps we are taking to train the Armed Forces of Latin America in controlling mobs, guerrillas, etc. . . . It has been suggested that we set up a camp in the United States similar to the FBI Academy which brings in police from all over the United States. We would bring up a good many officers from the different countries of Latin America for a period from 1 to 2 months; we would have FBI people there who could talk to them about the techniques they have developed to control Communism [and] subversion, and we could have our military coming in to teach them how to control mobs and fight guerrillas. . . .

Ultimately the counterinsurgency doctrine Kennedy advocated was promulgated through the departments of State and Defense, the Central Intelligence Agency, and the Agency for International Development (AID). The doctrine resulted in the revision of war college courses and field manuals and extensive training in counterguerrilla tactics and psychological warfare. Training camps were developed in the United States, Latin America, and Southeast Asia. South Vietnam became the ultimate "laboratory" for testing the effectiveness of this form of military operation.

On other fronts Kennedy fought a propaganda war. On July 14, 1961, in a National Security Action Memorandum to Secretary of Defense McNamara and the director of the U.S. Information Agency, Bundy wrote, "The President completely endorses the effort to combat the Soviet propaganda trap contained in the phrase 'Peaceful Coexistence' by the use of symbolic language that expresses our view of the nature of the conflict in which we are engaged. . . . The President has requested that immediate steps be taken to give this formulation the widespread currency and usage that would make it an effective countertheme to the Soviet formula."

One day after the border between East and West Berlin was closed (August 14, 1961), the President asked Secretary of State Dean Rusk, "What steps will we take this week to exploit politically propagandawise the Soviet/East German cutoff of the border? . . . It offers us a very good propaganda stick which, if the situation were reversed, would be well used in beating us. It seems to me this requires decisions at the highest level."

Throughout his term of office, Kennedy sought rallying words and bracing gestures that would improve the stature of the United States in the eyes of the world, yet he simultaneously pressed measures to promote cooperation. By giving defense-level ratings to the man in space program, the President accelerated the race to land an American first on the moon; at the same time he recommended that the United States and Soviet Union develop a joint space program. He vastly expanded the nuclear arsenal and increased the defense budget, but he also initiated productive disarmament talks in Moscow. Although cold war tension reached new heights during the Kennedy administration, he made strides toward opening trade with countries behind the iron curtain and established new channels of communication with Moscow—most dramatically, a private correspondence with Khrushchev himself.

There were gulfs between the symbolic gestures and the pragmatic actions, and since the memos focus on the pragmatic, the portrait that emerges from the memos is more of the warrior than the peacemaker. Nonetheless, there are ample signs that Kennedy did not give up hope of reaching new forms of compromise with the Soviet Union. In National Security Action Memorandum No. 239, written seven months after the Cuban missile crisis brought the United States to the brink of nuclear war, Kennedy said he was disappointed that the Eighteen-Nation Disarmament Conference at Geneva had not achieved any kind of agreement on either "general and complete disarmament" or "a nuclear test ban treaty." In that memo the President affirmed, "I have in no way changed my views of the desirability of a test ban treaty or the value of our proposals on general and complete disarmament. Further, the events of the last two years have increased my concern for the consequences of an unchecked continuation of the arms race between ourselves and the Soviet Bloc."

Still, his actions were fueled by internal contradictions. Two years before, he had initiated a military budget (to close a nonexistent "missile gap") that included provisions for nine hundred new nuclear missiles. He had responded to the Soviet resumption of atmospheric testing by ordering the resumption of U.S. tests. During the missile crisis, while arguing for peaceful settlement, he had issued an unconcealed threat to the Soviet Union, indicating that the United States would not hesitate to use its nuclear arsenal unless the Soviet Union withdrew its missiles from Cuba.

The memos and correspondence provide unfiltered questions that Kennedy wanted to have answered and direct actions he wished to take. They reflect his intelligence, his style, and, in some instances, his humor. But they also record the unresolved contradictions.

From these memos it is evident that Kennedy was prepared to use nuclear weapons, yet he believed that nuclear war was, in the words of his American University speech (June 10, 1963), "a strategy of annihilation." He believed that developing countries should determine their own destinies; at the same time he readily interceded with those nations to promote the interests of the United States. He endorsed the proAmerican policies of some dictatorial regimes, yet he was convinced of the inevitable downfall of regimes that continued to maintain authoritarian rule. He wanted open flow of information with the press and within his administration, yet he bridled at criticism and press attacks launched against his administration.

From the evidence here, John Kennedy seemed to have something more than the ability to see a question from all sides. He had a more fatalistic talent for seeing that almost any view might prove to be defensible in certain circumstances. Thirty years later it is impossible to completely reconstruct the cold war fervor, the fear of Khrushchev, or the ideals of American beneficence that preceded the Vietnam War. But one hopes this chronological view of the presidential files will reconstruct the circumstances surrounding the President as well as his views and actions.

Editor's Note

The majority of the memorandums and correspondence in this volume are from the John Fitzgerald Kennedy Library in Boston. A few items related to the Cuban missile crisis are from the National Security Archives in Washington, D.C. The selections that come from the Kennedy Library are in the National Security Files (including "Meetings and Memoranda") and the President's Office Files. The bracketed number after each document is a reference to the listing in "Sources" on page 285.

The format of the original memos is inconsistent. Informal memos in the White House office files were rarely signed, though some were initialed by Kennedy. Often the recipient was mentioned only by name; some were referred to only by title. There is little handwriting on the original memos, though in some cases the President or his secretary, Evelyn Lincoln, did make a few notations.

The National Security Action Memorandums adhere more closely to a format; but here, too, there are exceptions, and some of the NSAMs Kennedy signed resemble the more informal office memos in style and wording. Nearly all the NSAMs were originally classified documents marked "confidential," "secret," "top secret," or "top secret—sensitive." Declassification has occurred selectively, either upon request or as the result of a periodic review process. In the declassification process, certain passages still considered sensitive have been blacked out ("sanitized") upon release of the document.

In editing the memos, I have presented them in their original format rather than attempt to standardize the style. In the office memos I have corrected obvious misspellings and punctuation errors, and I have inserted words that were omitted during transcription whenever the intended usage was clear. In those few instances where meanings were ambiguous, I have explained the corrections or insertions. I have used "*sic*" as little as necessary.

Copies of the NSAMs were often sent to various personnel within the administration and were copied for filing. For the most part, I have retained only the names of departments and individuals listed in the headings of the memos. The lists following "cc:" have been dropped. Unlike the more informal memos, most of the NSAMs were obviously reviewed before being sent; there are few errors in spelling or punctuation.

A final editor's note—or, rather, editorial comment.

The fact that many United States government documents from the Kennedy years are still classified three decades after they were written is appalling. True, there is a Freedom of Information Act, and it has led to the release of many papers that might otherwise still be classified. But requests for declassification are handled at glacial speed. Requests for release are denied without explanation. To judge by the information contained in papers that were declassified as recently as 1988, there is generally little or no cause for suppressing the information they contain. This is something more than bureaucratic obduracy; it is the kind of overzealous censorship that leaves a gaping hole in our history.

John F. Kennedy himself fired off one fast round against this kind of stubborn nondisclosure. On September 6, 1961, in NSAM 91, he wrote: "The effectiveness of democracy as a form of government depends on an informed and intelligent citizenry. . . . In my view, any official should have a clear and precise case involving the national interest before seeking to withhold from publication documents or papers fifteen or more years old."

Thirty years after those words were written, the record of that President's administration remains incomplete. The case against publication of still-classified documents is neither clear nor precise, and it seems doubtful that the national interest is at stake. But as Presidents both before and after Kennedy have discovered, bureaucracies have the power of inertia on their side, and they use it.

—E. B. C.

The Kennedy Administration

Following is a partial list of officials mentioned by name in the Kennedy papers—those who either held senior administrative positions or served as aides or advisers. Government officials not listed here are identified in the editorial notes.

Dean G. Acheson—former secretary of state, 1949–53; foreign policy adviser to Kennedy (no official government title).

George W. Ball—undersecretary of state for economic affairs, January 1961–November 1961; undersecretary of state, November 1961–September 1966.

David E. Bell—director, Bureau of the Budget, January 1961–November 1962; administrator of the Agency for International Development, January 1963–July 1966.

Adolf A. Berle, Jr.—chairman, Interdepartmental Task Force on Latin America, January–July 1961.

Richard M. Bissell—deputy director of plans, Central Intelligence Agency, 1959–62.

Charles E. Bohlen—special assistant for Soviet affairs in the State Department, June 1960–August 1962; ambassador to France, August 1962–December 1967.

McGeorge Bundy—special assistant to the President for national security affairs, January 1961–February 1966.

William P. Bundy—deputy assistant secretary of defense for international security affairs, January 1961–October 1963; assistant secretary of defense for international security affairs, October 1963–February 1964.

Brigadier General Chester V. Clifton, Jr.—military aide to the President, 1961–63.

Frank M. Coffin—deputy administrator, Agency for International Development, 1961–64.

C. Douglas Dillon—secretary of the treasury, January 1961–March 1965.

Allen W. Dulles, director of central intelligence, 1953–61.

Ralph A. Dungan—special assistant to the President, January 1961–October 1964.

Frederick G. Dutton—special assistant to the President, January 1961–November 1961; assistant secretary of state for congressional relations, November 1961–December 1964.

Frank B. Ellis—director, Office of Civil Defense and Mobilization, March 1961–February 1962; U.S. district judge, eastern Louisiana, April 1962–65.

Myer "Mike" Feldman—deputy special counsel to the President, January 1961–April 1964.

Michael V. Forrestal—presidential assistant for Far Eastern affairs, January 1962–July 1964.

Orville L. Freeman—secretary of agriculture, January 1961–January 1969.

J. William Fulbright—Democratic senator, Arkansas, 1945–75; chairman, Foreign Relations Committee, 1959–75.

John Kenneth Galbraith—ambassador to India, March 1961–June 1963.

Roswell L. Gilpatric—deputy secretary of defense, January 1961–January 1964.

Arthur J. Goldberg—secretary of labor, January 1961–October 1962; associate justice, U.S. Supreme Court, October 1962–July 1965.

Richard N. Goodwin—assistant special counsel to the President, January 1961–November 1961; deputy assistant secretary of state for Inter-American affairs, November 1961–July 1962; director, International Peace Corps Secretariat, December 1962–January 1964.

Kermit Gordon—member, Council of Economic Advisers, January 1961–November 1962; director of the budget, November 1962–April 1965.

Fowler Hamilton—administrator, Agency for International Development, September 1961–November 1962.

W. Averell Harriman—ambassador-at-large, January 1961–November 1961; assistant secretary of state for Far Eastern affairs, November 1961–March 1963; undersecretary of state for political affairs, March 1963–February 1965.

Walter W. Heller—chairman, Council of Economic Advisers, January 1961–November 1964.

Martin J. Hillenbrand—director of the Office of German Affairs, Department of State, 1958–62; director of Berlin Task Force, 1962–63.

Chet Holifield—Democratic representative, California, 1943–75; chairman, Joint Committee on Atomic Energy, 1961–63.

Carl Kaysen—deputy special assistant to the President for national security affairs, November 1961–December 1963.

George F. Kennan—ambassador to Yugoslavia, May 1961–July 1963.

Foy D. Kohler—assistant secretary of state for European affairs, January 1959–July 1962; ambassador to the Soviet Union, July 1962–September 1966.

Robert W. Komer—senior staff member, National Security Council, 1961–65.

James M. Landis—presidential assistant on regulatory agencies, January 1961–September 1961.

Lyman L. Lemnitzer—chairman, Joint Chiefs of Staff, October 1960–July 1962; supreme allied commander, Europe, January 1963–June 1969.

John J. McCloy—presidential disarmament adviser, January 1961–October 1961; director, U.S. Arms Control and Disarmament Agency, September 1961–October 1961.

John A. McCone—director of central intelligence, November 1961–April 1965.

Edward A. McDermott—deputy director, Office of Civil and Defense Mobilization, 1961–62; deputy director, Office of Emergency Planning, 1961–62; director, OEP, 1962–65.

George C. McGhee—undersecretary of state for political affairs, 1961–63.

Robert S. McNamara—secretary of defense, January 1961–February 1968.

John T. McNaughton—special assistant for disarmament affairs, international security affairs, Department of Defense, July 1961–September 1961; deputy assistant secretary of defense for international security affairs, October 1961–June 1962; general counsel, Department of Defense, July 1962–June 1964.

Charles Maechling, Jr.—director for internal affairs, Department of State, 1961–63; special assistant to Averell Harriman, 1963–66.

Edwin M. Martin—assistant secretary of state for economic affairs, August 1960–May 1962; assistant secretary of state for inter-American affairs, May 1962–December 1963.

deLesseps S. Morrison—ambassador to the Organization of American States, June 1961–September 1963.

Teodoro Moscoso—ambassador to Venezuela, March–November 1961; coordinator, Alliance for Progress, November 1961–May 1964.

Edward R. Murrow—director, U.S. Information Agency, March 1961–January 1964.

Frederick E. Nolting, Jr.—ambassador to South Vietnam, March 1961–August 1963.

Lauris Norstad—supreme commander, allied forces, Europe, April 1956–January 1963.

Lawrence F. O'Brien—special assistant to the President for congressional relations and personnel, January 1961–August 1965.

P. Kenneth O'Donnell—special assistant to the President, January 1961–January 1965.

Abraham A. Ribicoff—secretary of health, education, and welfare, January 1961–July 1962; Democratic senator from Connecticut, 1963–80.

Walt W. Rostow—deputy special assistant to the President for national security affairs, January–December 1961; chairman, State Department Policy Planning Council, December 1961–April 1966.

Dean Rusk—secretary of state, January 1961–January 1969.

Arthur M. Schlesinger, Jr.—special assistant to the President, January 1961–January 1964.

Glenn T. Seaborg—chairman, Atomic Energy Commission, January 1961–August 1971.

David M. Shoup—commandant, Marine Corps, January 1960–December 1963.

R. Sargent Shriver—director, Peace Corps, March 1961–February 1964.

Adlai E. Stevenson—ambassador to the United Nations, January 1961–July 1965.

Maxwell D. Taylor—military representative of the President, July 1961–October 1962; chairman of the Joint Chiefs of Staff, October 1962–June 1964.

Llewellyn E. Thompson, Jr.—ambassador to the Soviet Union, April 1957–August 1962; ambassador-at-large and special adviser on Soviet affairs to the secretary of state, August 1962–October 1966.

James Tobin—member, Council of Economic Advisers, January 1961–August 1962.

James E. Webb—director, National Aeronautics and Space Administration, February 1961–October 1968.

Jerome B. Wiesner—special assistant to the President on science and technology and chairman of the President's Science Advisory Committee, February 1961–February 1964.

Robert F. Woodward—assistant secretary of state for inter-American affairs, 1961–62; ambassador to Spain, 1962–65.

1961

Mr. President,

On the memos that you read would you put a check mark up in the corner so we will know whether or not you have seen them.

Signed,

Evelyn [Lincoln]

[1]

One week after the inauguration President Kennedy signaled a new role for the Vice President in the redesigned National Security Council. Under Eisenhower the NSC staff had been highly bureaucratic and, in Kennedy's view, unwieldy. Following the recommendations of Senator Henry Jackson's Subcommittee on National Policy Machinery, Kennedy created a smaller NSC that could operate with more flexibility and respond more quickly to the President's requests for action.

January 28, 1961

The Honorable Lyndon B. Johnson
The Vice President

Dear Mr. Vice President:

Recognizing the need for a Vice President who is fully informed and adequately prepared with respect to domestic, foreign and military policies relating to the national security of the United States, and recognizing also the need for a closer working relationship between the President and Vice President in this vital area, I would like you to preside over meetings of the National Security Council in my absence and to maintain close liaison with the Council and all other departments and agencies affected with a national security interest.

In addition, I am hereby requesting you to review policies relating to the national security, consulting with me in order that I might have the full benefit of your endeavors and your judgment.

You will need, in fulfillment of this assignment, pertinent information concerning the policies and operations of the departments and agencies concerned with national security policies, including the Department of State, the Department of Defense, the Office of Civil and Defense Mobilization, the National Aeronautics and Space Administration, the Bureau of the Budget, and the Central Intelligence Agency.

I will expect the departments and agencies concerned to cooperate fully with you in providing information in order for you to carry out the responsibilities outlined above.

Sincerely,
John F. Kennedy

[2]

Two top secret National Security Action Memorandums on February 3 recorded the President's early actions on national security matters. As with many subsequent NSAMs, the presidential request was transferred to other department heads (in this case, to Secretary of Defense Robert S. McNamara) by McGeorge Bundy, special assistant to the President for national security affairs.

TOP SECRET

February 3, 1961

NATIONAL SECURITY ACTION MEMORANDUM NO. 2
TO: The Secretary of Defense
SUBJECT: Development of Counterguerrilla Forces

At the National Security Council meeting on February 1, 1961, the President requested that the Secretary of Defense, in consultation with other interested agencies, should examine means for placing more emphasis on the development of counterguerrilla forces. Accordingly, it is requested that the Department of Defense take action on this request and inform this office promptly of the measures which it proposes to take.

McGeorge Bundy

[3]

TOP SECRET

February 3, 1961

NATIONAL SECURITY ACTION MEMORANDUM NO. 4
TO: The Secretary of Defense
SUBJECT: Purchases of uranium from foreign countries

In the light of discussion at the National Security Council on February 1, 1961, the President requested the Secretary of Defense to consult with the Atomic Energy Commission about a review of the purchases of uranium from foreign countries. It is accordingly requested that this review be undertaken and that this office be informed whether in fact there is any hope of early savings of foreign exchange in this area.

McGeorge Bundy

[4]

During the presidential race Kennedy repeatedly emphasized the existence of a "missile gap" between the United States and Soviet Union. His commitment to an expanded defense program was repeated in his State of the Union address.

On February 3, in a personal letter to the President, Deputy Secretary of Defense Roswell L. Gilpatric wrote:

In accordance with your recent State of the Union Message to Congress, the Navy proposes to commence work immediately on five additional nuclear-powered Fleet Ballistic Missile submarines (SSBN). Funds for construction of these submarines are included in the Navy's budget estimates for Fiscal 1962 now before the Congress. . . . The success of POLARIS to date has exceeded expectations. The proven accuracy and range of this powerful weapon brings almost any target within reach from the sea.

Gilpatric recommended building five submarines of the *Lafayette* (SSBN-616) class at an estimated cost of $584,100,000. He reported that one of two naval shipyards was already heavily obligated to submarine construction. Hence the recommendation in the President's memo that the other four submarines be built at "qualified public yards."

February 3, 1961

The Honorable Robert S. McNamara
The Secretary of Defense
Washington, D.C.

Dear Mr. Secretary:
   In accordance with the provisions of the Act of March 27, 1934 (Public Law 135, 73rd Congress), the Secretary of the Navy is authorized and directed to construct five nuclear-powered Fleet Ballistic Missile submarines (SSBN). Further, as provided for by the above-mentioned Act (48 Stat. 504), I find it to be inconsistent with the public interest this year for more than one of these submarines to be constructed in naval shipyards and hereby direct the Secretary of the Navy to construct four of these vessels in private yards and one in a naval shipyard.

Sincerely,
/s/ John F. Kennedy

[5]

(On February 6 a story in *The New York Times* revealed an internal Kennedy administration study showing that no missile gap existed.)

⊕   ♣   ≡

Kennedy was already designing the Food for Peace program when he assumed office. In 1954 the Eisenhower administration had begun to send U.S. farm surpluses abroad. The Eisenhower initiative was later supported by George McGovern in the House and Hubert Humphrey in the Senate, who saw the program as a way to provide assistance to food-poor countries while also promoting goodwill toward the United States. Kennedy, however, did not want the program to be seen as surplus dumping. He reconceived it as "a food-for-peace act designed to use American agricultural capacity to the fullest practicable extent to meet human needs the world over and to promote world economic development."

Arthur Schlesinger, adviser to the President and chronicler of the administration, became an ardent supporter and promoter of the program.

February 3, 1961

MEMORANDUM FOR ARTHUR SCHLESINGER

The Food for Peace mission is going to every Latin American country on February 12. It is a technical mission. Would you be interested in going? The value would be that it would give you an insight into our ambassadors, USIA [United States Information Agency], and give you a feel of Latin America. Would you speak to me about this?

/s/ John F. Kennedy

[6]

Schlesinger was enthusiastic. "One good thing about my going to Latin America," he wrote in a reply memo on February 6, "is that my presence as your representative will help persuade the Latinos that the U.S. government is not run by money-grubbing materialists." Schlesinger encouraged Kennedy to enlarge the mission to allow Schlesinger to meet with "editors, professors, and other intellectual leaders as well as political leaders." Schlesinger noted that "intellectuals have become a dynamic political force through much of the world," and he encouraged the President to put over a "new image" that would impress Latin American leaders:

You are a writer, an historian, your wife is a patron of the arts. All this provides a splendid foundation to launch an image of America as a land which deeply values artistic and cultural achievement. . . . This new image wouldn't turn the tide of the Cold War, but it would confound Communist propaganda and increase our appeal to the intellectuals of both old and new nations.

In Latin American affairs one of Kennedy's key negotiators was Adolf Berle, a Roosevelt New Dealer who had been assistant secretary of state and ambassador to Brazil. Berle was generally an opponent of Eisenhower's stance in Latin America and a supporter of the Good Neighbor policy. Through his contacts Berle had kept in touch with popular parties and given diplomatic support to various Latin American movements.

2/4/61
TO: Mr. Bundy
FROM: The President

It is my understanding that there is a sharp difference of opinion between the defense CIA [*sic*] on what we should do about Cuba, and Berle. Can you find out if the differences of view have been settled; or, if they continue, I believe we should have an opportunity to have them placed before me and have them argued out again. Would you let me know right away on this?

[7]

Secretary of Defense Robert S. McNamara, a registered Republican, had become president of the Ford Motor Company in November 1960, just one month before Kennedy called him to Washington. McNamara, who became one of the chief architects of the Vietnam War, accepted the position under a Democratic President because he thought it would be a "greater challenge" than his former post.

NATIONAL SECURITY ACTION MEMORANDUM NO. 7
February 6, 1961
MEMO FOR SECRETARY OF DEFENSE

I note that Congress has once again criticized the Department of
Defense for not giving more contracts to small business. This is an
old complaint. I think it would be useful for you to have someone
look into exactly how this is handled and whether it is possible for
the Defense Department to put more emphasis on small business.
If it isn't possible for us to do better than has been done in the past,
I think we should know about it. If it is possible for us to do better,
we should go ahead with it, and I think we should make some public
statements on it. Would you let me know about this.

[8]

The Mutual Defense Assistance Control Act of 1951 had been
sponsored by Representative Laurie C. Battle, an Alabama Democrat. The Battle Act specified that U.S. aid to a foreign country
would be terminated if that country was found to be shipping arms
or munitions to Soviet-dominated areas. The ban could also extend
to nonstrategic goods if the President concluded that the foreign
nation's activities were detrimental to national security.
    In 1958 as a senator, Kennedy had sponsored a Battle Act amend-
ment that would modify the prohibition of aid to East European
satellites. After the amendment was rejected, Kennedy teamed up
with Vermont Republican George Aiken to introduce a similar
amendment in 1959. The Senate passed the amendment, but the
House took no action.

NATIONAL SECURITY ACTION MEMORANDUM NO. 8
February 6, 1961
MEMORANDUM FOR SECRETARY OF STATE

In our State of the Union address, we committed ourselves to
changing the Battle Act. This is a matter which I worked on when
I was in the Senate. George Aiken cosponsored the bill with me.
We should certainly discuss the matter with him when we are ready
to move on it. Arrange to have him if not sponsor the bill cosponsor

it if we can get a Democrat interested in it. Perhaps Mike Mansfield would introduce the bill as Mike handled it on the Senate floor last summer.

In addition, I would like to be informed as to what progress we are making on our negotiations with the Polish government in regard to use of zlotys that are accredited to us from the sale of surplus food.

[9]

Brigadier General Edward G. Lansdale, the air force officer who headed the U.S. Military Mission to Vietnam in 1954, later became head of the Saigon station for CIA activities in South Vietnam. He strongly backed South Vietnam's Premier Ngo Dinh Diem, and for a time he lived in the presidential palace, serving as one of Diem's closest advisers. (The main character in *The Ugly American* by William J. Lederer and Eugene Burdick was loosely based on Lansdale.)

Lansdale left Vietnam in 1956 but returned in early January 1961 on a mission for President Eisenhower, in whose administration he served as assistant to the secretary of defense for special operations. His report was sharply critical of U.S. actions in South Vietnam.

Lansdale stated that the United States had failed to give Diem the support the premier needed to stabilize the countryside. The officer urged implementation of economic, political, and military programs to help the South Vietnamese. He further recommended that the U.S. ambassador to South Vietnam, Elbridge Durbrow, be replaced. Supervision of American Vietnam policy, Lansdale said, should be appointed to a special team that would not be constrained by bureaucracy.

Kennedy was especially impressed by Lansdale's report about the work he had done in the Philippines, aiding Filipino defense minister Ramón Magsaysay to end guerrilla actions of the Communist-backed Hukbalahaps. Lansdale, sponsored by the CIA, had introduced counterinsurgency techniques that he called "psychwar." According to one State Department official, the President considered appointing Lansdale the next ambassador to Vietnam.

NATIONAL SECURITY ACTION MEMORANDUM NO. 9
February 6, 1961
MEMO FOR MR. BUNDY

I think General Lansdale's story of the counterguerrilla case study would be an excellent magazine article for magazines like the Saturday Evening Post. Obviously it could not go under Lansdale's signature but he might, if the State Department and the Department of Defense think it is worthwhile, turn this memorandum over to them and they perhaps could get a good writer for it. He could then check the final story.

It seems to me that they would find it interesting and it might serve as an example of what can be done. In any case, even if that is not considered to be a good idea, we should arrange for distribution of this article to the people who would find it most useful —CIA and perhaps the ambassadors in Africa and Asia. Certainly the military aid groups that are at fault in those countries. You should make sure that this type of material has good distribution.

[10]

In 1959 Eisenhower had made Richard M. Bissell the deputy director of plans of the CIA. As the official in charge of covert activities Bissell had supervised an unsuccessful attempt to assassinate the Congolese leader Patrice Lumumba, and he had authorized two attempted assassinations of Cuban leaders in the summer of 1960. (There is no evidence that either Eisenhower or Kennedy knew of these attempts.)

On March 17, 1960, Eisenhower had authorized Bissell to begin recruiting and training a force of Cuban exiles to plan an invasion of Cuba. On November 18 Kennedy had been briefed by the director of the CIA, Allen Dulles, as well as by Bissell. The CIA chiefs informed Kennedy that the exiles were currently being trained by the agency in Guatemala in preparation for an amphibious landing at an as yet undetermined place in Cuba.

NATIONAL SECURITY ACTION MEMORANDUM NO. 10
February 6, 1961
MEMO FOR MR. BUNDY

Has the policy for Cuba been coordinated between Defense, CIA, Bissell, Mann [assistant secretary of state for inter-American affairs], and Berle? Have we determined what we are going to do about Cuba? What approaches are we going to make to the Latin American governments on this matter? If there is a difference of opinion between the agencies I think [it] should be brought to my attention.

[11]

Kennedy entered office faced with a balance of payments deficit that had been growing for a number of years. There were various contributing factors. Since World War II the United States had made large payments through the Marshall Plan and had steadily increased foreign aid spending. The U.S. was also carrying a large share of the NATO military commitment in Europe. In order to reduce the deficit, Eisenhower and then Kennedy began to pressure the allies to carry a greater share of the defense burden.

February began with a preliminary government estimate that projected the annual trade deficit at about $3.8 billion. To help ease this deficit, Kennedy planned to pressure the West German foreign minister, who was to meet with Kennedy on February 17, to make a commitment of foreign aid.

NATIONAL SECURITY ACTION MEMORANDUM NO. 11
February 6, 1961
MEMORANDUM FOR SECRETARY OF STATE

I would like to have more information on the progress of negotiations with the Germans on increasing their participation in foreign aid to the underdeveloped countries and to NATO. Is there any interdepartmental committee set up for this purpose with a representative from Defense, from the Treasury, under the chairmanship of State which carries the responsibility of unifying our approach to West Germany and indeed to Europe in general on aid, defense, and the balance of payment problems generally? If you are not wholly satisfied with the way the matter is being handled now, perhaps you could talk to Dillon and McNamara about it and I would ask Walt Rostow from here to serve as a liaison with that committee.

[12]

The same day Kennedy sent a memo to General Lyman L. Lemnitzer, chairman of the Joint Chiefs of Staff, concerning the current strength of U.S. troops in Vietnam.

NATIONAL SECURITY ACTION MEMORANDUM NO. 12
February 6, 1961
MEMORANDUM FOR GENERAL LEMNITZER

Is it possible for us to distribute the available forces we now have in Vietnam more effectively in order to increase the effectiveness of anti-guerrilla activities? Are there troops stationed along the border who could be made available for this activity? It is my recollection that the Vietnam army now numbers 150,000 and that we are planning to add 20,000 more, making a total of 170,000. Reports are that the guerrillas number from 7,000 to 15,000. I would think that the redistribution of available forces immediately would make them more effective in this work and we would not have to wait for action during the training period of the new troops. Would you give me your judgment on this when we meet.

[13]

In one of his concluding campaign speeches on November 2, 1960, Kennedy had spelled out the urgent need "to have the best Americans we can get to speak for our country abroad." The President encouraged exchange programs with countries behind the Iron Curtain as one way to broaden U.S. influence.

NATIONAL SECURITY ACTION MEMORANDUM NO. 13
February 6, 1961
MEMORANDUM FOR SECRETARY OF STATE

I would like to get a memorandum on the exchange of persons, programs behind the Iron Curtain, particularly with Poland and with Russia. What could we do to step them up?

[14]

*　　　　*　　　　*

The "checklist" that Kennedy sent to his personal secretary, Evelyn Lincoln, on February 8 was typical of a number of memos that he dictated to her during his administration. Among those mentioned in the February 8 memo are Massachusetts Representative William H. Bates, a member of the Joint Committee on Atomic Energy, and George A. Smathers, the senator from Florida (a close friend of both Kennedy and Johnson). Dr. John Hannah was chairman of the Civil Rights Commission.

Teno Roncalio would be made chairman of the U.S. section of the International Joint Commission between the United States and Canada. Allen J. Ellender, a Democratic senator from Louisiana, was the chairman of the Agriculture and Forestry Committee.

Heinrich von Brentano was the foreign minister authorized by West German Chancellor Konrad Adenauer to meet with Kennedy in discussions of the U.S. balance of payments deficit.

On the original memo the President made checkmarks in the left margin in front of each entry.

2/8/61

Miss Lincoln,

Remind me to call Bill Bates and thank him for his vote.

Ask Larry O'Brien to speak to me about what progress they are making in hiring Gene Robinson, whom Smathers is interested in.

Ask Arthur Schlesinger to [let] me consider his proposal of improving the ways in which the White House could communicate "a sense of genuine cultural concern." He may want to wait for his return from South America before doing this. Arthur Schlesinger should also talk to Ed Murrow before he goes, because he may have some thoughts about how USIA could be improved.

Ask Ralph Dungan and Kenny O'Donnell to speak to me about a substitute for Dr. Hannah on the Canadian-American joint board. Also ask Ralph Dungan to speak to me about what progress has been made on the Teno Roncalio appointment. If Teno isn't going to do it, we should consider Joe DeGugliemo.

Remind him [Dungan] to talk to Sarge [Sargent Shriver].

I would like to have George Bundy look at the material which

Ellender brought me on our status of [*sic*] NATO. It seems to me to be in extremely poor shape. I think it would be worthwhile to have some analysis made before I see Brentano to the extent of the German contribution in NATO and our criticism of the effort.

[15]

In a speech at Wittenberg College in Ohio on October 17, 1960, Kennedy had said, "And if we are to open employment opportunities in this country for members of all races and creeds, then the federal government must set an example." Soon after the President took office, he met with John Hannah, who urged Kennedy to exercise his executive authority rather than wait for legislative actions.

On February 8 a memo from Kennedy on this issue was sent to Theodore Sorensen, the President's special counsel and speech writer. In the memo the President refers to "Title III" of the Civil Rights Act of 1960. Title III required that "voting records and registration papers for all federal elections, including primaries, must be preserved for 22 months." According to the Civil Rights Act, the Attorney General had the power to order that voting records be turned over to "the office of the records' custodian."

February 8, 1961
MEMORANDUM FOR MR. SORENSEN

Dr. Hannah recommends that I put out a report that in ninety days I will analyze what can be done to improve the employment of Negroes by the Federal government. He feels that it would indicate my interest and put the matter on ice for awhile. Would you think about this and perhaps talk to him. Dr. Hannah also says that his lawyers advise him that we have the legal power to give the attorney general the right to intervene in cases—it doesn't require passage of Title III by the Congress.

[16]

Although Louis Harris had started an independent public opinion and market research company in 1956, during the 1960 presidential campaign he worked for Kennedy. In the primaries Harris's advice had helped Kennedy win a critical victory in the state of West Virginia. Counseling Kennedy before the televised debates with

Nixon, Harris had suggested that the senator have a "friendlier and warmer manner." He remained a trusted adviser in the early administration.

February 14, 1961
MEMORANDUM FOR ARTHUR SCHLESINGER

I have asked Kenny O'Donnell to turn over to you a memorandum Lou Harris prepared on a proposed electoral commission. I think this has a good deal of merit. Would you consider how best this would be done and then speak to me about it. Who the personnel would be. What areas they would cover. When their reports should be due. How we can make it bipartisan.

[17]

In an address to Congress on February 6 Kennedy had asked for ways to "solve the balance of payments problem by strengthening the domestic economy and expanding U.S. exports." Another measure for reducing the drain on dollars was by limiting the duty-free goods that foreigners could bring into the United States.

NATIONAL SECURITY ACTION MEMORANDUM NO. 18
February 15, 1961
MEMO FOR THE SECRETARY OF TREASURY

What exactly is the effect of our reduction from 500 to 100 dollars on the amount a tourist can bring in duty free? How much money is involved in these purchases and how much will it save abroad?

[18]

Florida Senator George A. Smathers, representing southern interests, supported restrictions on importation of tobacco and fruit.

NATIONAL SECURITY ACTION MEMORANDUM NO. 19
February 15, 1961
MEMO FOR MR. BUNDY

I know that Senator Smathers has suggested that cutting the importations of tobacco, vegetables, fruits, etc. from Cuba to the United States involves about $70 million. What is George Ball's judgment of this? Would it save us valuable dollars in gold reserves? Would it make things more difficult for Castro? Would it be in the public interest?

John Kennedy

[19]

Senators Albert A. Gore and C. Estes Kefauver, both from Tennessee, were ardent New Deal Democrats who stood together on many issues. A reformer suspicious of the goals of big business, Gore became a watchdog of Kennedy's administration and a crusader on many issues. Kefauver, since 1957 the chairman of the Subcommittee on Antitrust and Monopoly of the Judiciary Committee, had been one of Kennedy's chief backers during the presidential campaign.

February 15, 1961
MEMORANDUM FOR MR. LANDIS

Senators Kefauver and Gore inform me that there have been five increases in rates in the Tennessee Gas transmission without any action by the Federal Power Commission. Are they getting away with murder? If so, what can we do about it?

[20]

Although he had a Democratic majority in both houses, Kennedy did not have strong congressional support for many of his programs. Senate Majority Leader Mike Mansfield of Montana was usually an ally, however, and the President solicited Mansfield's advice on most congressional matters.

The "depression legislation" mentioned in the President's February 16 memo included measures to increase construction, to increase payments of veterans' life insurance dividends and food stamp projects in distressed areas, and to help the unemployed and aged.

February 16, 1961
MEMORANDUM FOR MR. BUNDY

Mike Mansfield suggested that no foreign aid bill be sent to the Capitol until we have disposed of this depression legislation. I think that is a rather good suggestion and will you pass that on to the State Department, particularly to the undersecretary of state for economic affairs.

[21]

The following day Bundy passed along the President's views to George Ball with the additional note: "It is hoped that the depression legislation can be handled speedily, but in any case no foreign aid bill should be sent without the President's explicit approval."

In 1950 the Chinese leader Chiang Kai-shek, who had led Nationalist Chinese troops against the Communists, had been driven from mainland China to Taiwan (Formosa). The recipient of massive military aid from the United States, Chiang subsequently led a number of incursions against the Chinese Communists on the China coast and eventually into Burma.

After sending the following memo to his secretary of state on February 16, the President announced an investigation of rumors that American arms were going to guerrillas on Burma's northern frontier.

February 17, 1961
MEMORANDUM FOR SECRETARY OF STATE

I note in the newspapers that the Burmese government has publicly objected to the fact that the Chinese irregulars in Northern Burma have been using new American equipment. I understand that we have indicated to them that we have not been able to bring influence to bear on Chiang Kai-shek. Query:

1. Is this report true?

2. What protests have we made to Chiang Kai-shek?

3. Should these protests be renewed on a stronger and higher level?

[22]

In *A Thousand Days* Arthur Schlesinger noted that Kennedy considered the balance of payments deficit one of the two things that "scared him most." The other was nuclear war.

NATIONAL SECURITY ACTION MEMORANDUM NO. 22
February 20, 1961
MEMORANDUM FOR THE SECRETARY OF STATE

In the wake of our discussions last week with the Germans and the British, I hope we can press on, as a matter of high priority, development of formulas for fair sharing in both foreign aid and military partnership with our European allies as well as with the arrangements that will ease the balance of payments problem of the United States and other deficit countries. We need to make rapid progress with these ideas in order to prepare the way for our efforts on behalf of foreign aid in Congress and with our own people. I know that George Ball has been making good progress in this area, and all I am saying is that I hope he will keep it up as a matter of urgency.

JFK

[23]

On February 22, after meeting with three former ambassadors to the Soviet Union, Kennedy asked the current ambassador, Llewellyn Thompson, to arrange a Kennedy-Khrushchev meeting in Vienna or Stockholm later that spring. Following is the invitation that Thompson delivered to Khrushchev on March 19. (It was declassified in October 1984.)

February 22, 1961

His Excellency
Nikita S. Khrushchev
Chairman of the Council of Ministers
   of the USSR
The Kremlin, Moscow

Dear Mr. Chairman:

I have had an opportunity, due to the return of Ambassador Thompson, to have an extensive review of all aspects of our relations with the Secretary of State and with him. In these consultations, we have been able to explore, in general, not only those subjects which are of direct bilateral concern to the United States and the Soviet Union, but also the chief outstanding international problems which affect our relations.

I have not been able, in so brief a time, to reach definite conclusions as to our position on all of these matters. Many of them are affected by developments in the international scene and are of concern to many other governments. I would, however, like to set before you certain general considerations which I believe might be of help in introducing a greater element of clarity in the relations between our two countries. I say this because I am sure that you are as conscious as I am of the heavy responsibility which rests upon our two Governments in world affairs. I agree with your thought that if we could find a measure of cooperation on some of these current issues this, in itself, would be a significant contribution to the problem of insuring a peaceful and orderly world.

I think we should recognize, in honesty to each other, that there are problems on which we may not be able to agree. However, I believe that while recognizing that we do not and in all probability will not share a common view on all of these problems, I do believe that the manner in which we approach them and, in particular, the manner in which our disagreements are handled can be of great importance.

In addition, I believe we should make more use of diplomatic channels for quiet informal discussion of these questions, not in the sense of negotiations (since I am sure that we both recognize the interests of other countries are deeply involved in these issues), but rather as a mechanism of communication which should, insofar as is possible, help to eliminate misunderstanding and unnecessary divergencies, however great the basic differences may be.

I hope it will be possible, before too long, for us to meet personally for an informal exchange of views in regard to some of these matters. Of course, a meeting of this nature will depend upon the general international situation at the time, as well as on our mutual schedules of engagements.

I have asked Ambassador Thompson to discuss the question of our meeting. Ambassador Thompson, who enjoys my full confidence, is also in a position to inform you of my thinking on a number of the international issues which we have discussed. I shall welcome any expression of your views. I hope such exchange might assist us in working out a responsible approach to our differences with the view to their ultimate resolution for the benefit of peace and security throughout the world. You may be sure, Mr. Chairman, that I intend to do everything I can toward developing a more harmonious relationship between our two countries.

Sincerely,

John F. Kennedy

[24]

(Thompson delivered Kennedy's invitation to the Soviet premier on March 9. Khrushchev's reaction was positive, and the President began making preliminary plans for a summit in Vienna which took place in June.)

After meetings of the Joint Chiefs of Staff (JCS), one of the members often prepared a classified memorandum for the file. The following memo—recording the President's views on counterguerrilla activities and actions in Vietnam—was not declassified until 1987.

The MAAG mentioned in the memo stands for the military assistance advisory groups. Also mentioned is the report of Democratic Representative Chet Holifield (California), who was chairman of the Joint Committee on Atomic Energy. He presided over the Joint Atomic Energy Special Radiation and Research and Development subcommittees that had heard testimony on the nuclear test ban during April 1960.

SECRET
February 24, 1961
MEMORANDUM FOR THE FILE

Essential points arising from JCS meeting with the President on Thursday, February 23, 1961.

1. The President wishes to have the maximum number of men trained for counter-guerrilla operations put into the areas of immediate concern.

2. He wishes to have the matter of operations in Vietminh territory pressed.

3. The JCS ought to review policy guidance on Latin America and orient it towards a deterrence of guerrilla operations and counter-guerrilla operations.

4. The Departments of State and Defense ought to consider new instructions to the relevant ambassadors on the urgency of counter-guerrilla operations.

5. The JCS should insure that the MAAGs are orienting their work in the relevant areas towards counter-guerrilla operations, using maximum influence on the local military.

6. State and Defense should look into the character of forces in Iran and decide whether they are appropriate to the military dangers which exist there.

7. The SEATO [Southeast Asia Treaty Organization] meeting should be oriented around this problem; the matter should be discussed with Mr. Rusk.

8. The JCS should read the Holifield report and be prepared to discuss the problem of nuclear weapons control.

[25]

(During the April 1960 hearings Holifield made a closing statement in which he concluded that detection—and therefore control —of underground nuclear testing would be extremely difficult. Holifield said there was no current control network that could detect a "non-muffled bomb explosion of 20 kilotons or less" or "muffled tests of 100 kilotons or more set off deep underground within large cavities." He foresaw "a race between improved means of detection and identification, as against improved means of concealing and muffling nuclear tests." The Holifield report concluded that a "vigorous and sustained'' research and development program was needed.)

Kennedy was concerned about an economic crisis building in Iran, and he was eager to initiate long-term diplomatic planning. His memo of March 5, 1961, was in the form of a reminder— probably to Bundy.

3/5/61
REMINDER

1. Speak to Secretary Rusk about the Ambassador to Iran and Harriman's mission to Iran and what our future plans are in regard to that.

2. Also speak to Secretary Rusk about the advisability of his and others talking to Professor [Kenneth R.] Hansen who is coming down to assist Dave Bell as Assistant Director of the Budget and who has been in charge of our economic planning in Iran for the Ford Foundation and we ought to arrange to see him and see what his view is of the situation. I understand he considers it critical.

[26]

In the Congo fighting broke out in early March between Sudanese troops serving in the United Nations' armed forces and Congolese soldiers. Four U.S. Navy ships that had been part of a ''goodwill force'' headed toward Cape Town, South Africa, were diverted toward the Congo.

NATIONAL SECURITY ACTION MEMORANDUM NO. 26
March 6, 1961
MEMORANDUM FOR: Secretary of State
Secretary of Defense

Did Ambassador [to the Republic of the Congo, Clare H.] Timberlake notify the Department before he requested the Admiral to turn around with his ships? Did the Admiral notify the Navy department before he acceded to the request? Neither department was informed before action was taken. Is this because of faulty communications or because of the procedures that were followed in this case? In view of the importance that this decision has been given, it seems that we should take action in the future to have an opportunity to review these decisions before they are finalized.

/s/ John F. Kennedy

[27]

After Castro's overthrow of the regime of Fulgencio Batista in 1958, a stream of exiled pro-Batista Cubans fled to the United States. They formed a political group, the Batistianos, largely based in the Miami area, that was intent on overthrowing the Castro regime. The second wave of exiles included a number of political leaders who were professionals, businessmen, or racketeers but had no strong alliance to either Batista or Castro.

NATIONAL SECURITY ACTION MEMORANDUM NO. 31
March 11, 1961
MEMORANDUM OF DISCUSSION ON CUBA, MARCH 11, 1961

The President directed that the following actions be taken:

1. Every effort should be made to assist patriotic Cubans in forming a new and strong political organization, and in conjunction with this effort a maximum amount of publicity buildup should be sought for the emerging political leaders of this organization, especially those who may be active participants in the military campaign of liberation. Action: Central Intelligence Agency.

2. The United States government must have ready a white paper on Cuba and should also be ready to give appropriate assistance to Cuban patriots in a similar effort. Action: Arthur Schlesinger in cooperation with the Department of State.

3. The Department of State will present recommendations with respect to a démarche in the Organization of American States, looking toward a united demand for prompt free elections in Cuba, with appropriate safeguards and opportunity for all patriotic Cubans. Action: Department of State.

4. The President expects to authorize U.S. support for an appropriate number of patriotic Cubans to return to their homeland. He believes that the best possible plan from the point of view of com-

bined military, political, and psychological considerations has not yet been presented, and new proposals are to be concerted promptly. Action: Central Intelligence Agency with appropriate consultation.

McGeorge Bundy

[28]

In late March the Kennedy administration took steps to open commercial air agreements with the Soviet Union.

SECRET
March 21, 1961
NATIONAL SECURITY ACTION MEMORANDUM NO. 32
TO: Secretary of State
SUBJECT: US/USSR commercial air transport agreement

The draft US/USSR commercial air transport agreement enclosed with your memorandum of March 17, 1961, is approved for transmittal to the Soviet government for its consideration. Prior to the initiation of the US/USSR negotiations on the draft agreement, I would like to have prepared for my approval a statement of the objectives to be sought and the general principles to be followed in the negotiations. Such a statement would serve as a guide to the negotiators in responding to Soviet counter-proposals as well as ensure that the negotiations are closely linked to our over-all relations to the USSR. Because of the major importance of an air agreement with the USSR—the opportunities as well as the risks —I should like to be kept fully informed of developments as they take place.

[29]

In a final meeting with Eisenhower on January 19 before assuming the presidency, Kennedy had been briefed on the situation in Laos. It was Eisenhower's belief that Laos was "the key to all Southeast Asia," the gateway to Vietnam and Thailand.

The Communist Pathet Lao, occupying northeastern Laos, were led by Prince Souphanouvong, who was closely allied to Ho Chi Minh in North Vietnam. To build resistance and strengthen the

Laotian right-wing forces, the Eisenhower administration had poured economic and military aid into the country.

In late March, in preparation for his meeting with Khrushchev, Kennedy requested further background on Laos directly from Defense Department sources. (The following memo remained classified until 1988.)

March 28, 1961
MEMORANDUM FOR
THE SECRETARY OF DEFENSE

The President would like a brief memorandum giving the breakdown of what went into Laos, year by year from 1954 on, in the form of military aid and, if it is relevant, economic aid. He mentioned the sum of $340 million.

He does not need details of equipment and supplies, but he would like to know an approximate breakdown of ammunition, old weapons, new weapons (in groups) and the heaviest weapons that we have given them.

He understands that we gave them the weapons, but the training mission—except for the technical use and upkeep of the weapons —was a French responsibility.

C. V. Clifton

[30]

In 1958 Eisenhower's Federal Advisory Council on the Arts secured a charter from Congress for a national cultural center to be built in Washington. The charter specified that land worth five million dollars near the Potomac River would be donated for the building, and a thirty-member board of trustees would be appointed to raise the necessary funds to build the center.

As of 1961, little progress had been made. According to the charter, if sufficient money were not raised within five years, the law would lapse, no center would be built, and the funds already collected would be given to the Smithsonian Institution.

The following memo urging Kennedy to take action was written by Letitia Baldrige, Jacqueline Kennedy's social secretary. Mrs. Jouett Shouse was the wife of a Washington lobbyist.

April 10, 1961

Mr. President:

Mrs. Jewctt [Jouett] Shouse called again today re The National Cultural Center. It seems they are waiting anxiously on

a) The President's choice for a Chairman of the Committee, and

b) Permission to use Mrs. Kennedy's name as Honorary Chairman of the Sponsors' Committee

It seems everyone is itching to get to work on the project—but without White House action of some kind—all is stalemated.

I mentioned this to Mrs. Kennedy, and she said you would cope perhaps.

Tish B.

[31]

(By mid-1963 insufficient funds had been raised for the Center, and Kennedy introduced a bill, which was passed in July, to give the trustees three more years. In December 1963, following Kennedy's assassination, President Johnson introduced a bill providing $15.5 million for the Kennedy Center for the Performing Arts.)

Kennedy set off a controversy that affected a number of military suppliers when he canceled development of nuclear-powered aircraft. In the April 7 issue of *Time* magazine, a report cited General Electric as challenging the President's decision. GE claimed that it could build a nuclear engine that would be ready for a test flight by 1963 "for less than one-fifth of the additional billion dollars mentioned by Kennedy."

April 12, 1961

MEMORANDUM FOR

The Honorable Roswell Gilpatric
Deputy Secretary of Defense

Your account of the General Electric fudging on the ANP [aircraft nuclear power] is conclusive, and the President asked that someone in your Department, perhaps Arthur Sylvester, write a letter promptly to *Time* Magazine straightening out General Electric. He feels very strongly about this, and now that the evidence is conclusive, I hope such a letter can be written promptly.

McGeorge Bundy

[32]

(The following day Secretary of Defense McNamara drafted a letter to Roy Alexander, editor of *Time*, urging him to "present to your readers the full story." The defense secretary analyzed in detail why the two systems considered for aircraft power plant development "would present severe operational and ground handling hazards, particularly in the event of a crash.")

Walt W. Rostow, deputy special assistant to the President for national security affairs, was a supporter of General Lansdale on policy matters. He believed that the United States should use all diplomatic and military means to halt communist insurgency in Vietnam. On April 12 Rostow urged Kennedy to send Special Forces advisers to Vietnam and "gear up" the whole operation.

The following memo from the President was sent to Bundy on April 14, the same date the Cuban Brigade embarked at Puerto Cabezas, Nicaragua, for the Bay of Pigs. Although General Maxwell Taylor was not yet a member of the president's staff, Kennedy sought his advice on military matters.

April 14, 1961

MEMORANDUM FOR MR. BUNDY

1. I believe that you, General Taylor, and Walt Rostow are all dissatisfied with our organizational set-up on Southeast Asia.

2. An example of this is a military mission going to Southeast [Asia], the purpose of which is rather vague in our minds.

3. Should we not propose to the Secretary of State a more precise organizational set-up with specific missions to do the kind of job that was done by Dean Acheson?

4. Who should we get to do it?

[33]

*   *   *

On April 17 Cuban exile Brigade 2506, consisting of about fifteen hundred men, attempted to achieve "tactical surprise" by landing at the Bay of Pigs in Cuba. When the invasion faltered, the leaders requested air support, which Kennedy denied. Most of the brigade—whose operations were directed by the CIA—were either captured or killed.

On April 18 the President wrote the following letter to Soviet Premier Khrushchev:

April 18, 1961

Dear Chairman:

You are under a serious misapprehension in regard to events in Cuba. For months there has been evident and growing resistance to the Castro dictatorship. More than 100,000 refugees have recently fled from Cuba into neighboring countries. Their urgent hope is naturally to assist their fellow Cubans in their struggle for freedom. Many of these refugees fought alongside Dr. Castro against the Batista dictatorship; among them are prominent leaders of his own original movement and government.

These are unmistakable signs that Cubans find intolerable the denial of democratic liberties and the subversion of the 26th of July Movement by an alien-dominated regime. It cannot be surprising that, as resistance within Cuba grows, refugees have been using whatever means are available to return and support their countrymen in the continuing struggle for freedom. Where people are denied the right of choice, recourse to such struggle is the only means of achieving their liberties.

I have previously stated, and I repeat now, that the United States intends no military intervention in Cuba. In the event of any military intervention by outside force we will immediately honor our obligations under the inter-American system to protect this hemisphere against external aggression. While refraining from military intervention in Cuba, the people of the United States do not conceal their admiration for Cuban patriots who wish to see a democratic system in an independent Cuba. The United States government can take no action to stifle the spirit of liberty.

I have taken careful note of your statement that the events in

Cuba might affect peace in all parts of the world. I trust that this does not mean that the Soviet government, using the situation in Cuba as a pretext, is planning to inflame other areas of the world. I would like to think that your government has too great a sense of responsibility to embark upon any enterprise so dangerous to general peace.

I agree with you as to the desirability of steps to improve the international atmosphere. I continue to hope that you will cooperate in opportunities now available to this end. A prompt cease-fire and peaceful settlement of the dangerous situation in Laos, cooperation with the United Nations in the Congo and a speedy conclusion of an acceptable treaty for the banning of nuclear tests would be constructive steps in this direction. The regime in Cuba could make a similar contribution by permitting the Cuban people freely to determine their own future by democratic processes and freely to cooperate with their Latin American neighbors.

I believe, Mr. Chairman, that you should recognize that free peoples in all parts of the world do not accept the claim of historical inevitability for Communist revolution. What your government believes is its own business; what it does in the world is the world's business. The great revolution in the history of man, past, present and future, is the revolution of those determined to be free.

Sincerely,

John F. Kennedy

[34]

At his National Security Council meeting on April 22, after the invasion was over, the President created a panel headed by retired General Maxwell Taylor to analyze the CIA's role in the operation. Subsequently Kennedy issued a number of security action memos related to the NSC meeting.

NSAM 41 indicates that the President believed the Bay of Pigs would have immediate repercussions in Soviet relations, possibly in Berlin.

SECRET

NATIONAL SECURITY ACTION MEMORANDUM NO. 41

April 25, 1961

TO: The Secretary of Defense

SUBJECT: Military planning for possible Berlin crisis

In approving the record of actions of the April 22, 1961, meeting of the National Security Council, the President requested that the Department of Defense report to him promptly on current military planning for a possible crisis over Berlin (NSC Action 2407B). Accordingly it is requested that the Department of Defense prepare a report on the above subject as soon as possible for transmittal to the President through this office.

McGeorge Bundy

[35]

Kennedy's failure to provide second-wave support for the landing brigade brought condemnation from Cuban exile leaders in the United States. A memo directed to Abraham A. Ribicoff, secretary of health, education, and welfare, and to the director of the CIA, Allen Dulles, was concerned with future handling of refugee questions.

NATIONAL SECURITY ACTION MEMORANDUM NO. 42

April 25, 1961

TO: The Secretary of Health, Education and Welfare

The Director of the Central Intelligence Agency

SUBJECT: Assistance to Cuban refugees

In approving the record of actions of the April 22, 1961, meeting of the National Security Council, the President directed that levels of support for Cuban refugees should be reported to him for recommendations for their improvement (NSC Action 2406C). The President also expressed his desire that such support should be open and overt. In addition, he directed that the adjustment of Cubans to life in the United States should be given particular attention by the Department of Health, Education and Welfare. Accordingly it is requested that the Secretary of Health, Education and Welfare and the Director of the Central Intelligence Agency submit a report to this office on these matters as soon as possible together with such recommendations for the attention of the President as they deem appropriate.

McGeorge Bundy

[36]

In a later report on the Cuban exiles in the United States, Secretary of Defense Robert McNamara estimated that thirty-five hundred males were of "military ages of 17 to 26" and therefore eligible for the draft.

NATIONAL SECURITY ACTION MEMORANDUM NO. 43
April 25, 1961
TO: The Secretary of State
    The Secretary of Defense
SUBJECT: Secret training of Cuban nationals

In approving the record of actions of the April 22, 1961, meeting of the National Security Council, the President directed that the question of possible forms of large-scale open enlistment of Cuban nationals should be studied by the Departments of State and Defense (NSC Action 2406D). Accordingly it is requested that the above agencies undertake this study as soon as possible and present their recommendations to the President through this office.

McGeorge Bundy

[37]

(In a June 8 memorandum for the President, McNamara responded: "There are some legal barriers to the enlistment of aliens in the U.S. armed forces. These barriers, however, do not prevent their voluntary induction if they are between the ages of 18–26. It is therefore planned to make use of the existing mechanisms of the U.S. Selective Service System to provide special quotas for induction into the three services of Cuban volunteers in this age group as they become identified and available.")

Although Premier Fidel Castro clearly identified the United States and the CIA as the culprits in the Bay of Pigs invasion, Kennedy foresaw that the leader would step up Cuban efforts to make incursions into Caribbean nations.

NATIONAL SECURITY ACTION MEMORANDUM NO. 44
April 25, 1961
TO: The Secretary of State
   The Secretary of Defense
SUBJECT: Caribbean Security Agency

In approving the record of actions of the April 22, 1961, meeting of the National Security Council, the President directed that the possibility be studied of creating a Caribbean Security Agency to which we and other Caribbean countries would contribute forces and to whom any nation attacked could appeal for help (NSC Action 2046H). Accordingly it is requested that the Secretary of State and Secretary of Defense undertake this study as soon as possible, presenting their preliminary views at the next National Security Council meeting.

McGeorge Bundy

[38]

Kennedy also assumed that U.S. actions in the Bay of Pigs would lead to increased activity of pro-Castro Cuban agents inside the borders of the United States.

NATIONAL SECURITY ACTION MEMORANDUM NO. 45
April 25, 1961
TO: The Attorney General
   The Director of CIA
SUBJECT: Coverage of Castro activities in the United States

In approving the record of actions of the April 22, 1961, meeting of the National Security Council, the President noted that the Department of Justice and the Central Intelligence Agency would examine the possibility of stepping up coverage of Castro activities in the United States (NSC Action 2406I). Accordingly, it is recommended that the above agencies undertake this study as soon as possible and present their recommendations for the President's approval.

McGeorge Bundy

[39]

(In a memo on June 10 to Bundy, CIA Director Allen Dulles noted that "coverage of Castro activities in the United States is the primary responsibility of the Department of Justice." Dulles added that he had "supplemented" this coverage by "implementing action through CIA facilities abroad and in the United States." He told Bundy that the program had been coordinated with the Federal Bureau of Investigation, and "it is not anticipated that CIA implementation will entail recommendations requiring the President's approval.")

When it was confirmed in the United Nations that the CIA had backed the invasion, foreign reaction ranged from outrage to endorsement of U.S. actions. Kennedy took the reactions of Latin American neighbors as a sign of pro- or anti-U.S. sentiments.

NATIONAL SECURITY ACTION MEMORANDUM NO. 46
April 25, 1961
TO: The Secretary of State
SUBJECT: Attitude of various governments during the Cuban crisis

In approving the record of actions of the April 22, 1961, meeting of the National Security Council, the President requested that he and the Vice President be informed promptly as to which governments have been helpful in various parts of the Cuban crisis and which have been unhelpful (NSC Action 2406K). Accordingly it is requested that the Department of State present the above information as soon as possible to this office for transmittal to the President and the Vice President.

McGeorge Bundy

[40]

* * *

Though the possibility that war would result from the invasion seemed remote, Kennedy was concerned about the level of defense preparedness of the United States.

NATIONAL SECURITY ACTION MEMORANDUM NO. 48
April 25, 1961
TO: The Secretary of Defense
  The Director, Office of Civil and Defense Mobilization [OCDM]
SUBJECT: Level of U.S. efforts, military and foreign policy, civil defense, paramilitary

In approving the record of action of the April 22, 1961, meeting of the National Security Council, the President noted:

1. That the Department of Defense would review its military budget in the light of the discussion at the council meeting of possible changes in the level of U.S. effort in the fields of military activity, foreign policy, civil defense, and paramilitary activities, and;

2. That the Special Assistant to the President for National Security Affairs would expedite the study of the civil defense posture of the U.S. now being undertaken in consultation with the Department of Defense and the OCDM (NSC Action 2047A).

McGeorge Bundy

[41]

(On June 13 General Maxwell Taylor sent a letter to the President stating that Castro's "continued presence within the hemispheric community as a dangerously effective exponent of Communism and anti-Americanism constitutes a real menace capable of eventually overthrowing the elected governments in any one or more of weak Latin American republics." Taylor recommended "that the Cuban situation be reappraised in the light of all presently known factors and new guidance be provided for political, military, economic and propaganda action against Castro.")

At the executive meeting of the AFL-CIO in June, President George Meany was challenged by A. Philip Randolph, president of the Brotherhood of Sleeping Car Porters, the only African-American on the executive council. Randolph accused the AFL-CIO of "tokenism in human rights," and he made a motion to expel local unions that practiced discrimination against blacks. In the following letter from Kennedy to George Meany, the President cautiously suggested that the AFL-CIO support "the ideal of full equality in American society"—in other words, nondiscrimination in union practices.

June 28, 1961

George Meany
President
American Federation of Labor and Congress of Industrial
   Organizations
Unity House, Pennsylvania

Dear President Meany:

I have asked Secretary [of Labor Arthur] Goldberg to bring to you and to members of the Executive Council of the AFL-CIO my warm greetings and best wishes.

You meet together at an hour of great change and challenge, not only in affairs of traditional labor concern but in the broad structure of modern history itself.

As we in America seek to complete our own Revolution by dignifying human life with the material securities we produce and the spiritual freedoms we protect, the mass of the world's people embark on their own economic and social awakening from the long slumber of the past.

In such an era, the foreign policy of the United States is both a spokesman and an instrument for freedom. The support that the trade union movement has historically given to our foreign policy is one of the great satisfactions and strengths of our democratic government. In my meetings with the heads of state of many nations, including the Soviet Union, the knowledge that so powerful and important a segment of our society—and one that embodies many of the ideals most recognizable and appealing to the world's underprivileged—stood firmly for the policies enunciated on behalf of all Americans was a source of confidence.

Such unity of purpose and singularity of goal is a valuable asset to every free government. Patently necessary in our relations with other nations, such unity is equally desirable within our free institutions here at home.

I have welcomed and appreciated the support you have given to programs such as the Area Redevelopment Act, the Minimum Wage Law, the Temporary Extended Unemployment Compensation Act and others that are now law—as well as your announced support of proposals still before the Congress in the fields of unemployment compensation, manpower and training, housing, aid to education, medical aid to the aged, and others intended to improve our national life.

We have now emerged from the recession, but many economic problems will continue to confront us and demand our best efforts. In addition, the ideal of full equality in American society is still unattained.

We are moving toward an era of expanded economic growth and intensified individual effort to meet the demands of freedom in a gravely troubled world. This gathering of strength and marshalling of purpose demands, above all else, the shared conviction that the national welfare is the matter of first concern, and the shared belief that by recognizing a mutual interest, an individual interest can also be advanced.

> Sincerely,
> John F. Kennedy

[42]

During the Bay of Pigs operation Kennedy believed that he had been poorly informed by the Joint Chiefs of Staff. As it turned out, the Joint Chiefs were inaccurate about the preparedness of the U.S.-led Cuban brigade and the size of the Cuban Air Force. During the operation it became apparent that the President had also been misled about the terrain of the landing area and the probabilities of success.

NATIONAL SECURITY ACTION MEMORANDUM NO. 55
June 28, 1961
TO: The Chairman, Joint Chiefs of Staff
SUBJECT: Relations of the Joint Chiefs of Staff to the
            President in cold war operations

I wish to inform the Joint Chiefs of Staff as follows with regard to my views of their relations to me in cold war operations:

a. I regard the Joint Chiefs of Staff as my principal military adviser responsible both for initiating advice to me and for responding to requests for advice. I expect their advice to come to me direct and unfiltered.

b. The Joint Chiefs of Staff have a responsibility for the defense of the nation in the cold war similar to that which they have in conventional hostilities. They should know the military and paramilitary forces and resources available to the Department of Defense, verify their readiness, report on their adequacy, and make appropriate recommendations for their expansion and improvement. I look to the Chiefs to contribute dynamic and imaginative leadership in contributing to the success of the military and paramilitary aspects of cold war programs.

c. I expect the Joint Chiefs of Staff to present the military viewpoint in governmental councils in such a way as to assure that the military factors are clearly understood before decisions are reached. When only the chairman or a single chief is present, that officer must represent the Chiefs as a body taking such preliminary and subsequent actions as may be necessary to assure that he does in fact represent the corporate judgment of the Joint Chiefs of Staff.

d. While I look to the Chiefs to present the military factor without reserve or hesitation, I regard them to be more than military men and expect their help in fitting military requirements into the overall context of any situation, recognizing that the most difficult problem in government is to combine all assets in a unified, effective pattern.

John F. Kennedy

[43]

With increased tension in the Caribbean and in Southeast Asia, the President did not want to rely entirely on the CIA for paramilitary and counterinsurgency forces. NSAM 56 to McNamara authorized the Defense Department to begin building unconventional military forces.

SECRET
June 28, 1961
NATIONAL SECURITY ACTION MEMORANDUM NO. 56
TO: The Secretary of Defense
SUBJECT: Evaluation of paramilitary requirements

The President has approved the following paragraph: ''It is important that we anticipate now our possible future requirements in the field of unconventional warfare and paramilitary operations. A first step would be to inventory the paramilitary assets we have in the United States Armed Forces, consider various areas in the world where the implementation of our policy may require indigenous paramilitary forces, and thus arrive at a determination of the goals which we should set in this field. Having determined the assets and the possible requirements, it would then become a matter of developing a plan to meet the deficit.''

The President requests that the Secretary of Defense in coordination with the Department of State and the CIA make such an estimate of requirements and recommend ways and means to meet these requirements.

McGeorge Bundy

[44]

(In response to the memo, Deputy Secretary of Defense Gilpatric submitted three reports to General Taylor's office. The papers were ''Defense Resources for Unconventional Warfare,'' ''Unconventional Warfare Resources—Southeast Asia,'' and ''Indigenous Paramilitary Forces.'')

On June 28 Kennedy publicly declared that Soviet Premier Khrushchev must ''accept the principle of self-determination in Berlin and in all Europe if negotiation on the Berlin issue is to be 'profitable.' '' The same day an official gazette in East Germany decreed that all foreign aircraft flying over East Germany must register with an East German air safety center. The declaration was rejected by the U.S. State Department, which said East Germany could not impose curbs on air travel.

SECRET
June 30, 1961
MEMORANDUM FOR THE DIRECTOR, OCDM

In connection with current study of alternative courses of action regarding Berlin, the President wishes you to submit recommendations concerning additional measures which might be taken to reduce the vulnerability of the U.S. civilian population to nuclear attack, by March 15, 1961 [sic].

These recommendations should be submitted to the Secretary of State so that they may be coordinated with other studies relating to Berlin and fitted into an integrated timetable of actions designed for maximum deterrent effect.

Assumptions about the policy framework within which these recommendations are to be developed may be secured from Assistant Secretary of State Foy Kohler.

McGeorge Bundy

[45]

In a Bureau of Intelligence and Research report on Iran issued in June, the State Department noted that a nationalist regime in Iran would press for the withdrawal of that country from the Central Treaty Organization (CENTO) alliance. Simultaneously Pakistan, which was a member of the Southeast Asia Treaty Organization (SEATO), protested that the United States was increasing its military assistance to India while reducing aid to Pakistan. Pakistan's President Muhammad Ayub Khan was scheduled to visit Washington on July 11.

July 5, 1961
MEMORANDUM FOR SECRETARY OF STATE

I note that you have requested a study of any promises which may have been made or implied at the time of the formation of SEATO and CENTO. I understand Iran and Pakistan say they have received less support than they had been promised. Have you had any results of this study? This is particularly important because of the Pakistani visit.

[46]

In March David E. Bell, director of the Bureau of the Budget, had explained to the Congressional Joint Economic Committee that it would be impossible to avoid a $2.8 billion deficit. When the proposed 1962 budget drew fire from Congress, the budget director received the following memo from Kennedy:

July 5, 1961
MEMORANDUM FOR DAVE BELL

I would appreciate it very much if you would prepare a memorandum for the Members of Congress and the Democrats generally on the budget and the expenditures of money as compared with the Eisenhower administration. I am attaching a memorandum which I have received from Secretary Dillon on this subject.

[47]

When Guinea achieved independence from France in 1958, the independence movement was led by Sékou Touré, a left-wing trade union leader. Eisenhower subsequently withdrew all aid to Guinea, and Touré turned to the Soviet Union for assistance. Kennedy had met with Touré when he visited the United States in 1959, and the President hoped to improve future relations with Guinea.

MEMORANDUM FOR SECRETARY OF STATE

[Peace Corps Director Sargent] Shriver reported to me that Sékou Touré's government accepted without any qualifications 9 of the 10 points in our recent foreign aid package. The only point on which there was any hesitancy was the location of the proposed dam. Shriver believes it is essential for us to go through with the aid program for the following reasons:
1. Sékou Touré gave Shriver a completely enthusiastic reception and in three public speeches Touré himself pledged his independence

of Moscow and his enthusiasm for the United States. "Vive le Presidente," etc. were words he used at the end of his speeches. Sékou Touré's speeches, the reception he gave to Shriver, the radio and newspaper publicity in Guinea all are unprecedented changes in Guinea's attitude to our country.

2. Ghana has accepted 50 to 70 Peace Corps volunteers. Guinea is asking for 40 to 60 road builders and engineers from the Peace Corps. If we can successfully crack Ghana and Guinea, Mali may even turn to the West. If so, these would be the first Communist-oriented countries to turn from Moscow to us.

3. The President's [Touré's] reaction to Shriver in Guinea was enthusiastic, even in neighboring states. There seemed to be no animosity in the western-oriented African states.

4. Sékou Touré would definitely like to be invited to come to the United States. If the famous African ballet from Guinea could be invited simultaneously it might add a great deal to the invitation.

I have asked Shriver to talk to you, Senator Fulbright, and Senator Gore, Chairman of the Subcommittee on Africa.

[48]

(In October 1962 Touré visited the President, was introduced to Jacqueline and Caroline Kennedy, and attended a White House meeting and formal luncheon in his honor. Upon his return to Guinea, Touré reported that Kennedy was "a man quite open to African problems and determined to promote the American contribution to their happy solution.")

The increase of cold war tension, particularly linked to Berlin, prompted the President to send the following memo to his national security adviser.

July 5, 1961

MEMORANDUM FOR MR. BUNDY

I think we should ask the Civil Defense people to come next week with an emergency program. What could we do in the next six months that would improve the population's chances of surviving if a war should break out? What should we ask the citizens to do at this time and what should be required of them in case of attack?

[49]

(A memo was subsequently prepared for Bundy by Marcus G. Raskin, former adviser to the Congressional Liberal Project Group and a member of the Special Staff of the National Security Council. Raskin strongly objected to tying the civil defense buildup to the situation in Berlin. "After looking through the morass of suggestions that have been made on civil defense," wrote Raskin, "I think that we should be very hard nosed and stop kidding ourselves about the effects of certain kinds of civil defense programs." Noting that there were many reasons why civil defense would be inadequate and ineffective, Raskin concluded, "A large-scale civil defense program, rationally and comprehensively planned, would, in fact, change the character of our society so that it became an authoritarian and regimented one.")

In early July Kennedy began to examine the consequences of a rapid and massive troop buildup in Berlin.

SECRET
July 10, 1961
MEMORANDUM FOR THE SECRETARY OF DEFENSE

I don't know whether the President mentioned this to you during your visit to Hyannis Port on Saturday or not, but he has asked us to get him a prompt answer to the following questions:

"If we mobilize a million men (thinking of the Berlin situation), what would we do with them—how many would be combat troops, how many would be logistic support units, etc.? Would we send the million to Europe, how long would it take to get them over, how many ships, if by sea, how many would we plan to send by plane? How many days would it take to get all of them there? Where would they be positioned in Europe when they get there?"

The President does not desire a lengthy staff study, but understands that a good deal of this data is probably available, and, as he expressed it, "would like to have someone spend about a half day on the answers to these questions."

McGeorge Bundy

[50]

In the Dominican Republic on May 30, dictator Rafael Trujillo was gunned down by a group of disgruntled army officers. In the change of government, power fell into the hands of Joaquín Balaguer, who had served under Trujillo, and the dictator's son Ramfis Trujillo. The following memo was addressed to Robert F. Woodward in the Department of State.

July 10, 1961
MEMORANDUM FOR SECRETARY WOODWARD

Do we have any evidence of Communist activity or Castro activity in the Dominican Republic today? Have they infiltrated the "popular Dominican movement?" Which refugees have come back and what are their political histories? I want to make sure that our people there are the best people we can get, that their judgment is good, and that they are not emotionally committed to one group or another and not carrying out a crusade for anything but the United States. Would you check and give me your assurances that those are the kind of people we have, because a great deal will depend on their judgment. We don't want to have another Cuba to come out of the Dominican Republic.

Previous to your return, I stated that our objective was (1) have a democracy, and, (2) to continue the present situation.

I also said that if we could not have a democracy with some hope of survival, I would rather continue the present situation than to have a Castro dictatorship. That is our policy, and we want to make sure that in attempting to secure democracy we don't end up with a Castro Communist island.

We should indicate that we are opposed to permitting refugees to come back from Cuba or any Communist controlled country. I note this is what Balaguer said but we should indicate our approval. I want to watch this situation carefully and get a copy of all important reports coming in.

[51]

In early July the President sent messages to the rulers of Jordan, Saudi Arabia, Lebanon, Iraq, and the UAR stating: "The American government and people . . . are willing to help resolve the tragic Palestinian refugee problem on the basis of repatriation and compensation of property." He offered U.S. assistance "in finding an equitable answer to the question of Jordan River water-resource development." His letters received a very cool reception from leaders in the Middle East. In the wake of criticism, Kennedy fired off a memo to his national security adviser:

July 10, 1961
MEMORANDUM FOR MR. BUNDY

I want a report from the State Department. I asked Secretary Rusk about this, on whose idea it was for me to send letters to the Middle Eastern Arab leaders. The reaction has been so sour I would like to know whose idea it was, what they hoped to accomplish, and what they think we have now accomplished.

[52]

In May, during his fact-finding mission to Asia, Vice President Lyndon Johnson held talks in Taipeh, with Nationalist Chinese President Chiang Kai-shek. At a news conference on May 15 the Chinese leader said Johnson "had given him an unconditional pledge of continued U.S. support for Nationalist China."

July 10, 1961
MEMORANDUM FOR MR. BUNDY

I believe the proposed answer prepared for Lyndon Johnson by the State Department is hopeless. I am shocked that it could be approved by them. I can imagine nothing more irritating to Chiang Kai-shek and it indicates how careful we must be with their proposals. I think the proposed reply that I am sending Chiang Kai-shek is a good answer. Will you plan to go over it with me?

[53]

During his tour of Southeast Asia in May, Vice President Johnson repeatedly told leaders that the United States would stand by its commitments to honor military agreements. In Pakistan he reiterated the U.S. pledge of support "for Asian efforts to combat subversion, infiltration and terror." In Manila Johnson told a joint session of the Philippine Congress: "America will honor her commitments to the cause of freedom throughout the community of free nations."

In his memo to Bundy following Johnson's tour, Kennedy makes reference to Carlos P. Romulo, an elder statesman in the Philippine government who served under President Diosdado Macapagal.

July 10, 1961

MEMO FOR BUNDY

We have been consistently attacked by the Filipinos for our failure to "stand up to the Communists in Asia." This seems to be almost a campaign. It was particularly pronounced when Vice President Johnson was there and I notice that another statement is quoted by the Philippine ambassador to Nationalist China. These attacks may be part of a pattern. I am wondering if anyone has any suggestions as to what counter we could make, whether we could indicate to Romulo after we had collected all of them, with our displeasure with them.

I would like to know how many troops the Philippines contributed to the Korean war. My recollection is they offered only 180 to Planned 5 [sic] for Laos. I think we should find out (1) Why they are making these attacks and (2) Do something about them.

The New York Times story about the discontent in Asia, which mentions particularly Pakistan and Nationalist China as well as the Philippines, doesn't make as clear as I would like the reasons for the Nationalist China and the Pakistan attacks. This is a propaganda war against us and we ought to see how we could make that known. The only one that is somewhat more inexplicable is the Philippines.

[54]

Chinese Nationalists under Chiang Kai-shek were unalterably opposed to admission of both Communist China and Outer Mongolia to the United Nations. In late July after conferences at the White House, President Kennedy pledged to back Nationalist China's admission to the UN and to oppose that of the Red Chinese. Dr.

Thomas W. I. Liao, who is mentioned in the Kennedy memo, was an anti-Chiang Kai-shek, anticommunist Formosan nationalist who had requested an entry visa to the United States.

July 10, 1961

MEMORANDUM FOR MR. BUNDY

1. Adlai [Stevenson, U.S. ambassador to the UN] seems to endorse the idea of Maury Howard having Madame Chiang Kai-shek over here. I think she would be too tricky when she's here and would work against us. We should ask to have him send someone over direct.

2. I think we should try to hold up the Liao visit. We don't have to prove our point during this difficult summer. Will you talk to them over there in the State Department and if the visa hasn't been issued, let's just tell them we can't do it until later in the year or something. But let's not have him come now.

3. I think we should slow up on Outer Mongolia for the time being. We don't have to rush into that. It may be that we may not want to do the actual recognition until after the UN session, but our important job now is to persuade the Chinese Nationalists not to veto their admission to the UN. And it may be that we could do that better if we haven't already recognized them.

[55]

On June 10 John J. McCloy, Kennedy's special adviser on disarmament, began talks with Soviet Deputy Minister Valerian A. Zorin to consider the composition, date, and site of a proposed disarmament conference. On June 21 Khrushchev warned that the Soviet Union would resume nuclear testing immediately if the United States resumed its test program. A week after Khrushchev's warning, Kennedy ordered a scientific inquiry to explore for evidence that the USSR might have conducted tests in violation of the moratorium established in 1958.

July 10, 1961

MEMORANDUM FOR MR. BUNDY

What about the disarmament talks of McCloy? Should we break them off using the recent Soviet increases as our argument and ask that the matter be taken to the UN? Stevenson thinks that the UN emphasis on disarmament is most important. Can you arrange for me to see General Cline before he goes back?

[56]

(The reference is probably to Dr. Ray S. Cline, who served as director of the U.S. Naval Auxiliary Communications Center in Taipei from 1958 to 1962, when he was appointed deputy director for intelligence in the CIA. Though not a general, Cline had served in the OSS during World War II.)

As the Portuguese territory of Angola began to make strides toward self-determination, Portuguese Premier António de Oliveira Salazar implemented military measures to combat what he called "Angolan violence and savagery."

In a UN Security Council meeting, the United States voted with eight other nations to approve a resolution calling on Portugal to halt "severely repressive measures" in Angola.

SECRET
NATIONAL SECURITY ACTION MEMORANDUM NO. 60
July 14, 1961
TO: The Secretary of State
SUBJECT: U.S. actions in relation to Portuguese territories in Africa

The President reviewed the report of the Presidential Task Force on Portuguese territories in Africa dated July 12, 1961, and approved the following recommendations for action:

1. Send a special envoy to Portugal to talk with Salazar and inform him the U.S. is convinced Portugal must without delay institute basic and far-reaching reforms for her African territories. The scope of these reforms should be such as to lead eventually to self-determination. Inform the UK and Franco in advance and Spain when the action is taken.

2. Consult with the UK and France concerning further coordinated pressure on Salazar.

3. Explore with the Vatican, Spain and Brazil the possibility of their interceding with the Portuguese.

4. Begin immediately to formulate a U.S. course of action to be used in connection with the Portuguese African territories problem in the U.N.

5. Unless the results of step one above make it unnecessary or undesirable, raise the problem in the African subcommittee of NATO and subsequently in the NAC [North Atlantic Council] with the objective of impressing upon Portugal the importance attached by its NATO allies to the need for a major change in its colonial policy.

6. Make all possible efforts to ensure that MAP [military assistance program] equipment supplied to Portugal is not being diverted to Africa in contravention of existing agreements.

7. Deny authorization of licenses for the commercial export of arms from the U.S. to either side.

8. Expand U.S. assistance to refugees suffering from the Angolan conflict.

9. Expand the U.S. educational programs for Africans from the Portuguese areas.

10. Provide U.S. economic assistance primarily in the form of manpower training to help develop the technical and administrative skills of the Africans essential in the event reforms are introduced.

11. If Salazar embarks upon a more liberal colonial policy, grant reasonable requests for economic assistance in accordance with existing commitments.

12. Implement the foregoing quietly insofar as possible and in a manner designed to bring about basic and far-reaching reforms in Portuguese colonial policy and to minimize the possibility of losing the Azores.

Accordingly it is requested that the Department of State initiate the appropriate actions in collaboration with the other responsible agencies to carry out the recommended actions. It is further requested that the President be kept informed through this office of significant developments in the implementation of these recommendations.

Signed,
McGeorge Bundy

[57]

The President asked his advisers' opinions for a slogan that would counteract "the Soviet Union's propaganda campaign."

NATIONAL SECURITY ACTION MEMORANDUM NO. 61
July 14, 1961
OFFICIAL USE ONLY
TO: The Secretary of Defense
   The Director, U.S. Information Agency
SUBJECT: An effective countertheme to "Peaceful Coexistence"

The President completely endorses the effort to combat the Soviet propaganda trap contained in the phrase "Peaceful Coexistence" by the use of symbolic language that expresses our view of the nature of the conflict in which we are engaged. The statements by the Secretary of State before the Senate Foreign Relations Committee and, more recently, at the press club, have provided the language we need to do the job. He has expressed the conflict as being between "The World of Free Choice and Free Cooperation" and "The World of Coercion." The President has requested that immediate steps be taken to give this formulation the widespread currency and usage that would make it an effective countertheme to the Soviet formula. It is requested that the facilities available to the Department of State and the U.S. Information Agency be employed in this effort. This request is also being passed along to the appropriate members of the White House Staff for action.

                              Signed,
                              McGeorge Bundy
                                                      [58]

(On July 19 Schlesinger discussed the possible use of "Peaceful World Community." He noted, "In Russian I understand the words for 'peaceful' and 'world' are identical, which would make our proposed slogan very clumsy indeed." Schlesinger also observed that the word "community" was too close to "communism" in many languages, and he recommended finding another countertheme.)

NSAM 62 on the deepening Berlin crisis provides a summary of decisions reached by Kennedy after the July 19 NSC meeting. The

European leaders named in paragraph one were Chancellor of the Federal Republic of Germany (West Germany) Konrad Adenauer, French President Charles de Gaulle, and British Prime Minister Harold Macmillan.

TOP SECRET
NATIONAL SECURITY ACTION MEMORANDUM NO. 62
July 24, 1961
TO: The Secretary of State
    The Secretary of the Treasury
    The Secretary of Defense
    The Attorney General
    The Director, Bureau of the Budget
    The Director of Central Intelligence
    The Director, U.S. Information Agency
SUBJECT: Berlin

Following the National Security Council meeting on Wednesday, July 19, the President approved the following for further guidance and instructions of the heads of the responsible departments and agencies:

1. *Political*

The President and the Secretary of State have carefully reviewed together the political situation relating to Berlin, and their position is being stated in Presidential messages to Macmillan, DeGaulle, and Adenauer. The President's views will be further developed in his address to the nation July 25.*

2. *Military*

The President has authorized a prompt strengthening of the United States military position in the light of the general international situation. While the steps immediately authorized are related to improvement of U.S. capabilities in the next twelve months, the President considers these decisions to be steps in a continuing pro-

---

*In the televised address to the nation on July 25, Kennedy said, "We cannot and will not permit the Communists to drive us out of Berlin, either gradually or by force. For the fulfillment of our pledge to that city is essential to the morale and the security of Western Germany, to the unity of Western Europe, and to the faith of the whole free world. . . ."

gram for strengthening the armed forces. He expects at a later date to review further proposals from the Secretary of Defense relating to the long-term military position of the U.S.

The President intends that all possible steps be taken without a present call for major ground units of the Reserve or the National Guard to give the U.S. the capability of deploying as many as six additional divisions and supporting air units to Europe at any time after January 1, 1962, that the international situation may warrant it. In connection with an operating decision to effect such a deployment, further measures will be taken to maintain adequate ground forces in the United States.

In pursuit of this decision, the President has directed the submission to the Congress of proposals for appropriative and other legislative authority necessary for this program without the present declaration of a national emergency.

In particular, the President has authorized a request for increases amounting to $3.2 billion in new obligational authority. The measure is approved. . . . The President directed that negotiations be undertaken immediately with our allies looking toward their parallel participation in such a higher level of military readiness. In these discussions there will be no initial indication of any U.S. willingness to increase military assistance to our allies for these purposes.

3. *Economic*

The President approved the policy set forth in Annex B of the report of July 18 with regard to economic sanctions in the event of interference with access to West Berlin and authorized immediate negotiations with our major allies on such a policy.

The President directed the preparation of a tax proposal to be presented first in his radio address of July 25. He decided that a decision on a request for stopgap control legislation should be deferred until the latter part of August.

4. *Information*

The President assigned to the director of the U.S. Information Agency the responsibility for coordinating the information activities of the U.S. government capable of advancing international understanding of the U.S. position on Berlin.

Signed,

McGeorge Bundy

[59]

A July 26 memorandum touched on five topics requiring the attention of the secretary of state.

Kennedy was preparing to send Edmund Gullion, a trusted Foreign Service officer, as ambassador to the Congo, where the Congolese leader Moise Tshombe was threatening the secession of mineral-rich Katanga Province.

In the Dominican Republic President Joaquín Balaguer demanded the extradition of General R. L. Trujillo, Jr., brother of the slain dictator. Kennedy considered sending Robert D. Murphy, a former State Department official, to negotiate with the new government.

The Tunisian ambassador to the United States, Habib Bourguiba, Jr., was challenging the United States to demonstrate its anticolonialist views by supporting Tunisia against France.

In Geneva a fourteen-nation conference of the International Control Commission had met to discuss "peace and neutrality" in Laos. Kennedy hoped that the talk would lead to assurances that General Phoumi Nosavan's government would remain neutral. (In a meeting with the President in late June, Phoumi had assured the President that he would not allow Laos to be brought "under communist domination.")

July 26, 1961

MEMORANDUM FOR SECRETARY OF STATE

1. I feel that we should review the situation in the Congo. I have asked the Senate Foreign Relations Committee to speed up the Gullion hearing. What should be our policy on the Parliamentary meetings? Should we talk to the Belgians in regard to Katanga?

2. The CIA had a report that the Balaguer [people] seemed distraught as they were counting on us to put pressure on Trujillo.

Should we ask Bob Murphy to go down there for a couple of days and talk to the powers that be and make a report on his findings?

3. I note in the New York Times that Bourguiba is extremely angry at the United States and at me on the ground that we have let him down. The Baker story in the Times said that our embassies had not received any instructions from us in the last few days. How could they have found out about this?

4. We should come to definite conclusions with the Red Chinese admission question this week as we are having conversations with the Formosa representatives next week. Should the UN Council make it an "important" question to be placed on the calendar in October, at the conclusion of our Paris meeting?

5. We should have a meeting at the top on the question of Laos and Vietnam. I am concerned about Phoumi. It now appears that the talks will break down.

I know you are on all these matters, but we should come to some conclusion on them shortly.

JFK

[60]

In August Rusk was to meet in Paris with French Foreign Minister Maurice Couve de Murville and Lord Alec Douglas-Home, the British foreign secretary. The original purpose of their meeting was to decide on a coordinated Western response to Soviet moves in Berlin. However, French relations in Tunisia had deteriorated seriously in the weeks before the meeting, and Kennedy was concerned about De Gaulle's recent military actions against the Tunisians.

Although French troops had been withdrawn from Tunisia under an agreement reached in 1958, the French still held an airstrip in Bizerte. In June the French began extending the main runway of the airstrip for use by new Mystère jet fighters. Tunisian demonstrators blockaded the airstrip, and on June 19 the Tunisian National Guard opened fire on a French helicopter. In retaliation the French fired on demonstrators, then attacked the Tunisian barricades, bombed military barracks, and mortared the medieval Arab Casbah. In the end, thirteen hundred Tunisians were killed, and another eleven hundred wounded or captured, including women and children who were machine-gunned in the streets. The French lost twenty-one men.

SECRET

NATIONAL SECURITY ACTION MEMORANDUM NO. 64
July 28, 1961
MEMORANDUM FOR THE SECRETARY OF STATE

My last letter from de Gaulle as you will have seen contains another gentle hint about the need for improving our machinery for worldwide consultation on political as well as strategic matters. I understand that you will be talking with Couve and [Douglas-]Home about this general problem in Paris and I hope some practical progress will be made.

It does seem a little quixotic for de Gaulle to make this point in a paragraph about Bizerte—a topic on which consultation has not been equally sought by the French. Still we agreed at Paris to make a start in this direction, and I myself would like to make real improvements in our communications with the French on both political and military questions. May I hear from you after Paris on this.

[61]

After independence was declared in the Congo (July 1960), the divided nation became a battleground for UN, Soviet-backed, and Belgian forces. From Stanleyville (now Kisangani), Antoine Gizenga controlled the eastern sector of the Congo and received vigorous backing from Nikita Khrushchev. UN troops, Khrushchev believed, were acting entirely in the interests of the United States. Their official role, however, was to "protect a united coalition government."

August 2, 1961

MEMORANDUM

The President notices in his daily intelligence reports that the UN troops in the Congo seem to be much more active in other areas than they are in relation to Gizenga's part of the country. He would be glad to have a memorandum explaining whether in fact this difference exists, and if so, whether there is anything that can be done about it.

McGeorge Bundy

[62]

Pakistan was an ally of the United States and therefore a direct recipient of U.S. military aid, while India was ostensibly a "neutralist pacifist" country that received only economic aid. With Pakistan and India locked in a bitter dispute on the Kashmir border, Pakistan's president, Field Marshal Muhammad Ayub Khan, claimed that Prime Minister Jawaharlal Nehru's government was receiving U.S. weapons. During his three-day visit to the United States in June, when he appealed for increased aid, Ayub said in a speech to the National Press Club (July 13) that any U.S. arms aid to India would make Pakistan feel "more insecure" and "put a tremendous strain" on Pakistan's relationship with the United States.

August 7, 1961

MEMORANDUM FOR MR. BUNDY

In regard to the differences between Pakistan and India as I understand it, some of the economic aid that we give to India is used to purchase military equipment while we give the military equipment directly to Pakistan. Would there be any objection to our giving economic assistance to buy military equipment to Pakistan so we wouldn't have this difficulty we have had over these F104s. Perhaps someone who is informed about all of this would talk to me about this some time.

[63]

In his August 7 memo to McGeorge Bundy, the President referred to the Brookings Institution, a think tank focusing on statistical, economic, and government research.

August 7, 1961

MEMORANDUM FOR MR. BUNDY

You will remember our conversation about preparing an analysis of what we would expect to do in the next ten years. Your brother Bill may have some thoughts on how this could be done. It might be done through the U.S. government Council of Economic Advisers or it could be done by Brookings. I would lean towards the Council of Economic Advisers doing it at my request. Why don't you have someone talk to Dr. Heller and see if we can plan to do something about this in the fall, which would be a counter to the Soviet statements coming out of their October [Soviet Party Congress] meeting, and what a wonderful society they are going to have.

[64]

During August 1961 the President considered increasing the size of nuclear tests on the basis of information from his science advisers.

August 7, 1961

MEMO FOR MR. BUNDY AND WIESNER

Seaborg recommends that we lift our laboratory experiments to one ton in his letter of August 4th. It seems to me that we should consider that.

[65]

The International Control Commission (ICC), originally formed at the end of the French-Indochina War in 1954, was reconvened to deal with the situation in Laos. Though the communist-backed Pathet Lao were overpowering Laotian troops backed by U.S. aid, Kennedy—on the advice of the Joint Chiefs—was determined to keep U.S. troops out of Laos. He was convinced that a settlement could be negotiated by the ICC.

August 7, 1961

MEMO FOR WALT ROSTOW, GENERAL TAYLOR

1. Would you prepare a memorandum of the situation at Geneva—the bargaining position taken by both sides on ICC matter and the other basic questions which are now before the conference. Should we ask Harriman to come home?

2. I presume that we are going to receive shortly a military plan for action in the panhandle of Laos and also for military pressure against Northern Vietnam.

3. By what means can we bring to world public opinion the action of North Vietnam and Laos in Southern Vietnam? I agree with you that groundwork has to be laid or otherwise any military action we take against Northern Vietnam will seem like aggression on our part.

[66]

Piqued by the coverage that his administration had received in *Time* magazine, Kennedy asked Sorensen to look at an essay submitted by a student comparing *Time*'s treatment of the Eisenhower and Kennedy administrations during their first six months. In a six-point memo summarizing the essay Sorensen noted that the magazine's coverage of the Kennedy administration was "far more critical and skeptical than the glowing plaudits consistently given to Eisenhower during a period when actually little was done." Sorensen noted that Eisenhower's problems were blamed on his predecessors and his statements were "accepted and praised" while Kennedy's were "criticized or rebutted."

Kennedy sent the student essay to Henry Luce, editor in chief of *Time*, with the following cover letter.

August 8, 1961

Mr. Henry R. Luce
Editor in Chief
Time
Rockefeller Center
New York 20, New York

Dear Mr. Luce,

Shortly after our very enjoyable conversation, a member of the White House staff brought to my attention the attached student essay on one of the topics we discussed—a comparison of *Time*'s treatment of the first six months of this administration and the first six months of my predecessor. I found it both interesting and persuasive—and while you may only find it interesting, I thought you might want to pass it along to Mr. Furth [assistant editorial director]. I will be very interested to learn of the results of your inquiry and hope we have more opportunities to talk in the coming months.

> With every good wish,
> Sincerely yours,
> John F. Kennedy

|67|

A month later, when relations with *Time* were somewhat improved, the President confidentially informed Luce that General Maxwell Taylor was available to talk about Cuba. On September 12, Kennedy sent the editor in chief the following note:

I must emphasize the need for keeping the fact that this discussion has even taken place completely in the bosom of your official family. If it should become known that General Taylor has discussed the Cuban affair with you, the press as well as the Congress will immediately descend on us en masse demanding equal treatment.

Although there were fifty-three thousand foreign students in the United States during 1960 and 1961, Kennedy learned that only five thousand were under government programs. He regarded the education of foreign students as an opportunity to provide a new generation of U.S.-influenced leadership in foreign countries.

NATIONAL SECURITY ACTION MEMORANDUM NO. 66

MEMORANDUM FOR THE SECRETARY OF STATE

August 8, 1961

I again have been reminded that we do not have an office in the government which concerns itself solely with the guidance and welfare of some 50,000 foreign students in this country. I am sure you agree with me that this is a serious shortcoming on our part and one that should be remedied as swiftly as possible. Since you have already been thinking about the problem in the department, I wonder if we can't now move fast enough to perform at least some services for the students during the 1961–62 academic year. I feel very strongly that we must not allow these students—especially the Africans and Asians—to leave this country disappointed any longer. I do not think we can leave their welfare entirely to uncoordinated private enterprise. Would you let me know what we will be able to do for them during the upcoming academic year.

J. F. Kennedy

[68]

(A six-page, three-point reply prepared on September 2 by Secretary of State Dean Rusk recommended gathering and updating information about all foreign students and increasing the budget for the exchange program. He urged the President to send a special message to Congress in January 1962 "stressing the need to strengthen international educational and cultural affairs as a vital component of U.S. foreign policy.")

National Security Action Memorandum No. 65 on the subject of a joint program of action with the government of Vietnam was to have far-reaching implications for U.S. involvement. Though written by Bundy, the memo describes in detail actions that were approved by the President.

SECRET

August 11, 1961

NATIONAL SECURITY ACTION MEMORANDUM NO. 65

SUPPLEMENT TO NSAM #52 DATED MAY 11, 1961 TO THE

SECRETARY OF STATE

SUBJECT: Joint program of action with the Government of Viet-Nam

Following his review of the "Joint Action Program proposed by the Viet-Nam United States Special Financial Groups to President Ngo Dinh Diem and President John F. Kennedy," the President on August 4 made the following decisions:

1. The President agrees with the three basic tenets on which the recommendations contained in the joint action program are based, namely:

   a. Security requirements must for the present be given first priority.

   b. Military operations will not achieve lasting results unless economic and social programs are continued and accelerated.

   c. It is in our joint interest to accelerate measures to achieve a self-sustaining economy and a free and peaceful society in Viet-Nam.

2. The United States will provide equipment and assistance in training for an increase in the armed forces of Viet-Nam from 170,000 to 200,000 men. In order to make this increase as effective as possible, the United States and Viet-Nam should satisfy themselves before the time when the level of 170,000 is reached on the following points:

   a. That there then exists a mutually agreed upon geographically phased strategic plan for bringing Viet Cong subversion in the Republic of Viet-Nam under control.

   b. That on the basis of such a plan there exists an understanding on the training and use of these 30,000 additional men.

   c. That the rate of increase from 170,000 to 200,000 will be regulated to permit the most efficient absorption and utilization of additional personnel and matériel in the Vietnamese armed forces with due regard to Viet-Nam's resources.

3. In view of the fact that the force level of 200,000 will probably

not be reached until late in 1962, a decision regarding the further increase above 200,000 will be postponed until next year when the question can be reexamined on the basis of the situation at that time. Meanwhile the buildup in equipment and training of the Civil Guard and Self-Defense Corps within already agreed levels should be expedited. . . .

[Points 4–9 of the memo provided details of the joint action program.]

10. Make clear to Diem that we hope that one consequence of our new joint efforts will be an effective projection to the nation, its friends and its enemies, of our confidence in a long-range future for an independent Viet-Nam. In this connection the Ambassador should seek discreetly to impress upon President Diem that he should see the total U.S. program for the greatest political effect in his achievement of maximum appreciation of his government by the people of Viet-Nam and the people of the world. (It is hoped that the Ambassador will continue his efforts to persuade President Diem to engage more fully in his civic action program [word missing] non-Communist elements now in political opposition.)

11. The Parallel Committees should be given the maximum delegation of authority to assure follow-up action, approve modifications of the program and "recommend measures to improve and adapt the Special Action Program as the situation changes." In this connection the President has emphasized that the chief responsibility for the planning and execution of the U.S. share of the program will, more than ever, rest with the ambassador and, under his direction, with MAAC and USOM.

12. The President shall be informed of matters arising in the implementation of this Joint Program requiring his attention so that they may receive his immediate consideration.

McGeorge Bundy

[69]

Three days later Kennedy addressed questions about the fitness of U.S. recruits to Timothy J. Reardon, Jr., his administrative assistant. The President mentioned Lieutenant General Lewis B. Hershey, director of the Selective Service System.

August 14, 1961

MEMORANDUM FOR MR. REARDON

It is still not clear to me whether our physical standards are going up or down. The Selective Service is turning down more people than it did in World War II; however, this may be due to the fact that standards are higher today. Can Hershey tell us whether we are more physically fit or less than during World War II [and whether we are] using the same standards [as] in World War II?

Have they made any judgment as to what actions could be taken in the schools, etc. in order to lessen the number of turn downs?

J. F. K.

[70]

On August 13 the border between the Western and Soviet sectors of Berlin was closed by troops, police, and militia of the East German government, halting a flow of refugees that had swelled to four thousand per day. Within four days the Berlin wall began to go up. After consulting with Kennedy, Secretary of State Rusk charged that the East Germans had violated two statutes of the four-power Paris agreement of 1949 governing free travel between East Germany and all parts of Berlin.

August 14, 1961

MEMO FOR SECRETARY OF DEFENSE

1. With this weekend's occurrences in Berlin, there will be more and more pressure for us to adopt a harder military posture.

2. I do not think we can leave unused any of the men or money that we're offered by the Congress, with the exception perhaps of the bomber money.

3. I would appreciate it if you would plan to discuss this matter with me this week after you have made a judgment on it.

4. I am concerned that we move ahead as quickly as possible on Civil Defense. Perhaps we could get a report on that before the week is out.

/s/ John F. Kennedy

[71]

* * *

Kennedy was aware that his actions in Berlin had the support of the majority of the American people. A George Gallup opinion poll, circulated through the White House, indicated that 85 percent of those polled were in favor of keeping U.S. troops in West Berlin, even at the risk of war, while 67 percent wanted the United States to fight if East Germany tried to close all roads to Berlin. A majority (58 percent) said that the United States and its allies should back Berliners' rights to free elections "even if it means going to war."

August 14, 1961

MEMORANDUM FOR SECRETARY OF STATE

1. What steps will we take this week to exploit politically propagandawise the Soviet/East German cutoff of the border?

2. This seems to me to show how hollow is the phrase "Free city" and how despised is the East German government, which the Soviet Union seeks to make respectable.

3. The question we must decide is how far we should push this. It offers us a very good propaganda stick which, if the situation were reversed, would be well used in beating us. It seems to me this requires decisions at the highest level.

/s/ John F. Kennedy

[72]

The President considered sending immediate reinforcements for U.S. troops already stationed in the divided city. Kennedy learned that McNamara had not yet carried out measures that had been authorized in July.

August 14, 1961

MEMORANDUM FOR SECRETARY OF DEFENSE

Item 26 of your memorandum to me of August 9, 1961, in regard to actions taken to implement our July 19th decision I notice that you have not as yet called up the 29 Air National Guard Squadrons or the group described in Item 29, the five Air Force Reserve C-124 Squadrons. At what date do you intend to call them up? How much prior notice and training would they need before they could be sent to Western Europe?

[73]

(In a reply dated August 15, McNamara summarized "the action I have taken to implement your decision that we be prepared to deploy as many as 6 additional divisions to Europe by 1 January 1962." McNamara had taken steps to reduce the number of combat ready troops in the Strategic Army Forces (STRAF) divisions and the number of men who would replace European civilians employed by the United States Army Europe (USAREUR). He concluded, however, that "the Army's plans provide for utilization of the full increase of 133,000 men which you proposed in your July 25 Report To The Nation.")

On August 14 the President issued numerous memos addressed to Bundy regarding foreign affairs matters. Among them:

August 14, 1961

MEMORANDUM FOR MR. BUNDY

Can you find out where the newspaper stories came [from] this weekend on the Vietnam military intervention into southern Laos. Those stories were harmful to us. Probably exaggerated. Makes it very difficult for us now to attack the Vietminh for its intervention in Laos.

[74]

August 14, 1961

MEMORANDUM FOR MR. BUNDY

Check with the Department of State and find out exactly how many French African states we are going to get to vote with us on the Chinese Communist admission if we work out the Outer Mongolian matter. Up to now we have just been going on theory.

[75]

August 14, 1961

MEMORANDUM FOR MR. BUNDY

At the meeting on Southeast Asia last week, I suggested that we secure an increase in the number of Filipino troops available in order to fill the gap left by the delay in the arrival of Pakistani troops. Because of the necessity of moving by sea, suggest we ask the Philippine government to increase the number from 180 to several thousand. I wonder if we could find out what progress is being made on this.

[76]

Most European nations responded favorably to Kennedy's actions in Berlin. But he wanted firm evidence of support from the Western allies.

NATIONAL SECURITY ACTION MEMORANDUM NO. 70

August 15, 1961

MEMORANDUM FOR THE SECRETARY OF STATE, SECRETARY OF DEFENSE

In relation to the Berlin situation I should appreciate a report on how we are progressing in obtaining commitments from our NATO allies to increase their military forces.

/s/ John F. Kennedy

[77]

(Three days later Taylor replied, "Mr. Kohler informs me that agreement has now been received for the Berlin reinforcement from the British, French and Germans.")

When Kennedy placed Dean Rusk in position of secretary of state, he hoped that the former head of the Rockefeller Foundation could improve relations between the departments of State and Defense. The President also hoped for a State Department that would be more responsive to the White House.

August 16, 1961

MEMORANDUM FOR SECRETARY OF STATE

I would appreciate it if you would prepare a memorandum on the present assignment of responsibility within the Department of State. We discussed this at breakfast this morning, but I think if we could get it down on paper all concerned on the White House staff, as well as the State Department, would have a better idea of how they should conduct their responsibilities.

[78]

In the wake of the Berlin crisis, White House and national security staff reviewed emergency planning procedures that had been established during the Eisenhower administration. As part of the single integrated operational plan (SIOP) that would be used by the U.S. government and armed forces in the case of nuclear attack, Eisenhower's staff and advisers had also designed civil defense contingency plans for civilians.

An essential element in Eisenhower's military planning was the National Command Authority (NCA)—a "release authority" that would have decisive control over the use of nuclear weapons if the President were disabled or killed. According to Thomas B. Allen, author of *War Games*, the "release authority passes from a disabled or missing President to the Secretary of Defense, and then, if necessary, to the Deputy Secretary of Defense." Allen was unable to determine who would be next in the chain of command since "no two authorities I consulted agreed on the passing of authority beyond the Deputy Secretary of Defense."

The following memo of August 19, 1961, from White House Assistant Fred Dutton to Bundy reveals that Eisenhower had set up a parallel but separate "contingency" structure to exercise civilian authority in the event of a national emergency. The reply to Dutton's memo has not been released; it is not known whether Kennedy terminated or continued the "contingent authority" set up by Eisenhower.

August 19, 1961

MEMORANDUM FOR HONORABLE MCGEORGE BUNDY

You may recall that in late May, I wrote advising of the existence of classified letters from President Eisenhower to ten private citizens throughout the country giving them authority over various parts of the economy and total society in the event of a declaration of a national emergency. The President subsequently asked that letters from him to the individuals involved terminating their contingent authority be held up until reorganization of the civil defense structure and related operations to take effect in the event of a national emergency.

I would appreciate notification by you as to whether that outstanding authority should be terminated, as I recommend; continued under new letters of instruction from the President; or what course you may desire to have taken. This matter merely relates to cleaning up prior conditional operations in the field of national security and should, I presume, be routed to you before any action is taken.

Frederick G. Dutton

[79]

Despite Poland's enforced alignment with the Communist bloc, Kennedy was eager to use U.S. aid "to develop whatever differences in attitude or in tempo may take place behind the Iron Curtain."

August 21, 1961

MEMORANDUM FOR THE SECRETARY OF STATE

Is there anything we can properly do to persuade the Polish government to lift their present restrictions in taxes which Polish recipients of a relief package must pay? I understand that shipment of used clothing makes up the bulk of the traffic.

[80]

Carl Kaysen, a former economist in the Office of Strategic Services and Harvard economics professor, did not officially join the White House staff until November 1961, when he was made deputy special assistant for national security affairs. However, he played an important behind-the-scenes role even before his official appointment, acting as liaison between the White House and State Department. Kennedy's memo of August 21 refers to Kaysen's work on PL480, the Agricultural Trade Development and Assistance Act that became the Food for Peace program.

August 21, 1961

MEMORANDUM FOR MR. BUNDY

I understand Carl Kaysen has been following the negotiation on PL480 with Poland. The State Department has offered 500,000 tons of grain. The Poles want 700,000 tons and an agreement to reopen the negotiations in the light of the Polish harvest. I understand that the State Department wants to be generous, but the ambassador in Warsaw feels a little like George Kennan does in Yugoslavia in regard to the tone of the Polish press. I would like to see what exactly is being said. I am not sure that we are not pursuing a will-o-the-wisp in regard to hoping that we can ever change the Polish government in any substantial way. I think we want to help the Polish people, but I think we should be a little tougher with the government and also the Yugoslav government. Will you take a look at this and then you and Kaysen could speak to me about it.

[81]

During World War II Polish units fought with Allied forces under U.S., Canadian, and British command. Though many of the Polish soldiers later emigrated to the United States, they were technically ineligible for veterans benefits.

August 21, 1961

MEMORANDUM FOR
ADMINISTRATOR, VETERANS ADMINISTRATION

Could you give me the reasoning behind opposition to permitting Polish ex-patriots who participated in battle during World War II with Allied Armed Forces and who are now residents of the United States for more than 10 years to receive medical care through the Veterans Administration? I understand such arrangements have been made in the United Kingdom [and] in Canada.

[82]

*   *   *

Kennedy saw Cyprus as a potential trouble spot in the eastern Mediterranean. If fighting erupted between Turkish and Greek Cypriots, the conflict was likely to draw intervention from Greece and Turkey—and possibly open the door to Soviet influence.

August 21, 1961

MEMORANDUM FOR MR. BUNDY

I read the Cyprus report. It seems to me that if the situation is as desperate as we hear it is, that we cannot continue to rely upon our policy of hoping that the guarantor powers will shoulder the principal share of the western burden. Shouldn't we have this more carefully reviewed?

[83]

The United States was interested in maintaining political stability in Saudi Arabia, a source of oil. Kennedy was especially concerned that the Saudis might turn to Moscow for military aid, and he looked to the Defense Department for prompt action. In the memo he refers to Ernesto "Che" Guevara, the Communist guerrilla leader and Castro lieutenant who wrote *Guerrilla Warfare* (published in 1961).

August 21, 1961

MEMORANDUM FOR
SECRETARY OF DEFENSE

A recent report to me from the Department of State in regard to the request from the Saudi Arabian government for arms stated and I quote "The Defense Department estimated that from six weeks to six months would be needed to determine definitively availabilities to all items on the extensive Saudi list and that deliveries would vary with type of equipment, but might take a minimum of eight months and [in] some cases longer." Why does it take from six weeks to six months to determine availability of equipment and why does delivery take a minimum of eight months and in some cases longer? Guevara said in Montevideo the other day that everything that the United States does is strangled in the Washington bureaucracy. It seems to me that we could speed this up and it is the sort of thing that we should pay particular attention to in all the departments dealing with foreign governments. Would you let me have your thoughts on this?

[84]

(In his reply memo on August 26 McNamara wrote, "Mr. L. A. Kane, ACS [assistant chief of staff] #14 in the Defense Department, who is alleged to have made the statement to Mr. [Hermann F.] Eilts of State, is on vacation and cannot be located. Regardless of whether or not such a statement was made, I would not condone such practices and have taken positive steps to ensure that such delays not be tolerated." Eilts was the officer in charge of Arabian Peninsula Affairs in the Bureau of Near East and South Asian Affairs.)

United Nations Ambassador Adlai Stevenson spoke out in opposition to the proposed admission of Red China to the UN. However, the Chinese Communists had substantial support from Eastern bloc and developing nations.

August 21, 1961

MEMORANDUM FOR MR. BUNDY

I think we should get an up to date report on the Communist Chinese admission question. What is the latest word from Stevenson? Do we have a strategy? Is it going to be successful? We can't permit ourselves to get beaten. If we are not going to be able to win it on this basis, we'd better think of another one. Would you speak to me about this?

[85]

Looking ahead to further Berlin negotiations, the President wrote an extensive memo to the secretary of state. The "Acheson paper," prepared at Kennedy's request "to undertake special studies of the problems of NATO and Germany," was delivered to the President three weeks after he met with Khrushchev in Vienna. Acheson's thesis was that Khrushchev would use Berlin as a general test of America's will to resist communist expansion.

SECRET
August 21, 1961
MEMORANDUM FOR THE SECRETARY OF STATE
SUBJECT: Berlin Political Planning

I want to take a stronger lead on Berlin negotiations. Both the
calendar of negotiation and the substance of the Western position
remain unsettled, and I no longer believe that satisfactory progress
can be made by Four-Power discussion alone. I think we should
promptly work toward a strong U.S. position in both areas and
should make it clear that we cannot accept a veto from any other
power. We should of course be as persuasive and diplomatic as
possible, but it is time to act. My initial views on both subjects are
set out below.

1. *The Calendar*
I like your plan to issue, before September first, an invitation to
negotiations. I think this means that we should this week make it
plain to our three Allies that this is what we mean to do and that
they must come along or stay behind. I shall be glad to write to
General de Gaulle myself if desirable.

I also like your idea that the four Foreign Ministers, at New York
for the United Nations, should be empowered to work out a place
and a time for negotiations. If there is a better way, I'd be glad to
accept it. In general, I like the idea of an announcement before
September first, discussion of ways and means before October first,
and formal negotiation about November first.

Within the category of "discussion of ways and means," I place
the possibility of preliminary private talks between appropriate US-
USSR diplomats. I like Chip [Charles] Bohlen for this, on our side.
Obviously such talks would have to be based on a clear and solid
sense of our policy, and so I do not think they can begin for about
a month—say around September 25th.

I do not think well of the plans for a three-Ambassador call upon
Khrushchev to try to smoke him out. Until we have something to
suggest ourselves, we shall not get any more out of him than we
have been getting since Vienna.

2. *The Substance of Our Policy*

The Acheson paper is a good start, but it is *not* a finishing point. What you and I need is a *small* group of hard workers who can produce alternatives for our comment and criticism on an urgent basis. This, in my judgment, should be a labor separated from the day-to-day operations work and planning under Kohler. I think of such people as Bohlen, [David] Owen and [Martin] Hillenbrand from State and Bundy and Sorensen over here. Maybe there should be fewer; probably there should not be more. This group should be as nearly invisible as possible, and it should report directly to you and me. Most of the elements of a firm policy are standing around now—and I believe a group with orders from the two of us could prepare a clear paper for my decision in one long session on August 31st. We shall need a paper by that time if we are to talk with our allies and get something like an agreed position from them by the end of September. I would suggest that such a group bring in preliminary proposals on Friday of this week—August twenty-fifth.

In general, what I think we should say to such a small group as guidelines is this:

1. Make the framework of our proposals as fresh as possible—they should *not* look like warmed over stuff from 1959.

2. Protect our support for the *idea* of self-determination, the *idea* of all-Germany, and the *fact* of viable, protected freedom in West Berlin.

3. Do *not* insist on maintenance of occupation rights if other strong guarantees can be designed. Occupation rights are a less attractive base, before the world, than the freedom and the protection of West Berliners.

4. Consider well the option of proposing parallel peace treaties. If we table our own drafts, we might do a lot with this; and Khrushchev would have to look at what we say, because he has invited just this course.

5. Examine all of Khrushchev's statements for pegs on which to hang our position. He has thrown out quite a few assurances and hints here and there, and I believe they should be exploited.

6. Do not put too much distance between our initial proposals and our fall-back position. Indeed it may be well not to have any

fall-back position. Our first presentation should be, in itself, as persuasive and reasonable as possible.

Can I have your prompt reaction to this?

[86]

Kennedy believed it would be advantageous for Britain to enter the Common Market, but there was some risk that a European trade bloc would erect tariff barriers to American goods and farm products.

NATIONAL SECURITY ACTION MEMORANDUM NO. 76
August 21, 1961
MEMORANDUM FOR UNDERSECRETARY OF STATE GEORGE BALL

I am concerned about what will be the economic effect upon the United States if England joins the Common Market. I believe we should have a realistic detailed study made by State, Treasury, and the Council of Economic Advisers. I have been informed that the effect will be extremely serious. Could you consider the matter and talk to me about it and suggest what action we should properly take. We have been in the position, of course, of encouraging the expansion of the Common Market for political reasons. If it should have an extremely adverse effect upon us, a good deal of responsibility would be laid upon our doorstep.

[87]

In March 1961 the Kennedy administration had taken a stand against Portugal's abuses of its colonial power. At the UN the United States voted in favor of an investigation of the situation in Portuguese Angola. Kennedy was sensitive to charges that the Portuguese were using American-made weapons against the African country.

NATIONAL SECURITY ACTION MEMORANDUM NO. 77
August 21, 1961
TO: Secretary of State
    Secretary of Defense
SUBJECT: Use of American-made arms in Angola

I understand that we have cautioned the Portuguese government against the use of American equipment in Portugal. I also understand that a recent story in a London newspaper reported the finding of a "Made in America" mark on part of a bomb dropped on an Angolan village. This is going to present problems to us both in Angola and in Portugal. Have we considered (1) whether we can be successful in persuading the Portuguese of this, or (2) whether this will have an adverse effect upon the use of the Azores base? I wonder if we should perhaps content ourselves with a public statement in regard to the matter.

/s/ John F. Kennedy

[88]

(In an undated reply McNamara wrote, "For the immediate future the success of our efforts to restrain the Portuguese from the use of U.S. matériel already in Angola is indeed problematical. However, I believe that a quiet, persistent, but unpublicized campaign appealing to the Portuguese understanding of our position might in time be successful. The critical military importance of our rights and continued use of our facilities in the Azores, and of securing extension of our rights in negotiations which must be undertaken in 1962, are such that any further public pressure on the Portuguese regarding the use of U.S. military matériel in Angola should be avoided.")

From the beginning of the Berlin crisis the President had stressed the unity of the NATO alliance in meeting "our commitments to Berlin." In his television speech on July 25 Kennedy had stated, "We in the West must move together in building military strength. We must consult one another more closely than ever before. We must together design our proposals for peace, and labor together as they are pressed at the conference table. And together we must share the burdens and the risks of this effort."

A month later Kennedy urged the secretary of defense to take steps to secure commitments from NATO allies.

August 21, 1961

MEMORANDUM FOR SECRETARY OF DEFENSE

1. I wonder if we could get a report by the end of August on what military buildup in conventional forces we are going to get from the NATO countries for the Berlin crisis. If you are not satisfied with it, should you go to Europe and meet with the defense ministers of the countries involved, or what other steps would you suggest taking?

2. I think we should have a review of our contingency plan for Berlin and also see whether we have reached any understanding with the governments for the implementation of these plans. We have to assume that some time in the fall there may be a blockade of a formal or informal kind. Have we decided with the British and the French and the Germans what our response will be?

3. If the Communists block West Berlin and we begin an airlift, should we not be readying some decision as to what other steps we could take against them besides economic. Could we expect our Navy to carry out any blockade of the Soviet Union for example in the Eastern Mediterranean or the northern seas.

4. Would you talk to me about these matters at your convenience?

/s/ John F. Kennedy

[89]

In his speech to the nation on the Berlin crisis on July 25, Kennedy had addressed the threat of nuclear war: "Now, in the thermonuclear age, any misjudgment on either side about the intentions of the other could rain more devastation in several hours than has been wrought in all the wars of human history." Subsequently Kennedy felt compelled to reassure homeowners that they could take measures to ensure their personal safety in the event of nuclear attack.

August 21, 1961

MEMO FOR SECRETARY OF DEFENSE

I would appreciate receiving a weekly report on what progress we are making on civil defense. Do you think it would be useful for me to write a letter to every homeowner in the United States, giving them instructions as to what can be done on their own to provide greater security for their family? Or should we look into this at a later date after your organization has been completed?

[90]

(On September 15, 1961, the cover of *Life* magazine bore the headline HOW YOU CAN SURVIVE FALLOUT—97 OUT OF 100 PEOPLE CAN BE SAVED. DETAIL PLANS FOR BUILDING SHELTERS AND A LETTER TO YOU FROM PRESIDENT KENNEDY.

(In his letter to the American people, Kennedy said that all public buildings would be surveyed within the next year and a half and stocked "with enough food, medical supplies and water for two weeks." He said that an improved warning system "will make it possible to sound an attack warning on buzzers right in your homes and places of business."

(Promising that "more comprehensive measures than these lie ahead," Kennedy concluded by asking readers to consider seriously the contents of *Life*. "The security of our country and the peace of the world are objectives of our policy . . ." he wrote. "But in these dangerous days when both these objectives are threatened we must prepare for all eventualities. The ability to survive coupled with the will to do so therefore are essential to our country."

(Jerome Wiesner, Kennedy's science adviser, later expressed his views about the *Life* fallout shelter issue in a confidential memo to the President. "In my opinion," he wrote, "this article gives the American people an entirely false and misleading estimate of the protection that would be provided by fallout shelters, and of potential mortalities in the event of large-scale thermonuclear attack on this country.")

At the President's urging, Bundy continued to stress the foreign student question with State Department officials.

August 23, 1961
MEMORANDUM FOR
The Honorable Philip H. Coombs, Assistant Secretary of State
Through: Mr. Lucius Battle

The President has read with interest your report on recent actions
on African students. He continues to think that this is a most important problem and hopes that your office is getting necessary
support for the work which you describe.

He remembers with pleasure the meeting with foreign students
which occurred at the White House last spring and would like to
know whether you would think well of having another meeting
sometime in the fall. The President's hope is that he might extend
some sort of general invitation to foreign students—or conceivably
more than one meeting would be arranged for students from different
parts of the world—and there might be a certain advantage in receiving Latin American students on one occasion and Africans on
another.

Obviously there are complexities in such an undertaking, and it
may be that there are also opportunities of which the President is
unaware. For example, it might be preferable to invite selected
representatives of foreign students for a somewhat more intimate
meeting if there were any good way of selecting them.

Will you think about this and let me have your advice.

McGeorge Bundy

[91]

In an extensive memo to the President on August 25, Secretary
of the Treasury C. Douglas Dillon enumerated "Immediate Steps
in Furthering the Alliance for Progress." Dillon expressed his concern about improving "the quality of U.S. personnel working on
our aid programs in Washington and in the field." The treasury
secretary urged that the White House form a committee that could
respond immediately to Latin American requests for funds. In the
same memo Dillon also described for the President a number of
self-help and reform measures that would require "continuous rep-
resentational efforts and negotiations by our field personnel."

August 28, 1961

MEMORANDUM FOR SECRETARY OF TREASURY

I received your memorandum of August 25th on the steps that should be forthcoming in furthering the Alliance for Progress. These recommendations are extremely important. Who would you suggest should be in charge of implementing them? How much time can you give it or should it be put in the hands of [Robert] Woodward or [deLesseps] Morrison? I hope during this first period while our manning of the new aid program is incomplete that you will be able to give it as much of your attention as possible. In any case I would appreciate your letting me know what we should do in the White House and what specifically should be assigned to other departments of the Government.

[92]

Following the August meeting of the Inter-American Economic and Social Council in Punta del Este, Uruguay, Richard N. Goodwin, assistant special counsel to the President, was closely questioned by members of the Senate Foreign Relations Subcommittee on Latin America. Goodwin was regarded with suspicion by some members of the subcommittee after it was reported that he had been seen meeting with Che Guevara. In his August 28 memo the President acknowledged that "political steps" would be necessary to convince Congress that the progressive measures of the Alliance for Progress did not mean that the U.S. was going "soft on communism" in the Caribbean or Latin America.

August 28, 1961

MEMORANDUM TO RICHARD GOODWIN

What are we going to do about the Caribbean Defense Council? What are we going to do about political action following the Punta del Este meeting? Are we finished here or is there something we can do? We are going to look a little weak if we do not follow it up with some political steps and it is going to become increasingly difficult to get the money from Congress unless we can find some interest on the part of other Latin American countries to do something about Communism.

[93]

In a speech on March 3 Treasury Secretary Dillon had predicted that the balance of payments deficit would disappear by 1963. By late 1961 outflow of gold from the United States had been reduced, but the deficit continued to mount. (The total deficit for 1961 reached $2.4 billion.)

NATIONAL SECURITY ACTION MEMORANDUM NO. 81
August 28, 1961
TO: SECRETARY OF THE TREASURY
(SUBJECT: U.S. Gold Position)

I would like to have as soon as the Treasury has made an analysis an up-to-date study of our gold position. How much we are losing. How this compares to other years. Whether we can look for a better result in the next six months. What should we do about it.

I gathered the other day that one of the reasons for the flow of gold was the investment by Americans of dollars in Western Europe. Should I before Congress leaves announce that we are going to put this on a must basis of legislation next year that will make it retroactive to September 1st of this year? Would that help discourage a flow in the next four months?

/s/ John F. Kennedy

[94]

(By October 1964 the U.S. gold supply had dropped to $15.6 billion against the short-term dollar claims of foreign countries that amounted to $20.6 billion.)

Among specific state visits mentioned in the National Security Action Memorandum No. 84, Kennedy referred to President Gamal Abdel Nasser of Egypt; President Roberto Chiari of Panama; President William V. S. Tubman of Liberia; Major General Park Chung Hee, chairman of the Supreme Council of South Korea; President

Alberto Lleras Camargo of Colombia; and President Romulo Betancourt of Venezuela.

NATIONAL SECURITY ACTION MEMORANDUM NO. 84
August 28, 1961
TO: MR. BUNDY
(SUBJECT: Specific State Visits)

It seems to me that if Nasser comes to the General Assembly that he should be invited to Washington to have lunch with me.

For the first minister of Indonesia, it seems to me that a light luncheon is sufficient. I don't want to get involved in an exchange of dinners with him.

Check in on what is going to happen on the visit of President Chiari on the renegotiation of the canal.

Evidently we should answer President Tubman who now wants to come in October as he can't come in November or December. If it involved only a luncheon it is all right with me.

We should proceed ahead with Chairman Pak [sic] of South Korea. Once again it should only involve a luncheon.

In the memorandum it mentions that I am interested in having President [Lleras] Camargo of Colombia come here. He has been so helpful that I think we ought to make some arrangements to see him. Teddy suggested that I might go to Venezuela on something tied up with the Alliance and then Camargo could come over there. Another thought was Camargo and Betancourt could both meet me in Puerto Rico for a weekend. Otherwise, I would be delighted to have Camargo come here on an informal visit. That would also be true of Betancourt. We ought to think about this and discuss it.

[95]

(In December 1961 Kennedy became the first American President to make an official visit to Venezuela, where he signed a joint communiqué outlining U.S.-Venezuelan cooperation within the Alliance for Progress framework.)

Although the situation in Berlin seemed to have stabilized, the President continued to prepare for contingencies. (The following declassified memo was reviewed and "sanitized" before release:

Words that have been censored from the document are indicated by brackets.)

August 28, 1961

MEMO FOR THE SECRETARY OF STATE

1. I should like to have a meeting [word sanitized] this week to go over the status of our Berlin contingency planning; in order to see what has been quadripartitely agreed and what is still under discussion. Are there any gaps in our planning which need to be covered? I am particularly interested in knowing what we are doing with regard to the following situations:

    a. Interference with the civil air traffic into Berlin. This is very much on my mind.

    b. Contingencies arising from the partitioning of Berlin (for example, conflicts between the West German population and the East German police).

    c. The extension of [word sanitized] planning to take into account a greater reliance on conventional forces.

    d. Actions to be taken in the case of an East German revolt.

2. Please let me know when you will be ready to have this meeting.

/s/ John F. Kennedy

[96]

At the ICC negotiations in Geneva, where the fate of Laos was under discussion, it was generally agreed that Prince Souvanna Phouma was the most feasible candidate to head a neutral government. Within Laos, however, military and political factions backed Phoumi Nosavan, a highly untrustworthy Laotian officer who had been supported by the CIA under Eisenhower. For the Souvanna government to succeed, the prince needed assurances of U.S. backing.

NATIONAL SECURITY ACTION MEMORANDUM NO. 80
August 29, 1961
DECISIONS APPROVED BY THE PRESIDENT AT THE MEETING ON
SOUTHEAST ASIA, AUGUST 29, 1961

PARTICIPANTS: The Secretary of Defense, The Secretary of
State, The Attorney General, Mr. Harriman, Mr. Allen Dulles,
General Lemnitzer, Mr. Edward Murrow, [Deputy
Undersecretary of State for Political Affairs] Mr. [U.] Alexis
Johnson, [Deputy Assistant Secretary] John [M.] Steeves,
Robert Johnson, General Taylor, Mr. Bundy

The President approved the following actions:
1. An intensification of the diplomatic effort to achieve agreement
to the Paris proposals on the part of Souvanna, especially by direct
conversations between Ambassador Harriman and Souvanna with
an emphasis not only upon the interlocking importance of the Paris
proposals, but also upon U.S. support of Souvanna in the event that
he accepts the Paris plan.
2. Authorization to undertake conversations with SEATO allies
both bilaterally and with the SEATO Council, exploring the possibility of an enlargement of the concept of SEATO plan 5. It must
be understood that this exploration was in the nature of contingency
planning and did not represent a flat commitment of the United
States to participate in such an enlarged enterprise.
3. An immediate increase in mobile training teams in Laos to
include advisers down to the level of the company, to a total U.S.
strength in this area of 500, together with an attempt to get Thai
agreement to supply an equal amount of Thais for the same purpose.
4. An immediate increase of 2,000 in the number of Meos being
supported to bring the total to a level of 11,000.
5. Authorization for photo-reconaissance by Thai or [sanitized]
aircraft over all of Laos. It is assumed that these actions will be
carried out under the general direction of the Southeast Asia Task
Force under the direction of Deputy Undersecretary Johnson.

McGeorge Bundy

[97]

*   *   *

According to a treaty signed in 1903, the Panama Canal Zone was leased "in perpetuity" by the United States from Panama. In 1955 the United States signed a new treaty that guaranteed an increase in annual payments to the Panamanians. In 1958 and 1960 further agreements granted more employment opportunities to Panamanians and promised increased wages. While the United States considered constructing a sea-level canal, many Panamanians were agitating for more restrictions on U.S. rights and greater control over the Canal Zone.

August 30, 1961

MEMORANDUM FOR THE SECRETARY OF DEFENSE

I understand that recent technical studies by the Department of Army and the Panama Canal Company indicate there is no immediate necessity to negotiate for the construction of a sea-level canal. I further understand that these surveys show that such a canal will not be needed until the year 2000.

As you know, we are currently in discussions with the Republic of Panama about our mutual arrangements concerning the Panama Canal. It will be most helpful to these negotiations if I could finally have a final recommendation as to the necessity for a sea-level canal.

Could you also look into what has been done to implement and carry out the "equal pay for equal work" provision of the 1955 Treaty? There have been some complaints from Panamanian officials that we have not lived up to our treaty obligations in this regard.

/s/ John F. Kennedy

[98]

(In a reply memo Deputy Secretary of Defense Roswell Gilpatric indicated that studies by the Panama Canal Company showed that overhaul and repair of the locks could double the capacity. In regard to the equal pay for equal work provision of the treaty, Gilpatric reported that the secretary of the army said "that there has been careful and conscientious compliance with each element of our commitment.")

*   *   *

When Ghana became an African republic in 1960, Kwame Nkrumah of the Convention People's party made himself president for life. Although Nkrumah had met with Kennedy and said he welcomed U.S. assistance, during a subsequent tour of the USSR, Eastern Europe, and Communist China, he issued a number of communiqués condemning Western imperialism.

September 5, 1961
NATIONAL SECURITY ACTION MEMORANDUM NO. 89
TO: THE SECRETARY OF STATE
(SUBJECT: Soviet Training of Ghanaian Troops)

I would like to determine whether Mr. Nkrumah is going ahead with his plan to send 400 of his troops to the Soviet Union for training.

/s/ John F. Kennedy

[99]

(In his reply on September 11 Rusk confirmed the report. He added, "Embassy Accra believes Nkrumah will defend his action by saying he is balancing Soviet and Western influence. . . . If the British remain reluctant to make a strong protest, we should do so unilaterally, and should not delay too long or it may become impossible for Nkrumah to reverse his decision.")

With the U.S. economy emerging from recession, Kennedy hoped to avoid strikes that were threatened by members of the United Auto Workers. On August 28, after the UAW membership voted "overwhelmingly" for a walkout, the head of the Federal Mediation and Conciliation Service asked for an extension of talks. Subsequently UAW President Walter P. Reuther agreed to extend contract negotiations six days beyond the deadline. The following telegram to Reuther was also wired to the president of General Motors:

September 5, 1961

(To be delivered by hand)
Mr. Walter P. Reuther
President
United Automobile, Aircraft and Agricultural Implement
  Workers of America
8000 East Jefferson Avenue
Detroit, Michigan

I wish to emphasize to you, the parties participating in the automobile negotiations, the high degree of responsibility you bear to the country to achieve a settlement before the deadline. While the hour is late, I am confident that you can, by exercising industrial statesmanship, achieve a settlement which is fair and reasonable to both shareholders and workers and which preserves price stability in the industry.

I urge that in the hours that remain before the deadline, you, the representatives of the General Motors Corporation and the UAW make an all out effort to achieve a just settlement. Our country at this juncture in our affairs can ill afford a shutdown in this important segment of our economy.

John F. Kennedy

[100]

(General Motors and the UAW reached a tentative economic agreement on September 6, but a week later there were walkouts at 92 of GM's 129 U.S. plants. Wildcat strikes continued, and on September 22 Reuther called both management and local UAW officials from 21 of the struck plants to a meeting in Detroit. Discussions there led to final contract settlements.)

On August 30, in a memo for the President, White House Social Secretary Letitia "Tish" Baldrige urged Kennedy to use the Air Force to fly performers for state entertainments to and from Washington. "After all," she wrote, "if we are serving American culture and doing honor to our artists here and abroad, while they themselves are donating their services, we should at least be able to fetch, carry, and return them from New York or wherever they may be."

September 5, 1961

MEMORANDUM FOR TISH BALDRIGE

It is agreeable with me if the Air Force flies the performers down to Washington as long as we do it exactly the same way the previous administration did, and as long as we minimize the publicity. In other words, the actors, etc. should not attempt to attract the press to their departure or arrival and we should work out some way of compensating the Air Force at cost. You can let me know about this, however.

[101]

With a session of the UN General Assembly to be held at the end of September, Kennedy learned that a majority of delegates would probably vote in favor of the admission of Red China. Whatever the outcome, the President hoped to remain on good terms with Nationalist Chinese leader Chiang Kai-shek. In his memo of September 5, Kennedy mentions Roy W. Howard, Chairman of the executive committee of Scripps-Howard newspapers, who had met with Nationalist Chinese premier Chen Cheng on August 5 when Cheng visited the UN and talked with U.S. businessmen. (The following memo to Bundy was not sent, probably because Kennedy discussed the issue with White House staff the same day.)

September 5, 1961

MEMO FOR MR. BUNDY

I want to talk to you about the Red China question to see whether we ought to write another letter to Chiang Kai-shek or whether we ought to see whether we can get Roy Howard and see if we can do anything with him. We ought to do a nose count on how we are going to do on the numbers, particularly if the neutralist conference goes on record in favor of the admission to Red China. We ought to check on maybe getting some of the Republicans in before the end of the session to explain what the problem is. It would be good if we could get [former UN Ambassador] Jerry Wadsworth's help.

[102]

(According to Schlesinger, when Kennedy discussed the U.S. position, he admitted to UN Ambassador Stevenson, "It really doesn't make sense—the idea that Taiwan represents China. But if we lost this fight, if Red China comes into the UN during our first year in town . . . they'll run us both out.'')

On August 25 Brazilian President Jânio Quadros had abruptly resigned, throwing Brazil into a constitutional crisis. This was particularly disappointing in light of the fact that Brazil was the nation in South America on which the United States had spent the most money. Kennedy and his advisers feared that without U.S. assistance, Brazil and its Latin American neighbors would readily come under Cuban influence. (The following memo to the secretary of defense remained classified until March 1988.)

SECRET
September 5, 1961
NATIONAL SECURITY ACTION MEMORANDUM NO. 88
TO: The Secretary of Defense
(SUBJECT: Training for Latin American Armed Forces)

I would appreciate hearing what steps we are taking to train the Armed Forces of Latin America in controlling mobs, guerrillas, etc. In addition, as the events of the past week have shown in Brazil, the military occupy an extremely important strategic position in Latin America. I would like to know how many officers we are bringing up from Latin America to train here and whether we could increase the number. Also, what other steps we are taking to increase the intimacy between our Armed Forces and the military of Latin America. It has been suggested that we set up a camp in the United States similar to the FBI Academy which brings in police from all over the United States. We would bring up a good many officers from the different countries of Latin America for a period from 1 to 2 months; we would have FBI people there who could talk to them about the techniques they have developed to control communism [and] subversion, and we could have our military coming in to teach them how to control mobs and fight guerrillas. In addition to [increasing] their effectiveness it would also strengthen their ties with the United States. Will you let me know your view of this?

/s/ John F. Kennedy

[103]

(An extensive report by Undersecretary of State Chester Bowles was dated September 30, 1961. Bowles noted that the current Agency for International Development (AID) "public safety program" operated in twenty-six countries. A main emphasis of the program was to provide "technical advice in police administration and training in crime detection, countersubversion techniques, crowd and riot control and related subjects. . . . A key element of the program is bringing to the U.S. selected groups of police chiefs and key police specialists for three to six months of indoctrination and training."

(In Latin America, according to Bowles, the AID Public Safety Division had programs in eight countries and provided U.S. training to police officers from ten other countries. An important part of the program was "civilianizing" internal defense—"shifting part of the internal defense burden to a civilian police force who are trained to maintain law and order without unnecessary bloodshed and an obtrusive display of tanks and bayonets.")

While the President worked on an economic recovery program, he also fought a public relations campaign with the press over government spending. The following memo comes from Evelyn Lincoln's "Notebook of Memoranda to Staff":

September 5, 1961

MEMORANDUM FOR MR. DUTTON

The President dictated the following to me this morning:

"Tell Fred Dutton to compose a letter to a fellow called Daniels, Readers Digest (copy to the President of the Readers Digest) challenging his statistics in the September Readers Digest on unemployment—that the program presented this year would cost the taxpayer $18 billion annually in a few years. It is wholly untrue and we ought to make him eat it."

Evelyn Lincoln

[104]

To Kennedy a knowledge of the history of U.S. foreign relations was one of the prerequisites of office. His father, Joseph P. Kennedy, had been ambassador to Great Britain, and as a senator John Kennedy had served on the Senate Foreign Relations Committee. In his September 6 security action memorandum regarding clearance of foreign relations papers "for the record," Kennedy attempted to set new standards of disclosure for the *Foreign Relations* series.

NATIONAL SECURITY ACTION MEMORANDUM NO. 91
September 6, 1961
FOR: The Secretary of State
    The Secretary of Defense
    The Secretary of the Treasury
    The Administrator of the General Services Administration
SUBJECT: Expediting publication of "Foreign Relations"

The effectiveness of democracy as a form of government depends on an informed and intelligent citizenry. Nowhere is the making of choices more important than in foreign affairs. Nowhere does government have a more imperative duty to make available as swiftly as possible all the facts required for intelligent decision.

As many of these facts as possible should be made public on a current basis, but because of the inherent need for security in the current conduct of foreign affairs, it is obviously not possible to make full immediate disclosure of diplomatic papers. However, delay in such disclosure must be kept to a minimum.

It has long been a pride of our government that we have made the historical record of our diplomacy available more promptly than any other nation in the world. The Department of State has the responsibility within the executive branch for putting out this permanent record in the series "Foreign Relations of the United States." The discharge of this responsibility requires the active collaboration of all departments and agencies of our government in the submission and clearance of papers necessary for the completeness of this record. In recent years the publication of the "Foreign Relations" series has fallen farther and farther behind in currency. The lag has now reached approximately 20 years. I regard this as unfortunate and undesirable. It is the policy of this administration to unfold the historical record as fast and as fully as is consistent with national security and with friendly relations with foreign nations. Accordingly, I herewith request all departments, agencies, and libraries of the government to collaborate actively and fully with the Department of State in its efforts to prepare and publish the record of our diplomacy. In my view, any official should have a clear and precise case involving the national interest before seeking to withhold from publication documents or papers fifteen or more years old.

[105]

(On September 22 Chester Bowles replied that he appreciated the action the President had taken in "requesting all departments and agencies and libraries to cooperate fully. . . . I am sure that your initiative will result in more expeditious handling, and more carefully-considered decisions, by all departments and agencies, on papers we desire for publication in the 'Foreign Relations' volumes.")

Arthur Schlesinger, in *A Thousand Days*, recalled that he sent a memo to Kennedy asking whether it would cause any "embarrassment" to the President if Schlesinger were to do film criticism on his "own time" for *Show* magazine. The following reply—with a reference to the President's brother-in-law Peter Lawford—came from Evelyn Lincoln:

September 8, 1961

MEMO FOR ARTHUR SCHLESINGER
RE: Film notes for *Show* [magazine]

The President says it is fine for you to continue to write for *Show* as long as you treat Peter Lawford with respect.

[106]

On August 18 President Kennedy had sent fifteen hundred troops to West Berlin to reinforce the five-thousand-man U.S. garrison. Some three weeks later the President discussed with his advisers the ramifications of sending additional reinforcements to the divided city.

TOP SECRET
NATIONAL SECURITY ACTION MEMORANDUM NO. 92
September 8, 1961
MEMORANDUM TO THE SECRETARY OF STATE, THE SECRETARY
OF DEFENSE

The following questions seem to me to emerge from our discussion yesterday, and I am sending this memorandum to both of you in the knowledge that many of the questions have both a political and a military component. You may prefer to make separate answers, or you may find it possible to produce a single agreed response. On Question 10, I am asking separately for the view of the Secretary of the Treasury, who was out of town during our meeting yesterday:

1. What will the presence in Europe of six additional U.S. divisions accomplish:

    a. In meeting the Berlin situation?

    b. In vitalizing NATO and strengthening the long-term defense of Western Europe?

2. Will an increase of our conventional forces in Europe convince Khrushchev of our readiness to fight to a finish for West Berlin or will it have the opposite effect? What other steps of all kinds may help to carry conviction on this point?

3. Supposing that we and our allies raise the ground strength of NATO to thirty effective divisions, what have we accomplished? Specifically:

    a. Can NATO then defend Western Europe against a massive conventional attack by the Soviet Bloc?

    b. Can we safely mount a corps-size probe to reopen access to Berlin and at the same time present an adequate ground shield?

    c. How long can thirty divisions be supported logistically in combat?

4. It has been my understanding that we would need to call additional divisions only as we actually decided to send existing divisions to Europe. Since our current plan is to send only one such division, why is it necessary now to call four divisions from the reserve?

5. If we call up four additional National Guard divisions now and

do not send them to Europe, how can they be usefully employed? How long would it take to convert them to Army of the U.S. Divisions? How long would it take to create effective A.U.S. [Army of the United States] Divisions by other means?

6. How much of the four division build-up would be justified in view of the overall world situation if Berlin were not an immediate issue?

7. What tactical air support is needed for the planned forces in Europe and what is the plan for providing such support?

8. The reduction in terms of days of combat of the supply backup of U.S. forces in Europe which will result from increasing our forces and from supplying the West Germans has been noted. Would this result in putting U.S. troops in a possible combat situation without adequate supplies?

9. If we add six divisions to NATO, may not Khrushchev add six or more divisions to the conventional forces facing NATO? Or will logistical problems, fear of attack by atomic weapons, and preoccupations in the satellites set a limit on the Soviet conventional forces available for immediate use against NATO?

10. What is the estimated net gold cost per year of the movement of six divisions to Europe and what can be done to reduce it?

/s/ John F. Kennedy

[107]

(In an extensive reply memorandum General Taylor described the logistics of sending four additional National Guard units immediately and sending six additional divisions to Europe in January 1962. He concluded: ''A great many time-consuming preparations should be started soon if there is any likelihood of sending this reinforcement to Europe in the next few months. It will be necessary to decide now about the call-up if these new divisions are to be available in the anticipated period of maximum tension over Berlin and Southeast Asia.'')

The two access routes to West Berlin were a road through East German territory and the air corridor to the West Berlin territory that had been used during Stalin's 1948 blockade. If the situation in Berlin remained unchanged, the President and his advisers had to consider the possibility that the Soviets might take action to impede or deny U.S. access to West Berlin.

September 11, 1961
MEMORANDUM FOR THE SECRETARY OF STATE,
THE SECRETARY OF DEFENSE

This week, I should like to resume our discussion of Berlin contingencies with a rundown of planned reactions—political, military and economic—to the most likely situations which may arise, and a review of the status of Allied agreement to these reactions. I have appended a list of a number of cases which I would like to cover in this review. You may wish to add others.

In considering these contingencies, I would like to be reminded of the length of time required to react effectively in the way we propose, the degree of acceptance of dealing with East Germans implicit in our plans, and the circumstances under which our armed forces will be authorized to use their weapons.

I am also interested in knowing when and under what circumstances we would expect to use West German forces if the East Germans confront us. What if it is the East German Air Force which obstructs air access?

/s/ John F. Kennedy

[108]

(On September 27 the secretary of defense sent the President, Joint Chiefs, and other agencies an analysis of Berlin contingencies that included three possible scenarios. The first was the possibility that a commercial plane en route to West Berlin was "buzzed" by East German military aircraft and crashed leaving no survivors. In the second scenario a convoy encountered interference from an East German convoy. Scenario 3 speculated on what would happen if the Soviets took the place of East German soldiers and attacked civilians in East Berlin. The memo outlined political and military responses that would be most appropriate in each case.)

On September 6 Kennedy had written to the heads of twelve U.S. steel companies asking that they "heed the clear call of national interest" and "forgo a steel-price increase in the near future." The President said that a rise in the price of steel would put an end to stable prices and further hurt the nation's balance of payments position with other countries. While making his request to industry leaders, Kennedy also appealed to the head of the steelworkers' union. The following letter is the President's response to a September 8 letter from David J. McDonald, president of the AFL-CIO United Steelworkers Union.

September 14, 1961

Dear Mr. McDonald:

I appreciate very much your letter of September 8 in which you pledge the cooperation of the Steelworkers Union in the negotiations next year with the steel industry, to make sure that full weight and recognition is given to the public interest.

I am sure that you agree with me that the public interest requires responsible price and wage policies in this basic industry and throughout the American economy. The Steelworkers Union can make a significant contribution to the public interest by following, in the forthcoming negotiations, policies that will ensure that their collective bargaining proposals are fashioned so that, in meeting the needs of workers in the industry, the interests of stockholders are safeguarded and the public interest in price stability is protected. This implies a labor settlement within the limits of advances in productivity and of price stability.

No one, including workers in the industry, can profit by inflation and by advances in the cost of living. Nor can America as a whole maintain its position in the world if our balance of payments is jeopardized by price and wage policies that make our goods less competitive in the world markets. The whole nation has benefited from the price stability in steel for the last three years. We count on all concerned to maintain this stability.

I am confident that on the basis of your letter, we can rely upon the leadership and members of the Steelworkers Union to act responsibly in the wage negotiations next year in the interests of all of the American people.

Sincerely,
/s/ John F. Kennedy

[109]

*   *   *

(After conferring with Kennedy on September 21, Roger M. Blough, chairman of the board of United States Steel, released a letter in which he criticized the Council of Economic Advisers for assuming "the role of informal price-setters for steel." Blough claimed that it was "unworkable" to try to control prices across the board by holding down the price of steel. "The causes of inflation," he noted, "are clearly associated with the fiscal, monetary, labor and other policies of government." The following April Blough bluntly informed Kennedy that U.S. Steel was ignoring the presidential request and raising its prices six dollars a ton.)

The president of Panama, Roberto Chiara, saw the Alliance for Progress as an opportunity to negotiate for increased U.S. aid and further concessions related to the Canal Zone treaty.

September 15, 1961
MEMORANDUM FOR THE SECRETARY OF STATE

As you know, the President of Panama has sent me a letter requesting that we re-negotiate our Panama Canal Treaties. It seems to me we should take a careful look at this problem with a view to analyzing what our basic interests are in the Canal Zone, what concessions we could make, and on what terms we could reasonably expect to get a long-term settlement. After we formulate our own views we should discuss them quietly with the Panamanians. We don't want to make a public announcement of negotiations until we have decided what the result of the talks will be.

I think we should establish a special working group with Assistant Secretary Woodward as Chairman, including respresentatives from Defense, the Budget Bureau, Jerry Wiesner and Dick Goodwin. I would like the recommendations of this group within the next two weeks. After that we can go ahead and begin some talks with the Panamanians. You might also bring [Ambassador Joseph] Farland up for consultation with the group.

/s/ John F. Kennedy

[110]

* * *

With the continued threat of the European Economic Community to raise protective tariff barriers, agricultural interests in the United States were pressuring the President to take preventive measures. Howard Petersen, special White House adviser on trade, had recommended some amendments to an existing trade expansion act.

September 18, 1961

MEMORANDUM FOR SECRETARY OF AGRICULTURE

I was interested in your report to me on the Common Market. I assume that you are in touch with Petersen as to how we might build up support in the agricultural areas for our reciprocal trade legislation next year. The Common Market could adversely affect American agriculture and I think we have a chance to build support among the Agriculture Congressmen for our policies in order to protect their interests.

/s/ John F. Kennedy

[111]

On September 13 UN forces in the Congo launched an attack against troops of President Moise Tshombe's separatist Katangan government. Though UN forces attacked government buildings and communications centers in Elisabethville, news services reported that the UN command's "apparent aim was to suppress the Katangan regime in conformity with UN resolutions calling for the preservation of the Congo as a unified state."

NATIONAL SECURITY ACTION MEMORANDUM NO. 97
September 19, 1961
TO: The Secretary of State
SUBJECT: Use of U.S. fighter aircraft in the Congo
FROM: Bundy

The President at 4 P.M. on September 19 authorized the dispatch of U.S. fighter aircraft with the necessary logistical support to the Congo on a contingency basis. This authorization would become effective only if no fighter aircraft of other nations were made available to the United Nations, and the President specifically directed that the mission of U.S. fighter aircraft would be to support and defend U.S. and U.N. transports or other U.N. forces that might come under air attack. There will be no effort to seek out and destroy Fouga Magister jets not attacking the U.S. or U.N. forces without further authority from the President. In the President's view it is of high importance that U.S. fighter aircraft be understood to intervene only in defense of beleaguered U.N. forces. He is not prepared to authorize their use at this time in offensive activities against Katangan forces.

[112]

On September 1 the Soviet Union broke the test ban moratorium with a series of fifty nuclear weapons tests that continued for the next two months. On September 15 Britain and the United States commenced underground testing.

29 September 1961
MEMORANDUM FOR THE SECRETARY OF DEFENSE

The attention of the President has been called to the fact that the United States has never test-fired a missile with a nuclear warhead. As there is always a possibility that the USSR may do some such thing, he would like your view as to the military desirability of checking out a missile system to this degree and, if your view is affirmative, whether such a firing should be considered for inclusion in our program for test firings.

Maxwell D. Taylor

[113]

When Kennedy appointed Henry R. Labouisse to be head of the International Cooperation Administration (ICA), the President also made him chairman of a task force to study the foreign aid program, organization, and legislation. The task force report became the basis for the Agency for International Development.

October 2, 1961

The Honorable Henry R. Labouisse
International Cooperation Administration
Washington, D.C.

Dear Harry:

Your memorandum on the termination of the Task Force on Foreign Aid Program reports with characteristic simplicity the execution of a major task. I have already written you of my appreciation for this work, but I cannot let this memorandum pass without another word. The Task Force accomplished its mission on foreign economic assistance, and it has earned the thanks of all who care for the effectiveness of American foreign policy. For your single-minded and unselfish service here, we are all in your debt. And it is therefore with gratitude and respect that I accept your recommendation for the disbandment, on September 30, of the Task Force which has worked with you on this assignment.

Sincerely,
John F. Kennedy

[114]

At the October 11 meeting on Vietnam the rationale for U.S. intervention hinged on the white paper mentioned in the memo of October 13. The State Department paper presented evidence that guerrillas operating in South Vietnam were being supplied with munitions by the North Vietnamese.

TOP SECRET
NATIONAL SECURITY ACTION MEMORANDUM NO. 104
October 13, 1961
SUBJECT: Southeast Asia

The President on October 11, 1961, directed that the following actions be taken:

1. Make preparations for the publication of the white paper on North Vietnamese aggression against South Vietnam which is now being drafted in the Department of State.

2. Develop plans for possible action in the Vietnam ICC based

upon the white paper preliminary to possible action under paragraph 3 [*sic*] above.

3. Develop plans for presentation of the Vietnam case in the United Nations.

4. Subject to agreement with the government of Vietnam which is now being sought, introduce the Air Force "Jungle Jim" squadron into Vietnam for the initial purpose of training Vietnamese forces.

5. Initiate guerrilla ground action, including use of U.S. advisers if necessary, against Communist aerial resupply missions in Tchepone area.

6. General Taylor should undertake a mission to Saigon to explore ways in which assistance of all types might be more effective.

The President also agreed that certain other actions developed by the task force and concurred in by the agencies concerned, but which do not require specific Presidential approval, should be undertaken on an urgent basis.

[115]

On September 28 Syrian Army officers led a rebellion directed against Egyptian troops under United Arab Republic President Gamal Abdel Nasser. The revolt, coming four years after Egypt and Syria were united, was directed against Nasser's nationalization and socialization programs. According to Syrian leaders, Nasser was attempting to "Egyptianize" Syria by giving Egyptians the controlling jobs in that country.

NATIONAL SECURITY ACTION MEMORANDUM NO. 105
[Undated]
MEMORANDUM FOR THE SECRETARY OF STATE
SUBJECT: Policy toward Egypt and Syria

The President is greatly interested in what policy we should pursue in the post-coup situation toward both Egypt and the new Syrian regime. Is the at least temporary loss Nasser has sustained likely to lead him to turn his energies more inward and to create opportunities for bettering U.S.-Egyptian relations via U.S. development assistance?

With respect to Syria, what policy does the Department of State propose that we pursue toward the new regime? What is our estimate of its staying power? Should we undertake any special measures to encourage its apparent pro-western tendencies or would such measures be likely to be counterproductive? A report, and if indicated a program of action, is requested by October 30, 1961.

McGeorge Bundy

[116]

During the Berlin crisis General Lauris Norstad, supreme commander of the allied forces in Europe, had stressed the importance of a shared nuclear force for NATO. On November 8, when Kennedy sent Rusk the following top secret memo, Norstad was already championing the concept of a multilateral NATO force to supplement U.S. nuclear weapons, but he also endorsed diplomatic moves to ease the crisis in Berlin.

November 8, 1961
TOP SECRET
MEMORANDUM TO THE SECRETARY OF STATE

I had a talk with General Norstad yesterday, and among the points which he made were the following:

He suggested that at a certain stage in Berlin contingency activity—perhaps along with the events described in Section II of National Security Action Memorandum No. 109—it might be desirable to summon Chairman Khrushchev to an emergency meeting in Berlin to discuss the crisis. Would such a direct meeting between the Chairman and myself be a good idea at this or at some other stage of the crisis? Would Berlin be a good place? Should other Western statesmen be included? Should we privately prepare a contingency plan?

I think this idea should be explored and I would like to have your comments on it.

JFK

[117]

Kennedy's top secret letter to Khrushchev concerning U.S.-Soviet relations in Southeast Asia was written on November 16, 1961. It was not declassified for release until 1984.

November 16, 1961
His Excellency
Nikita S. Khrushchev
Chairman of the Council of Ministers
    of the Union of Soviet Socialist Republics
The Kremlin
Moscow

Dear Mr. Chairman:

I have now had a chance to study your most recent two letters on the German problem and on Laos and Vietnam. I shall be writing you again about Germany and Berlin, but I do wish to give you my thoughts about Laos and Vietnam as soon as possible.

In writing to you, I am conscious of the difficulties you and I face in establishing full communication between our two minds. This is not a question of translation but a question of the context in which we hear and respond to what each other has to say. You and I have already recognized that neither of us will convince the other about our respective social systems and general philosophies of life. These differences create a great gulf in communication because language cannot mean the same thing on both sides unless it is related to some underlying common purpose. I cannot believe that there are not such common interests between the Soviet and the American people. Therefore, I am trying to penetrate our ideological differences in order to find some bridge across the gulf on which we could bring our minds together and find some way in which to protect the peace of the world.

Insofar as Laos is concerned, it has seemed to us that an agreement ought to be possible if you share our willingness to see that country genuinely neutral and independent, and are prepared to take, jointly, the necessary steps to that end. I have explained to you quite simply and sincerely that the United States has no national ambitions in Laos, no need for military bases or any military position, or an ally. You have stated your interest in a neutral and independent Laos which we assume means that you do not seek to impose a Communist regime upon Laos.

Considerable progress has been made in Geneva, although there are still some points which ought to be clarified. Further progress there will depend upon the composition of the neutral government in Laos itself through negotiation among the Laotian leaders. It is true that the United States has agreed to the formation of a coalition government to be headed by Prince Souvanna Phouma, but it is not accurate as you write that the formula four-eight-four derives from any agreement between our governments. This formula was suggested by Prince Souvanna Phouma himself. I can assure you that the United States is not attempting to determine the composition of such a government, and that we have most certainly not been exerting pressure through the Royal Laotian Government in any respect. We have, in fact, been pressing the leadership of the Royal Laotian Government to negotiate these questions in good faith with Prince Souvanna Phouma. Our efforts in this direction, therefore, correspond to the request contained in your letter as to how we should use our influence.

I wish I could believe that Prince Souphanouvong is prepared to enter into such discussions in a spirit of negotiation with a view to the creation of a genuinely neutral government. Prince Souphan ouvong has remained consistently at a distance from these discussions. We are hopeful that Prince Souvanna Phouma will show a willingness to take the initiative now incumbent upon him to search for a government which would be broadly representative of all elements in Laos and sincerely committed to a policy of nonalignment. We shall continue our efforts with the Royal Laotian Government for the achievement of this objective and I can only venture to hope that you, for your part, will likewise exert your influence in the same direction.

As to the situation in Vietnam, I must tell you frankly that your analysis of the situation there and the cause of the military action which has occurred in Southern Vietnam is not accurate. Precisely because of the visit of such Americans as Vice President Johnson and General Taylor we are, as you yourself recognize, well informed as to the situation in that country. I do not wish to argue with you concerning the government structure and policies of President Ngo Dinh Diem, but I would like to cite for your consideration the evidence of external interference of incitement which you dismiss in a phrase.

I would draw your attention to a letter sent by the Government of Vietnam to the International Control Commission concerning the North Vietnam subversion and aggression against Vietnam, dated

October 24, 1961. I would urge that you should read this document very carefully since it contains evidence of a planned and consistent effort on the part of the DRV [Democratic Republic of Vietnam] to overthrow by violence the legitimate government of South Vietnam. I would like to add that the evidence contained in this document is known to the United States to be accurate and sober. Many more incidents of the type outlined in this document could be deduced from our own experience and our own direct knowledge. I might point out here that in effect from 1954, the signature of the Geneva Accords, until 1959, the situation in Vietnam was relatively tranquil. The country was effecting a limited recovery from the ravages of the civil war from which it had just emerged. The Government enjoyed the support of the people and the prospects for the future appeared reasonably bright. However, in 1959, the DRV, having failed in the elections which had been held in Vietnam and in the attempt to arouse the people against their legitimate government, turned to a calculated plan of open infiltration, subversion, and aggression. During the Third Party Congress of the Lao Dong Party the Secretary General Le Duan stated: "There does not exist any other way outside of that which consists in the overthrow of the dictatorial and Fascist regime of the American-Diemist clique in order to liberate totally South Vietnam, with a view to realizing national unity." As indicated in the document to which I have referred, you will find this statement in the *Nhan Dan, Hanoi Daily* Number 2362 of September 6, 1960.

It is the firm opinion of the United States Government that Southern Vietnam is now undergoing a determined attempt from without to overthrow the existing government using for this purpose infiltration, supply of arms, propaganda, terrorization, and all the customary instrumentalities of communist activities in such circumstances, all mounted and developed from North Vietnam.

It is hardly necessary for me to draw your attention to the Geneva Accords of July 20–21, 1954. The issue, therefore, is not that of some opinion or other in regard to the government of President Ngo Dinh Diem, but rather that of a nation whose integrity and security [are] threatened by military actions, completely at variance with the obligations of the Geneva Accords.

Insofar as the United States is concerned, we view the situation in which the Republic of Vietnam finds itself with the utmost gravity and, in conformity with our pledge made at the Geneva Conference on July 21, 1954, as one seriously endangering international peace and security. Our support for the government of President Ngo Dinh Diem we regard as a serious obligation, and we will undertake such measures as the circumstances appear to warrant. Since there is no semblance of any threat to the DRV by the Government of Vietnam, it is clear that if the DRV were honorably to discharge the obligations it undertook in the Geneva Accords, the prospects for peace would be greatly improved. I would, therefore, venture to suggest that you, as the head of a government which was a signatory to the Geneva Accords, should use all the influence that you possess and endeavor to bring the DRV to the strict observance of these Accords. This would be a great act in the cause of peace which you refer to as the essence of the policies of the Twenty-second Party Congress. If the DRV were to abide by its obligations under the Geneva Accords, there would be no need for the United States to consider, as we must at the present, how best to support the Government of Vietnam in its struggle for independence and national integrity.

I have written you frankly about Laos and Vietnam for a very simple reason. Both these countries are at a distance from our own countries and can be considered areas in which we ought to be able to find agreement. I am suggesting to you that you use every means at your disposal to insure a genuinely neutral and independent Laos, as those words are commonly understood throughout the world, and to insure that those closely associated with you leave South Vietnam alone. On our part, we shall work toward a neutral and independent Laos and will insure that North Vietnam not be the object of any direct or indirect aggression. This would be a step toward peace; I am reluctant to believe that there is any necessary alternative to be imposed upon my country by the actions of others.

I am leaving for a few days for a visit to the western part of our country and will be in touch with you on other matters when I return.

Sincerely,
John F. Kennedy

[118]

On the campaign trail in November 1960, Kennedy had given a speech in San Francisco in which he deplored the fact that "seventy percent of all new Foreign Service officers had no language skill at all. . . . We cannot understand what is in the minds of other people if we cannot even speak to them. That is why we are given tongues." Noting that the United States was "in the most deadly struggle in which freedom has even been engaged," Kennedy asked how embassy officials who "do not even know how to pronounce the name of the head of the country . . . can . . . compete with Communist emissaries long trained and dedicated and committed to the cause of extending communism in those countries."

November 16, 1961

MEMORANDUM FOR ASSISTANT SECRETARY WOODWARD

I received a letter from a recent visitor to Peru who told me that the Peruvians were very pleased that our ambassador and his wife there spoke Spanish. However, the visitor understood that some of the personnel in the lesser positions in the embassy who have been there for some time did not know the language. Would you let me know how many of our personnel in our Latin American posts are able to speak Spanish? Also, what the degree of facility is of those in Spanish?

[119]

By October 18 South Vietnam's President Ngo Dinh Diem had issued an "emergency decree" empowering him to suspend constitutional processes and "take any action necessary for national security." In the wake of increased "Viet Cong attacks" and severe flooding in the rice-producing Mekong Valley, the decree was promptly ratified by South Vietnam's National Assembly.

On November 22 Kennedy gave his authorization for the "First Phase of the Viet-Nam Program." Although the memo was issued by Bundy, it provides a clear record of the President's decisions on all major points.

TOP SECRET
November 22, 1961
NATIONAL SECURITY ACTION MEMORANDUM NO. 111
TO: The Secretary of State
SUBJECT: First Phase of Viet-Nam Program

The President has authorized the Secretary of State to instruct our Ambassador to Viet-Nam to inform President Diem as follows:

1. The U.S. Government is prepared to join the Viet-Nam Government in a sharply increased joint effort to avoid a further deterioration in the situation in South Viet-Nam.

2. This joint effort requires undertakings by both Governments as outlined below:

a. On its part the U.S. would immediately undertake the following actions in support of the GVN [government of Vietnam]:

(1) Provide increased air lift to the GVN forces, including helicopters, light aviation, and transport aircraft, manned to the extent necessary by United States uniformed personnel and under United States operational control.

(2) Provide such additional equipment and United States uniformed personnel as may be necessary for air reconnaissance, photography, instruction in and execution of air-ground support techniques, and for special intelligence.

(3) Provide the GVN with small craft, including such United States uniformed advisers and operating personnel as may be necessary for operations in effecting surveillance and control over coastal waters and inland waterways.

(4) Provide expedited training and equipping of the civil guard and the self-defense corps with the objective of relieving the regular Army of static missions and freeing it for mobile offensive operations.

(5) Provide such personnel and equipment as may be necessary to improve the military-political intelligence system beginning at the provincial level and extending upward through the Government and the armed forces to the Central Intelligence Organization.

(6) Provide such new terms of reference, reorganization and additional personnel for United States military forces as are required for increased United States military assistance in the

operational collaboration with the GVN and operational direction of U.S. forces and to carry out the other increased responsibilities which accrue to the U.S. military authorities under these recommendations.

(7) Provide such increased economic aid as may be required to permit the GVN to pursue a vigorous flood relief and rehabilitation program, to supply material in support of the security efforts, and to give priority to projects in support of this expanded counter-insurgency program. (This could include increases in military pay, a full supply of a wide range of materials such as food, medical supplies, transportation equipment, communications equipment, and any other items where material help could assist the GVN in winning the war against the Viet Cong.)

(8) Encourage and support (including financial support) a request by the GVN to the FAO [UN Food and Agriculture Organization] or any other appropriate international organization for multilateral assistance in the relief and rehabilitation of the flood area.

(9) Provide individual administrators and advisers for the Governmental machinery of South Viet-Nam in types and numbers to be agreed upon by the two Governments.

(10) Provide personnel for a joint survey with the GVN of conditions in each of the provinces to assess the social, political, intelligence, and military factors bearing on the prosecution of the counter-insurgency program in order to reach a common estimate of these factors and a common determination of how to deal with them.

b. On its part, the GVN would initiate the following actions:

(1) Prompt and appropriate legislative and administrative action to put the nation on a wartime footing to mobilize its entire resources. (This would include a decentralization and broadening of the Government so as to realize the full potential of all non-Communist elements in the country willing to contribute to the common struggle.)

(2) The vitalization of appropriate Governmental wartime agencies with adequate authority to perform their functions effectively.

(3) Overhaul of the military establishment and command

structure so as to create an effective military organization for the prosecution of the war and assure a mobile offensive capability for the Army.

McGeorge Bundy

[120]

Rafael, Hector, and Arismondi Trujillo, three brothers of the former dictator of the Dominican Republic, threatened to "reassert dictatorial domination" in November 1961. When U.S. warships began patrolling the coast of the island on November 19, the Trujillo family finally left the country and the former dictator's political party was dissolved by President Balaguer.

Admiral George W. Anderson, Jr., was chief of naval operations during the Dominican maneuvers.

24 November 1961
Admiral George W. Anderson, Jr.
Chief of Naval Operations
Washington 25, D.C.

Dear Admiral Anderson:

I was interested to see a column by Mark S. Watson in the Baltimore Sun on November 21st in which he analyzed recent happenings in and around the Dominican Republic. I wholly agree with his appraisal of the value of seapower in support of diplomacy. Would you express my appreciation to those involved in this successful operation.

Captain [Tazewell T.] Shepard [naval military aide] also showed me your memorandum to Flag Officers dated 9 November. Speaking personally, I was most impressed by what you said and thought you stated the issue admirably. All officers should realize—particularly those in the senior grades—that the present provisions of law removing them from politics are for their own protection. Should either party start using Flag and General Officers for advancing their partisan causes, it will be the end of the career service.

As you know, I am always available, as are Secretary McNamara and Secretary [of the Navy John] Connally, to discuss with you any subject. I would particularly like to hear your views on any problem developing from this issue, which must be handled with greatest care.

> With every good wish,
> Sincerely,
> John F. Kennedy

[121]

Defoliant operations in Vietnam, approved by the President in National Security Action Memorandum No. 115, were initiated between January 13 and 16, 1962, along sixteen miles of Vietnamese Route 15 between Bien Hoa and Vung Tau.

TOP SECRET
November 30, 1961
NATIONAL SECURITY ACTION MEMORANDUM NO. 115
TO: The Secretary of State
　　The Secretary of Defense
SUBJECT: Defoliant Operations in Vietnam

The President has approved the recommendation of the Secretary of State and the Deputy Secretary of Defense to participate in a selective and carefully controlled joint program of defoliant operations in Viet Nam starting with the clearance of key routes and proceeding thereafter to food denial only if the most careful basis of resettlement and alternative food supply has been created. Operations in Zone D and the border areas shall not be undertaken until there are realistic possibilities of immediate military exploitation.

The President further agreed that there should be careful prior consideration and authorization by Washington of any plans developed by CINCPAC [commander in chief, Pacific] and the country team under this authority before such plans are executed.

> McGeorge Bundy

[122]

(On February 3, 1962, after conducting defoliant operations along twenty-one miles of highway, General Taylor promised to provide "effects data on diversified vegetation species, permitting a full evaluation of the merits of the defoliation program.'' On that date Taylor recommended that the President approve a proposal for additional defoliant operations ''with the understanding that the ground rules prescribed for the first operation remain valid for the new target areas.'')

At the end of the year President Kennedy sent via Western Union a message of greetings and goodwill to Premier Khrushchev and to Leonid I. Brezhnev, chairman of the Presidium of the Supreme Soviet.

Dear President Brezhnev and
Chairman Khrushchev:

As the year 1961 approaches its close I wish to extend to the people of the Soviet Union and to you and your families my most sincere wishes and those of the American people for a peaceful and prosperous new year. The year which is ending has been a troubled one. It is my earnest hope that the coming year will strengthen the foundations of world peace and will bring an improvement in the relations between our countries, upon which so much depends. It is our grave responsibility to fulfill that hope. As President of the United States, I can state on behalf of the government and the American people that we will do our best to do so.

John F. Kennedy

[123]

1962

Under Mortimer M. Caplin, commissioner of internal revenue, the Internal Revenue Service began to require strict accounting of allowable deductions and to scrutinize "lavish and extravagant" expenses closely.

January 5, 1962

MEMORANDUM FOR SECRETARY OF THE TREASURY

I believe that the Internal Revenue could usefully conduct an investigation of the charity balls in New York which have assumed great proportions and which I believe should be scrutinized. I think particularly the April and October balls, which cost the minimum of $50 per person. It would be interesting to see how much went to charity and how much is kept by those putting on the balls. Most of the persons attending these balls are in the high income bracket and therefore the federal government is being deprived of taxes. Likewise, the charitable theatre parties come in under the tax exemption.

We also might look into the foundations to see if they are sufficiently strict and whether they are withholding funds that should go to the federal government.

Perhaps you could talk to Kaplan [Caplin] and he might have some suggestions. Then we could discuss it.

[124]

In July 1961, after the Bay of Pigs, Kennedy put the nation's fallout shelter and civil defense programs under the Defense Department and created the Office of Emergency Planning (OEP) to oversee stockpiling of critical materials. Under Eisenhower the stockpiling accumulation had mounted to about $7.7 billion worth of strategic materials. In a news conference on January 31 Kennedy declared that this amount "exceeded our emergency requirements by nearly $3.4 billion." He called the "excessive stockpiling . . . a potential source of excessive and unconscionable profit."

February 7, 1962
NATIONAL SECURITY ACTION MEMORANDUM NO. 126
TO: Honorable Edward McDermott, Acting Director, Office of
    Emergency
    Planning
SUBJECT: Review of principles and policies guiding the
        stockpiling of strategic
        materials

To confirm our earlier discussions, I am designating you to serve as the chairman of a group of department and agency heads to review the principles and policies which should guide our program for the stockpiling of strategic materials. Any stockpiling must obviously be related to our nation's defense strategy and must ensure that materials necessary to our national defense and security will be available in the event of national emergency. I believe your committee should also give attention to specific goals as well as to basic principles, to the acquisitions and the maintenance of the material, and to the disposal of materials now on hand in excess of goals determined to be appropriate. This program is of vital importance to the nation, both in terms of our security and in terms of the Federal investment in these stockpiled goods. In addition, consideration should be given to the problems of our domestic minerals industry and to the international consequences of our programs of acquisition and disposal.

In the past, there may have been justification for classifying all or most of the information bearing on this program, but the changes in circumstances from the initiation of the program to the present call for review of the Secret classification. I expect, therefore, that your committee composed of the heads of those departments and agencies whose responsibilities bear heavily on whether classification is warranted promptly review this question and that you will take the steps necessary to declassify as much information as possible, consistent with national security. I am hopeful that your review will be completed by an early date and in any event no later than March 19. Those who will serve on the committee with you are the Secretaries of Defense, State, Interior, Commerce, and Labor, the Director of the Central Intelligence Agency, and the Administrator of the General Services Administration.

/s/ John F. Kennedy

[125]

Early in January 1962, British Prime Minister Harold Macmillan wrote an extensive letter to President Kennedy about the possible resumption of atmospheric tests by the United States and Britain and the prospects of reopening disarmament talks with Moscow. In his memoirs of that period (*At the End of the Day, 1961–1963*), Macmillan said that he "knew the strong pressure being brought upon him [the President] by the Pentagon and the atomic scientists to resume tests immediately. . . . At the same time I knew that Kennedy was desperately anxious to postpone the day of resuming tests, which he regarded as a confession of failure in the diplomatic field."

In his letter to Kennedy, Macmillan noted:

It has been agreed between us and the Russians that there will be an Eighteen-Power Conference on Disarmament beginning in the middle of March. We must build on this. . . . My idea would be that you and I, who are in the lead on the Western side, should take the initiative and invite Mr. Khrushchev to concert with us, before this committee meets, on the best methods of ensuring that practical progress is made.

On February 10 Khrushchev wrote to Kennedy about the direction of the proposed disarmament talks. The President's letter of reply was sent on February 13:

SECRET

Dear Mr. Chairman:

In reading your letter of February 10, 1962, I was gratified to see that you have been thinking along the same lines as Prime Minister Macmillan and myself as to the importance of the new disarmament negotiations which will begin in Geneva in March. I was gratified also to see that you agree that the heads of government should assume personal responsibility for the success of these negotiations.

The question which must be decided, of course, is how that personal responsibility can be most usefully discharged. I do not believe that the attendance by the heads of government at the outset of an 18-nation conference is the best way to move forward. I believe that procedure along the lines of that outlined in the letter which Prime Minister Macmillan and I addressed to you on February 7 is that best designed to give impetus to the work of the conference.

I agree with the statement which you have made in your letter that there exists a better basis than has previously existed for successful work by the conference. The Agreed Statement of Principles for Disarmament Negotiations which was signed by representatives of our countries on September 20, 1961, and which was noted with approval by the 16th General Assembly of the United Nations, represents a foundation upon which a successful negotiation may be built.

As you have recognized, there still exist substantial differences between our two positions. Just one example is the Soviet unwillingness so far to accord the control organization the authority to verify during the disarmament process that agreed levels of forces and armament are not exceeded.

The task of the conference will be to attempt to explore this and other differences which may exist and to search for means of overcoming them by specific disarmament plans and measures. This does not mean that the conference should stay with routine procedures or arguments or that the Heads of Government should not be interested in the negotiations from the very outset. It does mean that much clarifying work will have to be done in the early stages of negotiation before it is possible for Heads of Government to review the situation. This may be necessary in any case before June 1 when a report is to be filed on the progress achieved.

I do not mean to question the utility or perhaps even the necessity of a meeting of Heads of Government. Indeed, I am quite ready to participate personally at the Heads of Government level at any stage of the conference when it appears that such participation could positively affect the chances of success. The question is rather one of timing. I feel that until there have been systematic negotiations —until the main problems have been clarified and progress has been made—intervention by Heads of Government would involve merely a general exchange of governmental position which might set back, rather than advance, the prospects for disarmament. It is for these reasons that I think that meetings at the highly responsible level of our Foreign Ministers would be the best instrument for the opening stages.

A special obligation for the success of the conference devolves upon our two Governments and that of the United Kingdom as nuclear powers. I therefore hope that the suggestion made in the letter of Prime Minister Macmillan and myself to you, that the Foreign Ministers of the three countries meet in advance of the conference in order to concert plans for its work, will be acceptable to the Soviet Government.

[126]

In early 1962 a low-flying SC-47 carrying eight Americans and one Vietnamese crashed in the jungle near Da Lat, killing all aboard. Since journalists were barred from Bien Hoa, the active role of U.S. commandos and the crash of the SC-47 were not reported. (Jungle Jim/Farmgate activities were not disclosed until 1964, and by then U.S. troops were officially playing a combat role.)

In Kaysen's report on his breakfast meeting with the President, he mentions Sterling Cottrell, a State Department specialist. As early as 1961 Cottrell reported that the Vietnam War was being waged in villages where "foreign military forces themselves cannot win." He questioned whether the Diem regime could succeed, even with U.S. assistance.

2/14/62

Mr. Bundy
From Mr. Kaysen

Major things that came up at breakfast

1. South Vietnam—George Ball was preparing the statement and Cottrell was bringing it in.

2. The President asked about the crashed C-47 [SC-47]. All we know was that it was a Jungle Jim operation; that in addition to the usual crew of three Americans, two UNAF, there were 5 Army passengers. We still don't know why. These operations have never been made public.

3. The President commented on the amount of aid we have been giving to Egypt and wondered if we haven't overdone it. Possibly Komer ought to do a memo on this one.

[127]

In the Kennedy administration the Agency for International Development had a multitude of diverse functions related to foreign policy. It was designed to foster long-term development projects and to encourage the economic growth of developing countries by coordinating the work of such agencies as the International Cooperation Administration (ICA) and the Development Loan Fund (DLF) as well as the Food for Peace program. Part of the agency's mission was political: to support democracy in nations receiving grants or loans from the United States. Part was economic: to distribute U.S. technology, food surpluses, and aid to "deserving" countries. And as Kennedy's memo of February 19, 1962, makes clear, a large role of AID was military: to encourage counterinsurgency training and police assistance programs.

NATIONAL SECURITY ACTION MEMORANDUM NO. 132
February 19, 1962
TO: The Honorable Fowler Hamilton
     The Administrator, Agency for International Development
SUBJECT: Support of local police forces for internal
          security and counter-insurgency purposes

As you know, I desire the appropriate agencies of this Government to give utmost attention and emphasis to programs designed to counter Communist indirect aggression, which I regard as a grave threat during the 1960s. I have already written the Secretary of Defense "to move to a new level of increased activity across the board" in the counter-insurgency field.

Police assistance programs, including those under the aegis of your agency, are also a crucial element in our response to this challenge. I understand there has been some tendency toward de-emphasizing them under the new AID criteria developed by your agency. I recognize that such programs may seem marginal in terms of focusing our energies on those key sectors which will contribute most to sustained economic growth. But I regard them as justified on a different but related basis, i.e., that of contributing to internal security and resisting Communist-supported insurgency.

I am further aware that police programs, as a relatively minor facet of the functions of the aid agency, may have tended to receive little emphasis as a result. Therefore, I would like you to consider various ways and means of giving the police program greater autonomy within AID, if this seems necessary in order to protect it from neglect. I fully recognize that police programs must be looked at on a case-by-case basis and in some instances they can indeed be cut back or eliminated. I simply wish to insure that before doing so we have taken fully into account the importance of the counter-insurgency objective as I view it.

In sum, I should like AID to review carefully its role in the support of local police forces for internal security and counter-insurgency purposes, and to recommend to me through the special group (Counter-Insurgency) what new or renewed emphases are desirable.

/s/ John F. Kennedy

[128]

The President's February 20, 1962, meeting with General Clifton occurred at a critical time of military escalation in Laos and Vietnam, and the "Notes" dictated before the meeting give insight into Kennedy's planning, operations, and coordination of military and diplomatic personnel.

In the memo the President mentioned a ceremony for Richard M. Bissell, deputy director of plans for the CIA. Bissell was among those held responsible for the failure of the Bay of Pigs invasion.

He resigned on February 17 but received a secret intelligence medal for his years of service.

In Points 17 and 18 of the memo the President referred to the resumption of U.S. atmospheric testing of nuclear weapons. Kennedy planned to begin tests on Christmas Island, an atoll in the Pacific where Britain had conducted tests in 1947 and 1958.

In Britain the leader of the opposition Labour party, Hugh T. N. Gaitskell, had asked for Prime Minister Macmillan's assurances that no tests would be conducted until Great Britain, the Soviet Union, and the United States had a chance to negotiate at the disarmament conference that was to resume in Geneva in March. When Macmillan said he could give no such assurances, Gaitskell conferred directly with Kennedy.

On February 20, 1962, the date of this memo, astronaut John H. Glenn became the first American to orbit the earth.

February 20, 1962

NOTES ON GENERAL CLIFTON'S MEETING WITH PRESIDENT

1. The President wants to have a meeting at 9:00 AM. tomorrow in the Mansion prior to the bi-partisan meeting to rehearse for the 9:30 meeting. Following should be there: McNamara, Lemnitzer, Rusk, McCone, Harriman, General Taylor (if well), Bundy, Clifton. (McNamara and Lemnitzer know about this; others should be checked.) (Bundy)

2. The President wants from Mr. Bundy a summary of the troop situation in Viet-Nam and Laos. He wants to see it beforehand, and also wants it for the meeting. (Bundy)

3. He wants a copy of the message which said that the troops ran away in the last month. (General Clifton is getting this.)

4. He wants from Mr. Bundy a group of charts (which Mr. Bundy showed him before) showing number of incidents and casualties. He wants the charts big enough to show the Leadership. (Bundy)

5. He wants to know anything we have about the number of Viet-Minh prisoners taken by the RLG [Royal Laotian government]—if they were captured, what we have found about them. (Bundy)

6. He wants to know number of casualties at Nam Tha [Laos]. (Bundy)

7. Wants in addition all casualties since first of January in Laos. (Bundy)

8. Wants complete report on the number of U.S. casualties in Viet-Nam since the start. (Thinks most were those lost in helicopter.) (Bundy)

9. Wants a comparison of SNIE [special national intelligence estimate] 58–62 and SNIE 58/1–62—of the differences, and an explanation, and wants both for the meeting. (Bundy)

10. Secretary McNamara has been told to be ready on Viet-Nam and Laos. (Clifton)

11. The President wants Secretary Rusk to be prepared to give full run-down on Berlin negotiations. Mr. Bundy should decide whether Rusk or Lemnitzer will discuss the corridor in detail and what we have decided to do, and what plans have been made, and how much should we tell. (Mr. Bundy should tell Secretary Rusk.)

12. He wants Bundy to talk to McCone and have him round up any additional important intelligence matters, and wants McCone prepared to give it—no charts or handouts. He wants a fast, snappy briefing on this. (Bundy)

13. With regard to ceremony for Mr. Bissell, he wants Mr. Bundy to get the citation written up and the medal ready, and sent over here for approval. He thinks the ceremony will be Monday or Tuesday. He wants Mr. Allen Dulles invited plus lots of others, and wants it at the White House. Mr. Bundy should arrange. (Bundy)

14. He is having lunch with Ambassador Stevenson on Thursday. He asked that Dr. Wiesner and Dr. [Harold] Brown [director of research and engineering for the Department of Defense] stand by in ante-room but not attend lunch if needed for discussion. Mr. O'Donnell is to arrange. (O'Donnell)

15. The President wants before the meetings the analysis of Geneva accords [on Laos] that we have reached and those things that are still vague—being prepared by Mr. Bundy. He wants the analysis at his finger tips and wants to be well versed in it before hand.

16. Clifton will get for the President a wire from Souvanna that says he wants us to help lick the Pathet Lao.

17. Following the discussion with Gaitskell yesterday, he wants the pros and cons of our public announcement idea gone over again in light of this talk. One alternative would be to make a statement

before the fleets sail; second was to say nothing until April 5–8 when the fleet is there and everything is ready, and we have seen how things went. He wants the discussion of the pros and cons analyzed. He wants to have a feel for this problem before tomorrow when he discusses nuclear testing.

18. Mr.Bundy has already put out that we are going to have our final decision on testing at an NSC meeting next week. If we go with the second alternative, then we will have to get off this hook because it just won't hold water and we may have to change the NSC idea and the whole business next week to a discussion of the Disarmament Conference, and not even discuss nuclear testing or we will never be able to choose the alternative of waiting until April for an announcement.

19. If all is successful, Colonel Glenn will come in on Monday. The President is talking about a big parade and reception on Capitol Hill.

20. Wants to know from Mr. Bundy and State Department whether we should start preparing letters of thanks for the Attorney General's trip—especially those to Japan and Indonesia—or should this wait until he gets home. Are the Ambassadors sending drafts?

21. Mr. Bundy should get in touch with the President and set up a meeting next week with the Gold Outflow Group. He had a long talk with Dillon on the phone about this.

[129]

Under Fowler Hamilton AID moved away from a policy of making outright grants to developing nations. Instead, loans were granted with variable terms of repayment. In an AID memo sent to the President on February 9, Hamilton advocated forty-year loans, with a ten-year grace period and, in lieu of interest, a small (three quarters of 1 percent) credit fee. "Our objective of stimulating a greater degree of development," wrote Hamilton, "depends upon providing capital additional to that which is available from conventional sources. If this cannot be accomplished on a dollar-repayable loan basis, the alternative would appear to be to return to grant aid or local currency repayment."

March 2, 1962
NATIONAL SECURITY ACTION MEMORANDUM NO. 130
TO: The Administrator, Agency for International Development
SUBJECT: Terms of AID Development loans

I concur in your proposal in your memorandum of February 9, 1962, to establish liberal terms as a basis for development lending. Our fundamental purpose in offering these loans is to advance the development of countries who [sic] are already mobilizing their own resources extensively, whose needs are great but whose capacity to repay will come only with the long-run development of their national economy. Long-term low-interest loans will allow carrying out many high priority and worthwhile development projects and programs which meet the stiff standards set by Congress and the Executive Branch, but for which financing on conventional terms would be either unavailable or inappropriate.

At the same time, I agree that we must also maintain substantial flexibility in our loan term policies so that we can suit both interest rates and maturities to the individual situation. Countries have different repayment capacities justifying differing loan terms. Some kinds of loans, such as those for private and public revenue-producing projects or for short and medium-term economic requirements, should usually be made on terms considerably more strict.

As we expand our lending programs, I am concerned that we construct a lending strategy involving foreign assistance loans, the Export-Import Bank, and the Inter-American Bank Trust Fund which builds on the individual advantages and specialties of each agency, and which ties in closely with the international lending agencies. To this end, I would like you to investigate thoroughly the use of consortia as a means of correlating our programs with those of others and ways by which we can strengthen the organizational and administrative leadership of consortia.

I would further like to have your advice on other steps we might take to increase the coordination of the several U.S. and international lending agencies in major countries and on whether it might be possible to build up functional specialties in certain of these agencies to attack specific development problems. You should assume a primary part in examining these questions, and I look forward to your recommendations at such time as you have formulated them.

/s/ John F. Kennedy

[130]

On March 7 Kennedy sent to Premier Khrushchev a number of concrete proposals for cooperation between the United States and Soviet Union in scientific experiments and exploration of outer space. Andrei Gromyko was the Soviet foreign minister and a member of the Central Committee of the Communist party.

March 7, 1962

His Excellency
Nikita S. Khrushchev
Chairman of the Council of Ministers of
  the Union of Soviet Socialist Republics,
Moscow

Dear Mr. Chairman:

On February twenty-second last I wrote you that I was instructing appropriate officers of this Government to prepare concrete proposals for immediate projects of common action in the exploration of space. I now present such proposals to you.

The exploration of space is a broad and varied activity and the possibilities for cooperation are many. In suggesting the possible first steps which are set out below, I do not intend to limit our mutual consideration of desirable cooperative activities. On the contrary, I will welcome your concrete suggestions along these or other lines.

1. Perhaps we could render no greater service to mankind through our space programs than by the joint establishment of an early operational weather satellite system. Such a system would be designed to provide global weather data for prompt use by any nation. To initiate this service, I propose that the United States and the Soviet Union each launch a satellite to photograph cloud cover and provide other agreed meteorological services for all nations. The two satellites would be placed in near-polar orbits in planes approximately perpendicular to each other, thus providing regular cov-

erage of all areas. This immensely valuable data would then be disseminated through normal international meteorological channels and would make a significant contribution to the research and service programs now under study by the World Meteorological Organization in response to Resolution 1721 (XVI) adopted by the United Nations General Assembly on December 20, 1961.

2. It would be of great interest to those responsible for the conduct of our respective space programs if they could obtain operational tracking services from each other's territories. Accordingly, I propose that each of our countries establish and operate a radio tracking station to provide tracking services to the other, utilizing equipment which we would each provide to the other. Thus, the United States would provide the technical equipment for a tracking station to be established in the Soviet Union and to be operated by Soviet technicians. The United States would in turn establish and operate a radio tracking station utilizing Soviet equipment. Each country would train the other's technicians in the operation of its equipment, would utilize the station located on its territory to provide tracking services to the other, and would afford such access as may be necessary to accommodate modifications and maintenance of equipment from time to time.

3. In the field of the earth sciences, the precise character of the earth's magnetic field is central to many scientific problems. I propose therefore that we cooperate in mapping the earth's magnetic field in space by utilizing two satellites, one in a near-earth orbit and the second in a more distant orbit. The United States would launch one of these satellites while the Soviet Union would launch the other. The data would be exchanged throughout the world scientific community, and opportunities for correlation of supporting data obtained on the ground would be arranged.

4. In the field of experimental communications by satellite, the United States has already undertaken arrangements to test and demonstrate the feasibility of intercontinental transmissions. A number of countries are constructing equipment suitable for participation in such testing. I would welcome the Soviet Union's joining in this cooperative effort which will be a step toward meeting the objective, contained in United Nations General Assembly Resolution 1721 (XVI), that communications by means of satellites should be available to the nations of the world as soon as practicable on a global

and non-discriminatory basis. I note also that Secretary Rusk has broached the subject of cooperation in this field with Minister Gromyko and that Mr. Gromyko has expressed some interest. Our technical representatives might now discuss specific possibilities in this field.

5. Given our common interest in manned space flights and in insuring man's ability to survive in space and return safely, I propose that we pool our efforts and exchange our knowledge in the field of space medicine, where future research can be pursued in cooperation with scientists from various countries.

Beyond these specific projects we are prepared now to discuss broader cooperation in the still more challenging projects which must be undertaken in the exploration of outer space. The tasks are so challenging, the costs so great, and the risks to the brave men who engage in space exploration so grave, that we must in all good conscience try every possibility of sharing these tasks and costs and of minimizing these risks. Leaders of the United States space program have developed detailed plans for an orderly sequence of manned and unmanned flights for exploration of space and the planets. Out of the discussion of these plans, and of your own, for undertaking the tasks of this decade would undoubtedly emerge possibilities for substantive scientific and technical cooperation in manned and unmanned space investigations. Some possibilities are not yet precisely identifiable, but should become clear as the space programs of our two countries proceed. In the case of others it may be possible to start planning together now. For example, we might cooperate in unmanned exploration of the lunar surface, or we might commence now the mutual definition of steps to be taken in sequence for an exhaustive scientific investigation of the planets Mars or Venus, including consideration of the possible utility of manned flight in such programs. When a proper sequence for experiments has been determined, we might share responsibility for the necessary projects. All data would be made freely available.

I believe it is both appropriate and desirable that we take full cognizance of the scientific and other contributions which other states the world over might be able to make in such programs. As agreements are reached between us on any parts of these or similar programs, I propose that we report them to the United Nations Committee on the Peaceful Uses of Outer Space. The Committee offers a variety of additional opportunities for joint cooperative efforts within the framework of the mandate as set forth in General Assembly Resolutions 1472 (XIV) and 1721 (XVI).

I am designating technical representatives who will be prepared to meet and discuss with your representatives our ideas and yours in a spirit of practical cooperation. In order to accomplish this at an early date, I suggest that the representatives of our two countries who will be coming to New York to take part in the United Nations Outer Space Committee meet privately to discuss the proposals set forth in this letter.

Sincerely,

John F. Kennedy

[131]

The Senate Armed Services Committee, one of the most powerful committees in Congress, has powers to oversee allocations and to investigate. Those on the Special Government Information Subcommittee of the Committee on Government Operations feared that a liberal administration might be too eager to invoke "executive privilege," possibly withholding information from the Armed Services Committee. The following is the President's reply to a letter from John E. Moss, the California representative on the subcommittee who, in later years, pressed for passage of the Freedom of Information Act.

March 7, 1962

Honorable John E. Moss
Chairman
Special Government Information Subcommittee of the
    Committee on Government Operations
House of Representatives
Washington, D.C.

Dear Mr. Chairman:

This is in reply to your letter of last month inquiring generally about the practice this Administration will follow in invoking the doctrine of executive privilege in withholding certain information from the Congress.

As your letter indicated, my letter of February 8 to Secretary McNamara made it perfectly clear that the directive to refuse to make certain specific information available to a special sub-committee of the Senate Armed Services Committee was limited to that specific request and that "each case must be judged on its merits."

As you know, this Administration has gone to great lengths to achieve full cooperation with the Congress in making available to it all appropriate documents, correspondence and information. This is the basic policy of this Administration, and it will continue to be so. Executive privilege can be invoked only by the President and will not be used without specific Presidential approval. Your own interest in assuring the widest public accessibility to governmental information is, of course, well known, and I can assure you this Administration will continue to cooperate with your subcommittee and the entire Congress in achieving this objective.

> Sincerely,
> /s/ John F. Kennedy
>
> [132]

National Security Action Memorandum No. 131, issued with the President's approval just a week after the memo to Hamilton on AID, effectively tied in the new AID loan policy with extended counterinsurgency training that would be conducted for the Departments of State and Defense, AID, and USIA.

NSAM 131 was declassified in 1982.

MARCH 13, 1962
NATIONAL SECURITY ACTION MEMORANDUM NO. 131
TO: The Secretary of State
    The Secretary of Defense
    The Attorney General
    The Chairman of the Joint Chiefs of Staff
    The Director of Central Intelligence
    Administrator AID
    The Director, USIA
SUBJECT: Training objectives for counter-insurgency

1. The President has approved the following training objectives for officer-grade personnel of the departments and agencies indicated

above who may have a role to play in counter-insurgency programs as well as in the entire range of problems involved in the modernization of developing countries:

a. *The historical background of counter-insurgency*

Personnel of all grades will be required to study the history of subversive insurgency movements past and present in order to familiarize themselves with the nature of the problems and characteristics of Communist tactics and techniques as related to this particular aspect of Communist operations. This kind of background historical study will be offered throughout the school systems of the responsible departments and agencies beginning at the junior level of instruction and carrying forward to the senior level.

b. *Study of departmental tactics and techniques to counter subversive insurgency*

Junior and middle grade officers will receive instructions in the tactics and techniques of their particular departments which have an application in combating subversive insurgency. This level of instruction will be found in the schools of the armed services at the company/field officer level. In the case of the Central Intelligence Agency, this kind of instruction will be offered at appropriate training installations. The State Department will be responsible for organizing appropriate courses in this instructional area for its own officers and for representatives of the Agency for International Development and the United States Information Agency. Schools of this category will make available spaces in agreed numbers for the cross-training of other U.S. agencies with a counter-insurgency responsibility.

c. *Instruction in counter-insurgency program planning*

Middle grade and senior officers will be offered special training to prepare them for command, staff, country, team, and departmental positions involved in the planning and conduct of counter-insurgency programs. At this level, the students will be made aware of the possible contributions of all departments and of the need to combine the departmental assets into effective programs. This type of instruction will be given at the Staff College-War College level in the armed services. The State Department will organize such courses as may be necessary at the Foreign Service Institute for officials of State, Agency for International Development, and United States Information Agency. All schools of this category will make available spaces in agreed numbers for the cross-training of other U.S. agencies with a counter-insurgency responsibility.

d. *Specialized preparations for service in underdeveloped areas*

There is an unfilled need to offer instruction on the entire range of problems faced by the United States in dealing with developing countries, including special area counter-insurgency problems, to middle and senior grade officers (both military and civilian) who are about to occupy important posts in underdeveloped countries. A school will accordingly be developed at the national level to meet this need to teach general (including counter-insurgency) policy and doctrine with respect to underdeveloped areas, to offer studies on problems of the underdeveloped world keyed to areas to which the students are being sent and to engage in research projects designed to improve the U.S. capability for guiding underdeveloped countries through the modernization barrier and for countering subversive insurgency. In addition, this school would undertake to assist other more specialized U.S. Government institutions engaged in underdeveloped area problems (i.e., those conducted by the Foreign Service Institute, Agency for International Development, the Joint Chiefs of Staff, and the services including the Military Assistance Institute and the Central Intelligence Agency) to develop curricula on the nontechnical aspects of their courses of instruction.

e. *Training of foreign nationals*

It is in the interest of the United States to provide counter-insurgency training to selected foreign nationals both in the United States and in their own countries. The emphasis should be placed on those countries with an actual or potential counter-insurgency problem. This training will be given in the following places:

(1). In facilities operated by the Department of Defense and the Central Intelligence Agency which are available to foreigners;

(2). In special facilities operated by the Department of Defense and the Agency for International Development in Panama for the benefit of foreign nationals;

(3). USMAAG/missions and USOMs in countries with counter-insurgency programs.

2. It is desired that the Special Group (Counter-Insurgency) explore ways of organizing a school of the type described in Paragraph 1 (d) above as a matter of urgency and develop appropriate recommendations. This Special Group (Counter-Insurgency) should also examine the possibility of setting up interim courses at the Foreign Service Institute and/or at the National War College to fill the gap during consideration of a new school.

3. It is desired that the addressees examine the counter-insurgency training which is currently offered in their departments and agencies and to report by June 1, 1962, upon the adequacy with which it meets the training objectives above. If any deficiencies are determined to exist, the responsible department or agency will report its plan for correcting them.

McGeorge Bundy

[133]

(On April 23, in a memo to the President commenting on NSAM 131, Secretary of State Rusk replied, "We recognize the need for such a school. At the national level the academy would consist of a school of languages, a school of foreign relations, a center for international development studies. AID and USIA support it. General Taylor and Bundy and Rostow discussed this concept of an enlarged foreign service institute with you on March 17.")

On October 25, 1961, President Kennedy, Arthur Schlesinger, and other U.S. officials met with Dr. Cheddi Jagan, the prime minister of British Guiana. From that meeting Schlesinger concluded "Jagan was unquestionably some sort of Marxist. The question was whether he was recoverable for democracy."

In January 1962, after Guiana's minister of finance had introduced across-the-board tax increases and a compulsory savings plan, civil and government workers in the British colony mounted a protest. Events came to a crisis on February 16, when about fifty thousand workers went on strike, followed by looting and arson, resulting in a number of deaths. Jagan claimed that the rioting was part of a plot to overthrow the government. British naval and military forces were mustered, and the British Colonial Office called for an inquiry.

SECRET
March 8, 1962
NATIONAL SECURITY ACTION MEMORANDUM NO. 135
TO: The Secretary of State
SUBJECT: British Guiana

No final decision will be taken on our policy toward British Guiana and the Jagan government until: (a) Secretary of State has a chance to discuss the matter with Lord [Alec Douglas-] Home in Geneva and (b) Hugh Fraser completes his on-the-spot survey in British Guiana for the colonial office. The questions which we must answer before we reach our decision include the following:

1. Can Great Britain be persuaded to delay independence for a year?

2. If Great Britain refuses to delay the date of independence, would a new election before independence be possible? If so, would Jagan win or lose? If he lost, what are the alternatives?

3. What are the possibilities and limitations of the United States action in this situation?

/s/ JFK

[134]

The President was impatient with the Berlin Task Force, a group assigned by the State Department to help formulate policy decisions. In June and July 1961 it took the task force six weeks to draft a reply to the aide-mémoire on Berlin that Khrushchev gave to Kennedy in Vienna. In August 1961, when the Berlin wall went up, the task force took four days to draft a weak protest to Moscow.

March 15, 1962
NATIONAL SECURITY ACTION MEMORANDUM NO. 137
TO: The Secretary of State
SUBJECT: Restrictions on East German athletes

The President has reviewed the matter of travel bans on German athletes and while he recognizes that in the current round of negotiations we are pretty well committed to our present position, he would like it understood that he does not accept the premise of the argument in the Berlin Task Force Memorandum submitted on February 22. He believes that it is better to separate international athletic questions from political questions, and he hopes therefore that we can find ways and means of modifying our present position as circumstances permit. Furthermore no new initiative in the restriction of individual participation in international athletic events should be undertaken without his specific approval.

McGeorge Bundy

[135]

When Arthur Schlesinger and George McGovern visited Argentinian president Dr. Arturo Frondizi in February 1961, the U.S. envoys promoted the Food for Peace program and sought Frondizi's views on Cuba, Castro, and communism. In March 1962, after Frondizi lost an election against the Peronistas, he was arrested. The head of the Argentinian Senate, José María Guido, was installed as the new president. According to a memorandum from AID, Frondizi had accepted a $150 million loan from the Alliance for Progress at the time he was removed from office.

March 20, 1962
MEMORANDUM FOR ASSISTANT SECRETARY EDWIN MARTIN,
ASSISTANT ADMINISTRATOR TEODORO MOSCOSO

The President would like an analysis of the extent to which President Frondizi's recent political reverses were due to either:

(a) Exploitation by his opponent of the fact that he arranged to accept United States aid;

(b) Exploitation by his opponents of reforms undertaken or promised by him and associated with the Alliance for Progress.

The President would also like consideration given to the question as to whether it is advisable to channel more Alliance aid through Inter-American agencies.

I assume that Assistant Secretary Martin will wish to handle points (a) and (b) above, and that Assistant Administrator Moscoso will handle the point made in the last paragraph. I should welcome an opportunity to discuss these matters with you or members of your staff to whom they are assigned.

Signed,
F. H. R. Hamilton
[136]

(In a memo to the President a week later Hamilton cited reports that Frondizi's defeat would have been even worse if U.S. aid hadn't come when it did. "An important reason for Frondizi's defeat," Hamilton concluded, "was that his reforms and development program had not gone far enough or deep enough to reach the common man yet." Subsequently Ed Martin advised Kennedy to support Frondizi, but Senate leaders convinced Kennedy to recognize the new government.)

It was Kennedy's view that being the first nation to put a person on the moon would give the United States a clear political and psychological advantage over the Soviet Union. By establishing the highest priority rating in NSAM 144 for the manned lunar landing, the President placed the space program on the same footing as the Atlas ICBM, Titan ICBM, Polaris FBM, Minuteman ICM, Ballistic Missile Early Warning systems, and other military programs.

April 11, 1962

NATIONAL SECURITY ACTION MEMORANDUM NO. 144
TO: The Administrator, National Aeronautics and Space
     Administration
SUBJECT: Assignment of highest national priority to the Apollo
          manned lunar
          landing program

As recommended by the National Aeronautics and Space Council, I have today established the following program as having highest priority in the context of paragraph 6 of NSC 6021, which is amended accordingly: Apollo (manned lunar landing program) including essential space craft, launch vehicles, and facilities.

/s/ John Kennedy

[137]

In a top secret memorandum for the Special Group (Counter-Insurgency) written by Lyman L. Lemnitzer, chairman of the Joint Chiefs of Staff, on January 20, the general defended the level and quality of counterinsurgency training already provided by the military services. In his memo Lemnitzer noted that many training programs were being provided for "personnel selected for MAAG, Mission and Attaché duty."

He also informed the Special Group (CI) that "the Military Services are taking full advantage of the laboratory-type approach afforded by the current situation in Southeast Asia and other areas of the world."

The President referred to this previous work of the Special Group (CI) in his memo of April 16.

April 16, 1962

MEMORANDUM FOR THE SECRETARY OF STATE,
THE SECRETARY OF DEFENSE

You will recall that I discussed last week the possibility of improving the equipping and training of police forces in the capitals of many of the new emerging countries to assure that they can maintain order without the necessity of firing upon civilian demonstrators who are often composed of students. This consideration leads to the broader question of whether such training of foreign police forces should remain under AID or should be assigned to some other agency, possibly to a special group in the Pentagon. I would like you to organize a joint State/Defense study of this matter, to include an examination of the police techniques in Paris and Rome to assure that our technicians are aware and take advantage of the extensive police experience in these capitals. I would like your recommendations as soon as possible as to ways of improving the training and equipping of police forces in sensitive areas and the U.S. organization best adapted to this end. You will find that the Special Group (Counter-Insurgency) has done some work in this field which is available to you.

[138]

Secretary McNamara initially played the role of cost cutter in the Defense Department, bringing criticism from the Joint Chiefs of Staff and other officers who were advocates of special military programs. In late 1961 McNamara assigned the Defense Department comptroller and a weapons systems analyst to develop a planning-programming-budgeting (PPB) system within the Pentagon. The purpose of the new budgeting system was to eliminate the overlap of special weapons systems designed by different branches of the armed forces and to put an end to programs that had design flaws.

Since the acceleration of the man in space program required an additional twenty-billion-dollar allocation from Congress, Kennedy looked for cost cutting in other areas. He turned to McNamara to implement these measures in Defense.

17 April 1962

The Honorable Robert S. McNamara
Secretary of Defense
Washington, DC

Dear Mr. Secretary,

I have given considerable thought to the complexities of our modern weapons systems and their requirements for systems testing. I believe that the rapid advances in technology over the last ten years have thrust us very rapidly into a transition period during which these highly complex systems are coming into operational use. It seems to me that such a situation breeds danger. Through impatience, overselling of capabilities, testing only under ideal conditions, or public relations or budgetary problems, hasty or ill-considered action may be taken which will cause some systems to be unwisely expedited. If our defense dollars are to be spent judiciously and our national security properly protected, such situations must be avoided. These same thoughts have undoubtedly occurred to you, but I wanted you to know my personal concern on these matters. Would you please advise me whether you feel that any major weapons system gives evidence of not fulfilling its design objectives or failing to meet operational requirements under realistic conditions.

Sincerely,
John Kennedy

[139]

In March the newly appointed assistant secretary of state for Far Eastern affairs, Averell Harriman, informed the Laotian general Phoumi Nosquon that U.S. military troops would be pulled out of Laos unless the general accepted a coalition government under Prince Souvanna Phouma. Under pressure from the Thai government, Phoumi relented, and in early May he informed Harriman that he was willing to negotiate with Souvanna. (Agreement among Laotian leaders to the terms of the ICC was finally reached in June.)

The White Star teams referred to in NSAM 149 were U.S. mobile training teams that trained Meo and Kha tribesmen to battle the Pathet Lao and their North Vietnamese allies.

NATIONAL SECURITY ACTION MEMORANDUM NO. 149
April 19, 1962
TO: The Secretary of State
The Secretary of Defense
The Director of CIA
SUBJECT: Withdrawal of certain military units from forward positions in Laos.

1. The President has authorized the Secretary of Defense to plan for the withdrawal of those MAAG [Military Assistance Advisory Group] White Star teams in Laos which are located in forward field positions. Approximately seven or eight White Star teams would be withdrawn to the rear echelon and would remain in Laos until their normal tour of duty expired. Their replacement will be decided upon subsequently.

2. The withdrawal will take place at such time as the Secretary of State deems appropriate. It is not presently contemplated that this would occur before May 7, 1962.

3. The Secretary of State will prepare an appropriate public an-

nouncement of the action at the time the withdrawal takes place. Prior to such time every effort should be made to keep this matter confidential.

McGeorge Bundy

[140]

Using the code name Project Plowshare, Kennedy's science advisers were studying the possibility of creating a sea-level canal across Panama. Because nuclear explosives would be used to create the canal, the project involved the Department of Defense, the Atomic Energy Commission, and the CIA.

On December 12, 1961, the director of the Bureau of the Budget, David E. Bell, had attended a meeting with Glenn T. Seaborg and Leland Haworth of the Atomic Energy Commission to discuss the funding of Project Plowshare. Assistant Director of the Budget Kenneth R. Hansen noted that a proposed 1963 experiment in "cratering" would "involve massive venting to the atmosphere and the production of a large radioactive dust cloud." Hansen reported that Dr. Seaborg was primarily interested in "the scientific and basic research aspects of Project Plowshare rather than . . . the earth-moving aspects."

SECRET

NATIONAL SECURITY ACTION MEMORANDUM NO. 152

April 30, 1962

TO: The Secretary of State
    The Secretary of Defense
    Chairman Atomic Energy Commission
    The Director of Central Intelligence
    The Director, Bureau of the Budget

SUBJECT: Panama Canal Policy and relations with Panama

I have approved the following policy guidance governing the conduct of the United States relations with Panama and future actions related to the present Panama Canal and a possible new sea-level canal.

1. The United States will undertake further basic economic and technical investigations to provide the basis for examining the ques-

tion of the need for and the method of construction, location, and cost of a sea-level interoceanic canal in the isthmian region. Such investigations will include research to determine within approximately the next five years the feasibility, costs, and other factors involved in various methods of excavation.

2. Pending completion of such investigations, the United States is not now prepared to determine as a matter of policy nor [*sic*] to accept a commitment expressed or implied that it will at any particular time in the future actually construct a sea-level, interoceanic canal.

3. The United States will not accede at this time to a basic renegotiation of the existing treaties with Panama affecting the present canal. The government must recognize, however, that this question cannot be postponed indefinitely and may have to be faced before the studies discussed above are completed.

4. The United States will express a willingness and an earnest intent to consider with the Panamanians specific measures for adjusting our relationships through a liberal interpretation of the existing treaties in order to place U.S.-Panamanian relations on a more mutually satisfactory basis.

5. The United States will give serious consideration to accelerated assistance to Panama through the Alliance for Progress, particularly in support of projects which promise to develop new sources of livelihood for the Panamanian people and otherwise diversify the Panamanian economy.

[Point 6 detailed the responsibilities of the secretary of state, the chairman of the AEC, and the secretary of defense in coordinating and carrying out these policies.]

/s/ John F. Kennedy

[141]

With White Star teams in Laos and military advisers in South Vietnam, a "limited force" of U.S. Marines prepared to go to Thailand, as Pathet Lao troops began a drive toward the Thai border. On May 2 the President gave a briefing on Laos and Vietnam. Among others mentioned in the memo were Kenneth Young, ambassador to Thailand, and Winthrop G. Brown, ambassador to Laos.

SECRET

May 2, 1962

Memorandum of the President's Instructions
at the Laos/Vietnam Briefing

1. The President wishes to see the cables being drafted to Ambassadors Young and Brown on the current Laos negotiations.

2. The President asked Mr. [Roger] Hilsman [director of State Department Bureau of Intelligence and Research] to prepare a paper on Laos describing events in that country over the past few years.

3. The President asked that an effort be made to screen visitors to South Vietnam in order to limit any unnecessary trips there, especially by high ranking officers.

4. The President directed that the recent authorization for an operational experiment with defoliation on 7 kilometers of road in Vietnam be rescinded. Such an experiment would better be conducted in Thailand.

5. The President agreed that we should await the report of the ICC in Vietnam before considering indirect approaches to Hanoi on the Vietnam conflict.

[142]

With the Portuguese territories of Angola and Mozambique in some stages of revolt, Portugal's President Salazar renewed his threats to close down the Azores air base. This was the first item in Kennedy's May 21 memo.

The "Dutch-Indonesian problem" that Kennedy noted in the same memo had to do with Indonesia's leftist leader Achmed Sukarno, who intended to seize West New Guinea from the Dutch. After Robert Kennedy visited Sukarno in February, there were prolonged negotiations between Dutch and Indonesian representatives. U.S. diplomat Ellsworth Bunker played the role of mediator.

May 21, 1962

MEMORANDUM FOR SECRETARY OF STATE

1. I notice in the checklist this morning that Salazar recently told an American reporter that he would not agree to a renewal of the Azores base agreement and that Portugal would henceforth look to

Europe for economic support. It is possible that they might receive help from France. I think this bears out the necessity for us to work out a government position before we begin our negotiations and also explore the role that the NATO countries should play in these negotiations.

2. Should we begin to work out with the military an alternative in the Azores in case the base is withdrawn?

3. In reading the Washington Post this morning on the Dutch-Indonesian problem it sounded to me as if someone from the Dutch Embassy had been talking. I am wondering about the usefulness of the approach that is being made to resume peace talks inasmuch as no progress has been made for six months.

[143]

At the end of March a twenty eight-member committee headed by Dr. Franz Matsch of Austria had met at the UN to consider "Peaceful Uses of Outer Space." A scientific and technical subcommittee and a legal subcommittee were created at that time. Both were directed to start work in Geneva on May 28. On May 14 Charles C. Stelle, acting head of the U.S. delegation to the seventeen-nation conference in Geneva, appealed for conference action "to prevent the extension of the East-West arms race into outer space." Two days later Soviet Deputy Minister Zorin rejected Western suggestions for demilitarization of outer space.

In a top secret memorandum (NSAM 156) that was sanitized upon release in 1983, Kennedy refers to Project West Ford. The announced purpose of this program was to study the possibility of using orbiting copper-wire fibers to relay communications signals. (A container with 350 million copper fibers was ejected from a Midas IV spacecraft; but the package malfunctioned, and the test was reported to be a failure.)

TOP SECRET

May 26, 1962

[ENCLOSED WITH NATIONAL SECURITY ACTION MEMORANDUM NO. 156]

DRAFT TO THE SECRETARY OF STATE (Info to DOD, CIA, NASA, AEC and Science advisers)

The President is concerned about possible attacks on the U.S. Space Program at the forthcoming session of the U.N. Outer Space Committee and the General Assembly. Please develop positions on the following questions in consultation with DOD, CIA, NASA, AEC, and the science adviser:

1. How do we deal with charges the United States is seeking a military domination in space and plans to use space to launch weapons of mass destruction?

2. [Sanitized.]

3. How do we defend the past and prospective space experiments (high-altitude nuclear test Project West Ford) which may have lasting effects in space and impair the free use of space by other nations?

4. How do we dispel foreign misapprehensions arising from our bitter domestic debate over the communication satellite bill and charges that the legislation is somehow inconsistent with U.N. statements looking toward an international arrangement involving widespread foreign participation?

The President would like to see the positions developed to deal with these questions.

McGeorge Bundy

[144]

In Laos on May 6 Pathet Lao troops broke the ICC cease-fire by storming the village of Nam Tha in the Mekong Valley. After Phoumi's Royal Laotian Army fled, Harriman urged the President to send the Marines into Thailand. For a time the Pathet Lao advance was halted and cease-fire negotiations resumed. In late May, however, Pathet Lao guerrilla forces were reported mustering on the Laotian border. On May 25 two Pathet Lao guerrilla columns began their advance to Saravane, a provincial capital of southern Laos.

TOP SECRET

NATIONAL SECURITY ACTION MEMORANDUM NO. 157

May 29, 1962

TO: The Secretary of State
    The Secretary of Defense
    Director of Central Intelligence
    Chairman Joint Chiefs of Staff
    SUBJECT: Presidential meeting on Laos

The President has approved the following record of actions for the subject meeting. At the meeting on the situation in Laos held in the Cabinet Room at 4:30 P.M. today, the President requested contingency planning in the event of a breakdown of the ceasefire in Laos for action in two major areas:

a. The investing and holding by Thai forces with U.S. backup of Sayabouri [Sayaboury] Province (being that portion of northern Laos to the west of the Mekong River); and

b. The holding and recapture [of] the panhandle of Laos from Thakbok to the northern frontier with the Thai, Vietnamese, or U.S. forces.

In connection with the above contingency plans, the President desired an estimate of the military value of the Mekong River and Sayabouri Province as a defensive barrier in relation to the cost of taking and holding it. The President also asked that the above planning be undertaken unilaterally by the United States without discussion at this time with the Thais or the Lao. The President also indicated that he contemplated keeping U.S. forces in Thailand during the period of the three prince negotiations and the early days of the government of national union—i.e., as long as they serve the necessary purpose. The President observed that a cable would have to go in answer to Bangkok's 1844.

                                                        McGeorge Bundy

                                                                [145]

During the Kennedy presidency the autocratic director of the FBI J. Edgar Hoover lost the privileged connection to the presidential office that he had enjoyed under previous administrations. The attorney general and FBI director disagreed on their approaches to fighting organized crime. (Robert Kennedy believed that the Justice Department should have a separate unit devoted specifically to battling crime syndicates.) Both Kennedys were aware of Hoover's antipathy toward civil rights leaders, particularly Martin Luther King, Jr. And by February 1962 the Attorney General knew that Hoover was keeping a file on the President's relationship with Judith Campbell, the mistress of Salvatore "Sam" Giancana.

In June 1962 the President took action to divest some control of internal security matters from the FBI director and entrust operations of interdepartmental committees to the office of the attorney general.

June 9, 1962

NATIONAL SECURITY ACTION MEMORANDUM NO. 161

TO: The Secretary of State
The Secretary of Defense
The Secretary of the Treasury
The Secretary of Commerce
The Attorney General
The Director of Central Intelligence
Military Representative of the President
The Administrator, Federal Aviation Agency
The Chairman, Atomic Energy Commission
SUBJECT: U.S. Internal Security Programs

1. In line with my continuing effort to give primary responsibility for the initiative on major matters of policy and administration in a given field to a key member of my administration, I will look to the Attorney General to take the initiative in the government in insuring the development of plans, programs, and action proposals to protect the internal security of the United States. I will expect him to prepare recommendations in collaboration with other departments and agencies in the government having the responsibility for internal security programs with respect to those matters requiring presidential action.

2. Accordingly, I have directed that the two interdepartmental committees concerned with the internal security—the Interdepartmental Intelligence Conference (IIC) and the Interdepartmental Committee on Internal Security (ICIS)—which have been under the

supervision of the National Security Council will be transferred to the supervision of the Attorney General. The continuing need for these committees and their relationship to the Attorney General will be matters for the Attorney General to determine.

Signed,
John F. Kennedy

COPIES: J. Edgar Hoover, Chairman Interdepartmental Intelligence
Conference
John F. Doherty, Chairman Interdepartmental Committee
on Internal Security
A. Russell Ash, NSC staff
Mr. Hoagie

[146]

The breakthrough in the Laos accords at the ICC offered the promise of a neutralist government in Southeast Asia. On June 12 the President gave the following letter to Ambassador Llewellyn Thompson for delivery to Khrushchev.

June 12, 1962

His Excellency
Nikita S. Khrushchev
Chairman of the Council of Ministers of
the Union of Soviet Socialist Republics
Moscow

Dear Mr. Chairman:

I share your view that the reports from Laos are very encouraging. The formation of this government of national union under Prince Souvanna Phouma marks a milestone in the sustained efforts which have been put forward toward this end, especially since our meeting in Vienna.

It is of equal importance that we should now press forward, with our associates in the Geneva Conference, to complete these agreements and to work closely together in their execution. We must continue also to do our best to persuade all concerned in Laos to work together to this same end. It is very important that no untoward actions anywhere be allowed to disrupt the progress which has been made.

I agree that continued progress in the settlement of the Laotian problem can be most helpful in leading toward the resolution of other international difficulties. If together we can help in the establishment of an independent and neutral Laos, securely sustained in this status through time, this accomplishment will surely have a significant and positive effect far beyond the borders of Laos. You can count on the continued and energetic efforts of the Government of the United States toward this end.

Sincerely,

John F. Kennedy

[147]

National Security Action Memorandum No. 131 had contained an extensive outline of "training objectives for counter-insurgency," among them the creation of an academy that would instruct military personnel and advisers in police assistance programs and counterinsurgency techniques. The "seminar" subsequently approved by the President in NSAM 163 was a precursor of the training academy.

June 14, 1962

NATIONAL SECURITY ACTION MEMORANDUM NO. 163

TO: The Secretary of State
The Secretary of Defense
The Attorney General
Chairman Joint Chiefs of Staff
The Director of Central Intelligence
Administrator AID
The Director, USIA

SUBJECT: Training objectives for counterinsurgency

The President has noted with approval the establishment of an interdepartmental seminar on counter-insurgency at the Foreign Service Institute, entitled "Problems of Development and Internal Defense." This five-week course will commence on June 11 and will be repeated through the year.

The seminar has been established in accordance with paragraph 1D of the National Security Action Memorandum 131 to offer instruction on the problems faced by the United States in dealing with developing countries including special area counter-insurgency problems for the benefit of middle and senior grade officers (both military and civilian) who are about to occupy important posts in underdeveloped countries.

It is the wish of the President that key military and civilian personnel assigned to positions of responsibility at posts within Latin America, Africa, the Near East, and Southeast Asia attend this five week course prior to departing for their stations.

McGeorge Bundy

[148]

When Roberto Chiari paid a visit to Washington on June 12 and 13, the Panamanian president issued a joint communiqué with Kennedy in which the two leaders announced they would discuss "points of dissatisfaction" over the Panama Canal Treaty. Addressing a special session of the Council of the Organization of American States in Washington, Chiari warned against "drifting toward a new formula of eyes shut and hands off"—a reference to Cuban intervention in Latin American affairs. In exchange for the U.S. review of treaty matters, the Panamanians affirmed their solidarity with the United States.

NATIONAL SECURITY ACTION MEMORANDUM NO. 164
June 15, 1962
TO: The Secretary of State
    The Secretary of Defense
    The Secretary of the Army

1. As a result of President Chiari's visit, we are now committed to a continuing discussion of the problems arising out of our relations with the Republic of Panama from the Canal and the Canal Zone and a search for ways of dealing with them constructively. These discussions should over time produce an appropriate flow of concrete results in order to contain Panamanian pressures for immediate and radical treaty revision. This will require some extra attention by the responsible departments.

2. As our representatives for the discussions with Panama, I have decided to appoint the ambassador to Panama, Joseph Farland, and the Governor of the Canal Zone, Major General Robert Fleming.

3. I request the Secretary of State to take the leadership in organizing a small review group from the appropriate agencies to follow up the discussions between the two governments. This group should also be charged with the responsibility of examining what can be done on all the specific questions which the Panamanians have raised in their recent visit. In examining these questions, I think it important to distinguish what can be done by executive authority alone, what can be done by ordinary legislation, and what requires revision of the treaty. In considering specific problems I think it is desirable to explore methods of dealing with them which could bypass the traditional concern with the formalisms of sovereignty and concentrate on meeting legitimate Panamanian complaints while maintaining the practical arrangements necessary for the operation of the Canal and for our military activities in the Zone.

Some of the particular points on which the Panamanians have pressed us most are the flying of Panamanian flags on ships going through the canal, the use of Panamanian stamps in the Canal Zone postage system, change in the jurisdiction of American courts over Panamanian citizens, and the issuance by us of exequaturs* to permit Consuls accredited to Panama to function in the Zone. With the exception of the court question, these are largely symbolic matters. In addition, of course, we must continue to examine the more practical problems of U.S. commercial activity in the Zone, labor questions involving equality of treatment for Panamanians, unneeded lands, and direct Panamanian benefits from the Canal.

/s/ John F. Kennedy

[149]

Kennedy was acutely aware that the image of the United States overseas was of a wealthy, overbearing nation that spent lavishly on the rich and often ignored the poor. The most striking symbol of arrogance and power, especially in third world nations, were lavish U.S. embassies and official residences.

*Official documents recognizing consuls.

19 June, 1962

MEMORANDUM FOR THE SECRETARY OF STATE

I was concerned when I read the newspaper report of costs of embassy residences. Of course I believe that the residence of an American ambassador should reflect credit on him and his country. On the other hand I feel that excessive expenditures for such a residence will make us look ridiculous in the eyes of the people in the countries concerned. Knowing the type of house that $300,000 will buy in the United States, it is difficult for me to see the need for ambassadors' residences in that price range in such places as Senegal, Cyprus, and Seoul unless there are unusual factors involved. I believe that embassy residences should present an image of dignity and charm without being ostentatious or luxurious. Careful thought should be given and possibly some reexamination of plans made to assure that they reflect a proper impression of our ambassadors and of our country.

/s/ John F. Kennedy

[150]

Although the dollar drain abated somewhat in 1961 and 1962, it continued to be a leading concern of the President, who feared that the U.S. currency would become drastically destabilized if foreign governments continued to draw down American gold reserves.

June 20, 1962

MEMO FOR SECRETARY OF THE TREASURY
ADMINISTRATOR, AID

1. I would like in the future for all actions which affect our dollar drain or balance of payments to be brought to my attention before final decision is made.

2. Before any loan stabilization or AID agreement is made I would like to have an indication of what effect it would make on our dollar position.

[151]

June 20, 1962

MEMORANDUM FOR JAMES TOBIN
COUNCIL OF ECONOMIC ADVISERS

Pursuant to our recent conversation I would like to have a memorandum from the Council of dollar drains resulting from governmental actions, loans, exchange agreements, etc.

[152]

(In a reply memo on June 20 Tobin promised to "put together an analysis of the balance of payments impact of government programs." Tobin, who was responsible for international finance, money, and banking, was an advocate of an "aggressive monetary policy" with freer credit and more government spending. At the President's request, however, he noted, "We will also prepare a memorandum on the considerations of policy involved in squeezing government programs further, in comparison with alternative ways of meeting our balance of payments difficulties.")

On June 14 Dillon recommended that the President set up a committee to monitor the effect of the administration's budgetary actions on the balance of payments deficit. Dillon suggested a number of measures to control the deficit, including prepayment of debts by foreign nations, buying up of foreign currencies by the Treasury, and various strategies to increase exports.

June 22, 1962

MEMORANDUM FOR
THE SECRETARY OF THE TREASURY

I like the proposals in your memorandum of June 14th on the ways of carrying forward a small inter-Cabinet committee on the balance of payments. I agree with you that the Director of the Bureau of the Budget should be added, and I also believe that we should have representation from the State Department—presumably George Ball—and from the Council of Economic Advisers. I doubt if we would need any further White House representation at this stage.

I agree with your view that the group should begin to think hard about broad policy on the balance of payments, but I also want it to be a working committee that will keep a sharp eye on the management of our own disbursements within the Executive Branch. For this purpose I am asking Dave Bell to be prepared to bring to the new committee proposals for what might be called a "gold budget" for use in controlling all federal expenditures that affect the balance of payments. A number of instances in recent weeks have made it clear that our Executive control in this area is not what it ought to be, and I think the basic budgetary process provides an excellent analogy to the sort of thing we now need in the balance of payments field.

John F. Kennedy

Would you chair the committee and arrange for its frequent meeting.

[153]

By June 1962 the United States was attempting to push through the UN a Kashmir resolution that would put an end to fighting on the India-Pakistan border. The issue was particularly urgent because the Chinese, taking advantage of the dispute between Pakistan and India, were amassing troops in Ladakh in Kashmir. Kennedy learned that Indian Prime Minister Nehru was negotiating to buy MiG fighters from the USSR. In his June 23 memo the President specifically recommended manipulating AID money in order to win the compliance of other nations in the UN.

June 23, 1962

MEMORANDUM FOR
THE SECRETARY OF STATE
THE SECRETARY OF DEFENSE
ADMINISTRATOR, AGENCY FOR INTERNATIONAL DEVELOPMENT

I am greatly disturbed at the apparent lack of control and coordination between our various programs in the international field and our seeming inability to assure that our political objectives are advanced by actions taken by AID or other agencies. I have specific reference to the announcement from New Delhi of the signing of a $250 million loan with the Indians at the very time when, in the

United Nations, the Kashmir issue was being discussed and the MiG question was very much a live issue.

In these circumstances, I believe it essential that, under the leadership of the Secretary of State, a procedure is developed to guarantee that before any major action is announced, such as an economic or military aid agreement, to [sic] explore fully its coordination with our foreign policy objectives. This procedure should precede any actions. For example, I understand this week that Chile, Venezuela, Ireland and the UAR all abandoned an agreement that they had to sponsor the Kashmir resolution, leaving us holding the bag. It seems to me that some indication of our displeasure might be manifested by the slowing up of our AID agreements with those countries. Ireland finally came through.

I would appreciate it if you would develop this procedure at the earliest possible time.

[154]

(On June 25 the President followed up with a memorandum for Bundy requesting, "Would you let me know the results of your research on how the Indians persuaded Ireland, Chile, Venezuela and the UAR to abandon the Kashmir resolution leaving us holding the sack.")

Given that the international monetary system was gold-based, foreign nations could request a transfer of U.S. gold reserves for dollars whenever the balance of payments was in their favor. Since Kennedy did not want to erect punitive trade barriers, his recourse was to threaten to end other U.S. government programs that provided aid to these countries.

June 25, 1962
MEMORANDUM FOR
SECRETARY OF STATE
SECRETARY OF DEFENSE
SECRETARY OF THE TREASURY
ADMINISTRATOR, AGENCY FOR INTERNATIONAL DEVELOPMENT

It is my understanding that the Secretary of the Treasury has recommended a tightening of our Aid and Food for Peace Programs in Spain and an elimination of Spain as an off-shore procurement, because of their [the Spanish] raids on our gold.

I am also informed that there has been opposition to the Secretary implementing these recommendations.

If there is opposition I would appreciate knowing the reasons for this opposition and I would also like to know what steps have been taken to implement these recommendations.

[155]

Walter W. Heller, chairman of the Council of Economic Advisers, held the Keynesian view that prosperity could be stimulated by granting tax cuts and increasing federal spending. He argued that deficit spending would result in higher incomes and therefore greater economic growth.

June 25, 1962

MEMORANDUM FOR CHAIRMAN,
COUNCIL OF ECONOMIC ADVISERS

I note that the deficit of Canada is running approximately $600 million a year, which is comparable to about $20 billion a year for us. In spite of this, there has been no inflation and unemployment is not necessarily high. Does this suggest that if we ran a budget deficit similar to the one in Canada we would have similar results? What are your thoughts on this?

/s/ John F. Kennedy

[156]

Hans Bethe, the former director of the theoretical physics division of the Los Alamos Atomic Scientific Laboratory, was appointed in 1958 to the post of scientific adviser to the test ban talks in Geneva. On February 14 the *New York Herald Tribune* reported that Bethe made a speech in which he stated that "an effective anti-missile defense system was virtually unattainable." Since Bethe was a member of the Science Advisory Committee and therefore had access to classified information, his statement was considered a security regulation violation.

Kennedy's letter of July 9 was addressed to Representative Chet Holifield, an advocate of the fallout shelter program and of nuclear power in public utilities. Chairman Seaborg of the Atomic Energy Commission and John McNaughton of the Department of Defense were both proponents of atmospheric testing.

July 9, 1962

Honorable Chet Holifield
Chairman
Joint Committee on Atomic Energy
Congress of the United States
Washington, DC

Dear Chet:

The investigation into Dr. Hans Bethe's speech on Soviet testing and the earlier articles on the same subject which appeared in the *Washington Star* and *Newsweek* that were initiated in response to your inquiry of January 16 have now been completed.

Dr. Bethe has acknowledged his contravention of AEC security regulations and has been reprimanded by Chairman Seaborg of the Commission. It is Chairman Seaborg's judgment, which I share, that this is the appropriate measure in Bethe's case.

The investigations into the *Washington Star* article by Earl Voss and Richard Fryklund and the *Newsweek* article by Edwin Diamond were not fruitful. Thorough investigations were conducted by the FBI, the Department of Defense and the Atomic Energy Commission into possible leaks within the two latter agencies. The State Department and the Central Intelligence Agency, which had access to copies of the Bethe Panel Report, also examined whether or not there had been unauthorized disclosures of information by their staffs, and found no positive results.

I am glad to make available to you Mr. John McNaughton, the General Counsel of the Department of Defense, who has made himself thoroughly familiar with the facts of this situation, to answer in such further detail as is appropriate any questions you may have with respect to the nature and outcomes of the investigations.

For reasons you can understand, I think that my response and anything Mr. McNaughton has to say should be kept confidential.

Sincerely yours,

/s/ John F. Kennedy

[157]

After protracted negotiations led chiefly by Averell Harriman, an ICC agreement on Laos was set to be signed on July 23.

July 13, 1962

MEMORANDUM FOR
THE SECRETARY OF STATE

I spoke to the President about Mike Forrestal's suggestion that Averell might be invited to join with you in signing the Laos accords for the United States, and he asked me to tell you that he is for this if you are. He would be glad to do anything that will show his feeling that Averell has worked with great energy and skill on this very difficult affair.

McGeorge Bundy

[158]

As the President noted in NSAM 171, the United States was virtually supporting the foreign exchange currency needs of a number of nations in Southeast Asia. Although Kennedy needed to reduce the balance of payments deficits, he would not do so at the risk of withdrawing support from countries that were battling communist influence.

July 16, 1962
NATIONAL SECURITY ACTION MEMORANDUM NO. 171
TO: The Secretary of State
    The Secretary of Defense
    The Secretary of the Treasury
    Director Bureau of the Budget
SUBJECT: Department of Defense actions to reduce its overseas expenditures

1. I have reviewed the proposed actions of the Department of Defense directed toward reducing its overseas expenditures (see attached memorandum for Secretary of Defense). Subject to the qualifications set forth below, I approve these actions as interim measures until the Cabinet Committee recommends and I approve guidance for reducing government overseas expenditures in all departments.

2. In certain countries the actions proposed by the Defense Department may result in a need for compensating increases in aid. This appears especially likely to be the case in Korea, South Viet-Nam, and the Republic of China—countries whose foreign exchange requirements we, in essence, underwrite. In certain other countries including Iceland, the Philippines and Japan, which are not now major recipients of aid, the impact of reductions in U.S. military expenditures may also create demands for aid. The economic situation of these countries and our policy interests in them are such that we cannot simply ignore the possibility that savings on military account will be canceled or substantially offset by increased expenditures on aid account.

3. Accordingly, I request that the committee arrange for timely consideration of the interrelations among defense and aid overseas expenditures in these and similar cases. Any final decision to reduce one of the categories of expenditures should be made only after full consideration of its probable impact on the other as well as its budgetary costs. Issues which cannot be resolved by the committee should be referred to me.

/s/ John F. Kennedy

[159]

A program for international cooperation in the exploration of outer space was unanimously approved by the UN General Assembly on December 4, 1961. The program restricted national sovereignty in outer space and included agreements on scientific cooperation and noninterference. Still to be settled was the question of weapons in space. Although concerned about how deployments would be monitored, Kennedy wished to leave open the possibility of a total ban on weapons in outer space—a point of disagreement with Secretary of State Rusk. (The following sanitized memo was declassified in 1982.)

TOP SECRET
July 23, 1962
MEMORANDUM FOR: The Secretary of State
SUBJECT: Recommended U.S. position on the separate ban on
weapons of mass destruction in outer space

The President reviewed your memorandum of July 12 and asked me to report to you that he was not prepared to accept paragraphs 2, 3, and 6 of the recommended position insofar as they imply a total rejection of any possible declaratory ban on weapons of mass destruction in outer space. His present belief is that at a certain stage such a declaratory ban might be in our interest if nothing better can be achieved. He would like an examination of the possibilities of nationally operated systems for the detection and identification of any such weapons.

[Three lines sanitized.]

The President hopes that the matter will be reviewed in the light of these comments and that a further recommendation can be presented to him soon.

McGeorge Bundy
[160]

In the wake of his January announcement that the Office of Civil Defense and Mobilization had accumulated a stockpile that exceeded requirements by $3.4 billion, the President was dismayed when he heard from Congress in July that the stockpile figures were creeping upward again. These figures came to him from Congress rather than from the new director of the OCDM, Edward McDermott.

July 25, 1962

MEMORANDUM FOR ED MCDERMOTT

I notice that the joint House-Senate Committee on reduction of Federal Expenditures said that the acquisition value of critical materials inventories in our war preparedness stockpiles had crept up by $26.2 million since January 1st.

Will you send me an explanation on how this occurred. Also, would it not be useful for any announcements concerning the stockpiles to come out of your office rather than through the Congressional Committee as they usually put it in its worst light.

/s/ John Kennedy

[161]

With both the United States and Soviet Union testing nuclear weapons in the summer of 1962, there were occasional overlaps. Interestingly enough, Kennedy's information about Soviet tests did not come from confidential government sources. It came from the morning paper.

July 25, 1962

MEMORANDUM FOR SECRETARY OF DEFENSE

I note in this morning's paper that the Soviets might begin their nuclear testing around August 5. I believe our high altitude tests are to take place during the first few days of August and therefore the Soviets' renewal will occur about the same time. Does this present a problem for us, and should we attempt to speed up our high-altitude tests so that they will have gone off before they resume their testing?

/s/ John F. Kennedy

[162]

On July 18 Frank M. Coffin, deputy administrator for operations in the Agency for International Development, reported on the progress of staffing, training, and organizing for the counterinsurgency work of the agency. "A.I.D. is in the process of strengthening its organization in the police field," he wrote, "in order to provide the necessary guidance and evaluation of the effort within A.I.D., and to centralize and give adequate focus to the counter-insurgency aspect of the operation. . . ." Coffin outlined AID's "Public Safety" programs in "those areas where there is either current insurgency or an imminent threat."

In the broad scope of AID envisioned by the President, the program known as police assistance would be coordinated with the public safety programs in each country, all under the umbrella of counterinsurgency operations.

NATIONAL SECURITY ACTION MEMORANDUM NO. 177
August 7, 1962
MEMO FOR: The Secretary of State
              The Secretary of Defense
              The Attorney General
              The Administrator [of] AID
              The Director of Central Intelligence
SUBJECT: Police assistance programs

I hereby approve the recommendations of the Interdepartmental Committee on Police Assistance Programs and direct they be promptly put into effect as follows:

1. The U.S. should give considerably greater emphasis to Police Assistance Programs in appropriate less-developed countries where there is an actual or potential threat of internal subversion or insurgencies. To this end, all individual programs should be subject to normal review processes. AID should envisage very substantial increases in the global level of the FY1963 program with further increases in subsequent years where there is a demonstrated need. The DOD should also give, where appropriate, increased emphasis to the police aspects of existing MAP programs.

2. The Committee's statement of the role and function of police programs and criteria for their initiation in its report [should] be the basis for guidance from Washington and to the field. Using this guidance, AID should ensure that Washington agencies and country teams give appropriate priority to police assistance, including equipment where needed.

3. Subject to the general policy guidance of the Secretary of State in internal defense matters, the administrator of AID is charged in his capacity as coordinator of U.S. aid programs with responsibility for coordination and vigorous leadership of all police assistance programs; that he establish an interagency police group to be chaired by his designee to assist him in this responsibility.

4. AID is charged with operating and funding responsibility for all such programs, except for their covert aspects and for those programs which the administrator of AID in consultation with the Secretary of Defense decides should be carried out by the Department of Defense.

[In Points 5–9, the President gave specific departmental instructions for implementing the program.]

10. Wherever possible, we should coordinate our police effort with similar programs of other friendly western countries to assure that they are complementary; we should encourage such countries to provide similar assistance where appropriate, but not rely exclusively on them for this purpose; our aims in this respect should be to assure that adequate western assistance is available to any country which needs it and to deny the police assistance field to the Communist Bloc.

11. The Administrator of AID, as coordinator of U.S. aid programs, is charged with carrying out the above recommendations, and he should report to me no later than 1 December 1962 on progress made; this report should include his revised FY1963 and proposed FY1964 program level.

12. The Special Group (C-I) should review the implementation of the Police Committee Report in accordance with the responsibilities assigned under National Security Action Memorandum 124.

Signed,

John F. Kennedy

[163]

Kennedy covered the NSAM with a personal letter to the administrator of the Agency for International Development, emphasizing the importance of staffing the police assistance program.

August 7, 1962

The Honorable Fowler Hamilton
Administrator, Agency for International Development
Washington, D.C.

Dear Fowler:

Today I approved the recommendations of the inter-agency committee created under NSAM 146 to study our foreign police assistance program. As I wrote you on February 19, I consider this program an important part of our effort to help the less-developed countries achieve the internal security essential if our major economic development aid is to help create viable free nations.

I regard the committee's report as an excellent guide to the course we should follow in this field. However, policy on paper will not get us very far unless we get able and enthusiastic people to carry it out. I hope that you and Frank Coffin will give your personal attention to hiring the best professionals you can find to launch this re-invigorated effort and will give them every support in making the program count.

Sincerely,
/s/ John F. Kennedy

[164]

On August 11 and 12 two Soviet cosmonauts in separate five-ton spacecraft were launched from sites in the Soviet Union. Andrian Nikolayev completed more than sixty-four orbits, and Pavel Popovich completed forty-eight. Both cosmonauts landed on August 15, the day Kennedy sent his congratulatory message to Khrushchev.

August 15, 1962

MEMORANDUM FOR
   Mr. William Brubeck
   Executive Secretary
   Department of State

Will you please have the following message sent in the fastest way possible, and notify my office of the approximate time of delivery.

"Dear Mr. Chairman:

I send to you and to the Soviet people the heartiest congratulations of the people and government of the United States in the outstanding joint flights of Major Nikolayev and Colonel Popovich. This new accomplishment is an important forward step in the great human adventure of the peaceful exploration of space. America's astronauts join with me in sending our salute to Major Nikolayev and Colonel Popovich.

JOHN F. KENNEDY"
McGeorge Bundy

[165]

On August 15 the President also sent a memo to the head of the U.S. space program questioning expenditures. After the National Aeronautics and Space Administration program had received a congressional appropriation of $1.671 billion for 1962, Director Webb announced plans to build the Apollo Command Center in Houston.

August 15, 1962

MEMORANDUM FOR JAMES E. WEBB

I notice [in] an article in the Washington Post this morning that the subcommittee is considering appropriations for the National Aeronautics and Space Administration [center] that had been put at from $50 million to $60 million, but the final figure may reach $123 million. Is this correct? Who are the architects and builders, and under whose control is the Space Center building to be put up? I would appreciate your comment on this.

/s/ John F. Kennedy

[166]

By late August UN representatives were formulating a resolution intended to end the dispute between Indonesia and the Netherlands over the Dutch colonial territory of West New Guinea (West Irian). According to the pending agreement, Indonesia would become administrator of the colony with the understanding that open elections would be held before 1970, when the West Irians would be free to decide whether they wanted national independence. (The final resolution passed on September 21.) Knowing that Indonesian President Sukarno had close ties to Communist China, Kennedy hoped that U.S. intervention in the settlement would influence Sukarno to lean toward the West.

NATIONAL SECURITY ACTION MEMORANDUM NO. 179
August 16, 1962
MEMO FOR: The Secretary of State
The Secretary of Defense
The Administrator AID
The Director of Central Intelligence
The Director, USIA
SUBJECT: U.S. policy toward Indonesia

With the peaceful settlement of the West Irian dispute now in prospect, I would like to see us capitalize on the U.S. role in promoting this settlement to move toward a new and better relationship with Indonesia. I gather that with this issue resolved the Indonesians too would like to move in this direction and will be presenting us with numerous requests.

To seize this opportunity, will all agencies concerned please review their programs for Indonesia and assess what further measures might be useful. I have in mind the possibility of expanded civic action, military aid, and economic stabilization and development programs as well as diplomatic initiatives. The Department of State is requested to pull together all relevant agency proposals in a plan of action and submit it to me no later than September 15th.

/s/ John F. Kennedy

[167]

(In a reply from Deputy Undersecretary of State Charles Maechling, Jr., on October 2, the President learned that the Soviet bloc had given Indonesia an estimated $1 billion in military aid and $650 million in economic credits. Maechling recommended quadrupling the Food for Peace commitment to Indonesia as well as Export-Import Bank loans and military and police assistance. He also urged greater involvement on the part of the Peace Corps and AID. "Indonesia's geo-political position and magnitudes make it important to the U.S.," Maechling noted. "Our commitments on the Indo-China peninsula could be lost if the bottom of Southeast Asia fell out to Communism.")

On August 17, two East German youths tried to cross the border into West Berlin near the Friedrichstrasse crossing point, Checkpoint Charlie. One of the youths, Peter Fechter, was gunned down. According to news reports, he "was left bleeding to death unattended for more than an hour despite his groans and cries for help." Police on both sides threw tear gas grenades and smoke bombs, but neither the West Berlin police nor U.S. military police were able to help Fechter. West Berlin crowds jeered the American police, and West Berlin newspapers later criticized U.S. troops for failing to act.

In an earlier episode (August 13), East Berlin guards were bombarded by stones and beer bottles thrown by West Berlin crowds. On other occasions that month—the first anniversary of the Berlin wall—Soviet Army vehicles were stoned when they crossed the border carrying sentries to a Soviet monument in West Berlin.

August 21, 1962

MEMORANDUM FOR
SECRETARY OF STATE

While I recognize the difficulties the Commandants face in Berlin, I would appreciate a detailed report on the refugee incident last Friday. I would like to know how long it was before the Commandant was informed on what was happening and what action he took.

Secondly, the stoning of the Russian troops is most unfortunate. I would like to get a report on the handling of this situation by the Commandant and whether he took any action in the matter.

[168]

After Kennedy sent his inquiry about expenditures on the space center (August 15), the reply from James Webb was forwarded to the director of the Bureau of the Budget with the following memo from the President:

August 23, 1962

MEMORANDUM FOR DAVE BELL

I am enclosing a copy of a letter from James Webb relative to the Manned Spacecraft Center in Houston, Texas. In spite of his explanation it seems to me that the cost is excessive for this center, and it does raise the question of the funding of the entire program. This needs the most careful continuing scrutiny. I would like to have your suggestions on the recent appropriations for the space program—what programs are essential and desirable, and how we can make them meet the cost estimates more precisely. This program has so much public support that unless there is some restraint, there is a possibility of wasting some money.

/s/ John F. Kennedy

[169]

On August 23 Theodore Sorensen had a luncheon meeting with Soviet Ambassador Dobrynin at the Soviet Embassy. At the meeting Sorensen informed Dobrynin that the United States had observed large shipments of Soviet personnel, arms, and equipment into Cuba. With congressional elections coming up, Sorensen noted, the Soviet actions had "caused turmoil in our internal political affairs." In reply the ambassador read a conciliatory message from Khrushchev and insisted that the buildup of arms in Cuba was "nothing new or extraordinary."

The same day the President sent NSAM 181 to the departments of State, Justice, and Defense, the CIA, and the Joint Chiefs. The memo referred to Jupiter missiles that the United States had based in Turkey, which became a major issue in the Cuban missile crisis. (Khrushchev later demanded that the United States withdraw its Jupiter missiles before the Soviet Union pulled its nuclear weapons out of Cuba.)

Portions of the top secret, sensitive White House memo of August 23 were sanitized.

NATIONAL SECURITY ACTION MEMORANDUM NO. 181
August 23, 1962
Individual items to be reproduced for further assignment only
by personal decision of addressees. Full reproduction
prohibited.
TOP SECRET AND SENSITIVE
TO: The Secretary of State
    The Secretary of Defense
    The Attorney General
    Acting Director, CIA
    General Taylor

The President has directed that the following actions and studies be undertaken in the light of evidence of new [Soviet] Bloc activity in Cuba.

1. What action can be taken to get Jupiter missiles out of Turkey? (Action: Department of Defense)

2. What information should be made available in the U.S. and abroad with respect to these new Bloc activities in Cuba? (Action: Department of State in consultation with USIA and CIA)

3. There should be an organized effort to bring home to governments of our NATO allies, in particular, the meaning of this new evidence of Castro's subservience to the Soviets, and the urgency of action on their part to limit their economic cooperation with Cuba. (Action: Department of State)

4. [Sanitized.]

5. An analysis should be prepared of the probable military, political, and psychological impact of the establishment in Cuba of either surface-to-air missiles or surface-to-surface missiles which could reach the U.S. (Action: White House in consultation with Department of State, Department of Defense, and CIA)

6. A study should be made of the advantages and disadvantages of making a statement that the U.S. would not tolerate the establishment of military forces (missile or air or both?) which might launch a nuclear attack from Cuba against the U.S. (Action: Department of State, in consultation with Department of Defense with respect to the study in Item 7 below.)

7. A study should be made of the various military alternatives which might be adopted in executing a decision to eliminate any

installations in Cuba capable of launching nuclear attack on the U.S. What would be the pros and cons, for example, of pinpoint attack, general counterforce attack, and outright invasion? (Action: Department of Defense)

8. [Four lines sanitized.]

. . . To facilitate coordination of these efforts, I should like to receive an immediate report from action Departments indicating which officer of the Department will be directly responsible for items in which action is assigned to that Department.

[Three lines sanitized.]

There will be a further meeting with the President about September 1 to review progress on all these items. In the event of important new information an earlier meeting will be called. The President emphasizes again the sensitive character of these instructions.

McGeorge Bundy

[170]

On August 24 the President approved the final work of the special counterinsurgency group, creating "a national counterinsurgency doctrine" linking diplomatic and military missions.

SECRET

August 24, 1962

NATIONAL SECURITY ACTION MEMORANDUM NO. 182

TO: The Secretary of State
   The Secretary of Defense
   The Attorney General
   Chairman of the Joint Chiefs of Staff
   The Director, CI
   Administrator AID
   The Director, USIA
   Military Representatives of the President

SUBJECT: Counter-insurgency doctrine

The President has approved the document entitled "U.S. Overseas Internal Defense Policy," which sets forth a national counter-insurgency doctrine for the use of U.S. departments and agencies by subversive insurgency and has directed its promulgation to personnel to serve as basic policy guidance to diplomatic missions, consular personnel, and military command abroad; to government departments and agencies at home; and to the government educational system. The addressees of this NSAM will take action to ensure that the policies set forth in the document are reflected in departmental and agency operations and in such additional instructions and guidance as may be required to ensure uniformity of effort. They will also initiate the formulation of the internal doctrine, tactics, and techniques appropriate to their own department or agency based upon "U.S. overseas defense policy." These studies when completed will be reviewed by the Special Group (CI). The Department of State in consultation with the other addressees of this memorandum is assigned the task of keeping the "U.S. overseas internal defense policy" up to date making such modification as changes in policy or practical experience may require, and publishing revised editions as necessary.

McGeorge Bundy

[171]

Air Force Secretary Eugene M. Zuckert objected to the budgetary restrictions imposed on him by McNamara. Zuckert also criticized the U.S. space program, which de-emphasized the military role in outer space. The successful flights of Soviet Cosmonauts Popovich and Nikolayev prompted Zuckert to voice further criticism of the Kennedy space program.

August 27, 1962

MEMORANDUM FOR
EUGENE ZUCKERT

Thank you for your memorandum to me on space.

I am not so much interested in quotations from my previous speeches as I am in finding out exactly what programs the Air Force recommended to us for fiscal 1963 which were not approved by the Defense Department or by me.

Secondly, I would like to find out if there were any programs which were proposed by the Air Force between our budget and the recent Soviet flight.

Thirdly, I notice that TIME Magazine of this week, August 31st, has a quotation ascribed to you taken from a conversation between you and McNamara—"but the tone and the pace of our program [are] not right." I do not know how TIME secured this quotation, but I would be interested in having your suggestions as to how we can improve the tone and pace of our program.

[172]

Kennedy wished to maintain the position with the UN Outer Space Committee that the United States opposed nuclear tests in outer space. Since the U.S. space program was funded in part from the military budget, the President had to specify that the military presence in the program did not necessarily mean that spacecraft would be used for "aggressive" purposes.

TOP SECRET
NATIONAL SECURITY ACTION MEMORANDUM NO. 183
August 27, 1962
TO: The Secretary of State
    The Secretary of Defense
    The Director of Central Intelligence
    The Administrator, NASA
    Director, Arms Control and Disarmament Agency
    Chairman, Atomic Energy Commission
    Director, Office of Science and Technology

The President desires that the space program of the United States be forcefully explained and defended at the forthcoming sessions of the U.N. Outer Space Committee and the General Assembly. The Department of State is requested to consult with the Department of Defense, CIA, NASA, AEC, ACDA [Arms Control and Disarmament Agency], and the Office of the Science Adviser to develop positions which meet the following objectives:

1. To show that the distinction between peaceful and aggressive uses of outer space is not the same as the distinction between military and civilian uses, and that U.S. aims to keep space free from aggressive use and offers cooperation in its peaceful exploitation for scientific and technological purposes.

2. To build and sustain support for the legality and proprietary of [sanitized]. This position should proceed from the approved recommendations of the report submitted on this subject on June 30, 1962.

3. To make it plain that neither U.S. nuclear tests nor other U.S. experiments in space were undertaken without a proper sense of scientific responsibility and that in the case of the nuclear tests these were a response to previous Soviet tests.

4. To demonstrate the precautionary character of the U.S. military program in space.

5. To show that U.S. policies for communication satellites are fully consistent with cooperative international arrangements.

McGeorge Bundy

[173]

Peace Corps Director Shriver was assured both by Kennedy and by Allen Dulles, director of the CIA, that neither would attempt to turn the Peace Corps into a political organization. Nonetheless, the President kept an eye on the strategic placement of Peace Corps volunteers.

August 29, 1962

MEMORANDUM FOR SARGE SHRIVER

I note that you have plans of increasing the number of Peace Corps volunteers in various parts of the world, such as North Borneo. I would like for you to keep in mind the importance of Latin America which I think would be the primary area. At the present time, do we not have as many in the Philippines as we have in all of the Latin American countries?

[174]

More than a month before the onset of the Cuban missile crisis, the President considered the possibility of a confrontation between U.S. destroyers in the Caribbean and Soviet-made torpedo boats from Cuba.

September 7, 1962

MEMO FOR SECRETARY OF THE NAVY

I would like to get a report on the ability of our destroyers to deal effectively with the new motor torpedo boats of the Komar Class that the Cubans now possess. I understand these Soviet missiles have a range of fifty miles with an accuracy of one hundred feet. If these vessels should attack an American destroyer at that range, what means do we have to insure the destroyer's success?

/s/ John F. Kennedy

[175]

On July 9 the United States conducted a nuclear weapons test at an altitude of 250 miles above Johnston Island in the Pacific Ocean. The explosion was the equivalent to 1.4 million tons of TNT. On September 10 the U.S. Atomic Energy Commission and the Department of Defense announced that the test had produced an unanticipated "radiation belt" that, among other effects, rendered satellite communications inoperable. Five days after the AEC-DOD announcement the President drafted a letter to Khrushchev welcoming prospects for negotiation of a new test ban treaty. Originally intended for "eyes only," the letter was declassified in December 1989.

SECRET—EYES ONLY

September 15, 1962

I am happy to note your suggestion that you are prepared to negotiate a treaty banning nuclear tests in the atmosphere, in outer space and under water in the immediate future. Now that the subcommittee on nuclear test ban is continuing in session throughout the recess in the 18-Nation Disarmament Conference, I think we should make a serious effort to work out such an agreement in time to meet the target date of January 1, 1963, which both sides have mentioned in the Geneva negotiations. We have prepared such a treaty, and our representatives and those of the United Kingdom will be working with yours in the subcommittee to get the earliest possible agreement on a final text.

While we are negotiating toward a limited ban of this type we should at the same time be negotiating towards a treaty for banning nuclear weapons tests in all environments. As part of this effort we could be working to eliminate the difference of view as to a question of scientific fact which has so far kept our negotiators apart. Our scientists advise me that although substantial progress has been made in detecting and identifying nuclear explosions on the basis of instrumentation, it is not possible to do so on a basis which renders the requirement of on-site inspections unnecessary. Your delegation has taken the opposing view but has not supplied any scientific information which may have led your government to hold this view. A joint working party of your scientists together with ours and scientists from the United Kingdom might be able, finally, to dispel the differences which have so far blocked our efforts to obtain agreement.

I believe that when we have prepared and put into effect a treaty banning tests in the atmosphere, in outer space and under water, we can then look at the problem of continued testing under ground and take such steps as we may then determine seem most likely to be helpful in arriving at a comprehensive treaty in the light of the progress which has been made at that time.

In your message you mention the role that France should play in the treaty. Of course, our comprehensive treaty draft provides that the United States, the United Kingdom, and the Soviet Union shall cooperate in encouraging other states to become parties to the treaty. For its part, the United States would work in close consultation with France and would hope that France would adhere to the treaty. Indeed, both you and we have a great interest in assuring the adherence to the treaty of all states or authorities capable of conducting a nuclear weapons test. Without their adherence the treaty could not endure.

A test ban agreement, together with an agreement on the non-dissemination of nuclear weapons of the kind which Secretary Rusk has discussed with Ambassador Dobrynin, would have a powerful effect in deterring the spread of nuclear weapons capabilities to other countries. I firmly believe that obtaining this objective is in our mutual interest. It cannot be in the security interest of any of us if the present small number of nuclear powers is expanded, for, to the extent this is the case, the possibilities of war by accident or by design can only increase. There is still time to put an effective end to this threat.

[176]

Two months after the signing of the Declaration on the Neutrality of Laos in Geneva, the Southeast Asian nation was under the coalition government of Prince Souvanna Phouma. As the United States moved to implement the final measures of the agreement, Deputy Special Assistant Kaysen recorded the executive actions.

SECRET
NATIONAL SECURITY ACTION MEMORANDUM NO. 189
September 28, 1962
TO: The Secretary of State
    The Secretary of Defense
    The Chairman, Joint Chiefs of Staff
    The Director of Central Intelligence
SUBJECT: Presidential meeting on Laos, September 28, 1962

At the meeting to review the situation in Laos held in the Cabinet Room at 11:30 A.M. on September 28, 1962, the President took the following action:

1. Authorized the withdrawal by October 7, 1962, of the remaining elements of MAAG Laos in accordance with the Geneva Agreements;

2. Authorized a special U.S. contribution to the Royal Lao Government for the month of September not to exceed two million;

3. Approved a review of intelligence data concerning Viet Minh withdrawals from Laos in order to ascertain what information could be given to the RLG and the ICC in Laos without jeopardizing the integrity of intelligence collection;

4. Accepted the retention of U.S. combat forces in Thailand pending a further review of developments in Laos.

Carl Kaysen

[177]

In Honduras, under a labor code adopted in 1955 and a new constitution that became effective in 1957, the Hondurans elected

Ramón Villeda Morales. Villeda Morales backed an agrarian reform law that went into effect in 1961. The reforms threatened the United Fruit Company, which held enormous banana plantations on the north coast. (Bananas accounted for 50 percent of Honduran exports.)

October 2, 1962

MEMORANDUM FOR
ED MARTIN

I have received some complaints about the new land reform law in Honduras. It is alleged that this will adversely affect the American interests and that one of the justifications of its passage was the Alliance for Progress. It is possible that other countries may take similar actions.

Will you give me your thoughts on this.

[178]

At a news conference on August 29 President Kennedy declared that the United States would "watch what happens in Cuba with the closest attention." He was already aware that the Soviet Union was shipping arms to Castro, but so far the weapons were identified as "defensive" rather than "offensive." On the day of the President's news conference a high-altitude U-2 spy plane was taking photographs of military sites on Cuba. More photographs were taken on September 5. When the photos were analyzed, they revealed the presence of antiaircraft surface-to-air missiles (SAMs), missile-equipped torpedo boats, and MiG-21 fighter jets. There was also a significant increase in military personnel.

None of these weapons was defined as "offensive." However, in a September 13 news conference, the President warned, "If at any time the Communist build-up in Cuba were to endanger or interfere with our security in any way . . . then this country will do whatever must be done to protect its own security and that of its allies."

On October 14 a U-2 flying over western Cuba took a series of photographs that were analyzed on October 15 and shown to the President the following day. Interpretation of the photographs indicated the presence of motor pools, erector launches, and missile transporters for medium-range ballistic missiles capable of carrying nuclear warheads. Military experts estimated that the missile site near San Cristóbal was two weeks away from being operational.

Numerous high-level strategy meetings took place between the President and what came to be known as Excom (Executive Committee of the National Security Council). On the morning of October 22, prior to making a televised address to the nation on the Cuban missile situation, the President wrote to Khrushchev:

October 22, 1962

His Excellency
Nikita S. Khrushchev
Chairman of the Council of Ministers
   of the Union of Soviet Socialist Republics
Moscow

Sir:

A copy of the statement I am making tonight concerning developments in Cuba and the reaction of my Government thereto has been handed to your Ambassador in Washington. In view of the gravity of the developments to which I refer, I want you to know immediately and accurately the position of my government in this matter.

In our discussions and exchanges on Berlin and other international questions, the one thing that has most concerned me has been the possibility that your Government would not correctly understand the will and determination of the United States in any given situation, since I have not assumed that you or any other sane man would, in this nuclear age, deliberately plunge the world into war which it is crystal clear no country could win and which could only result in catastrophic consequences to the whole world, including the aggressor.

At our meeting in Vienna and subsequently, I expressed our readiness and desire to find, through peaceful negotiation, a solution to any and all problems that divide us. At the same time, I made clear that in view of the objectives of the ideology to which you adhere, the United States could not tolerate any action on your part which in a major way disturbed the existing over-all balance of power in the world. I stated that an attempt to force abandonment of our responsibilities and commitments in Berlin would constitute such an action and that the United States would resist with all the power at its command.

It was in order to avoid any incorrect assessment on the part of your Government with respect to Cuba that I publicly stated that if certain developments in Cuba took place, the United States would do whatever must be done to protect its own security and that of its allies.

Moreover, the Congress adopted a resolution expressing its support of this declared policy. Despite this, the rapid development of long-range missile bases and other offensive weapons systems in Cuba has proceeded. I must tell you that the United States is determined that this threat to the security of this hemisphere be removed. At the same time, I wish to point out that the action we are taking is the minimum necessary to remove the threat to the security of the nations of this hemisphere. The fact of this minimum response should not be taken as a basis, however, for any misjudgment on your part.

I hope that your Government will refrain from any action which would widen or deepen this already grave crisis and that we can agree to resume the path of peaceful negotiation.

Sincerely,

John F. Kennedy

[179]

In his address to the nation the same evening Kennedy announced that the United States had been closely watching the military buildup in Cuba. "Within the past week," he said, "unmistakable evidence has established the fact that a series of offensive missile sites is now in preparation on that imprisoned island." Announcing his determination to secure the withdrawal "or elimination" of the missiles from the Western Hemisphere, the President stated: "We will not prematurely or unnecessarily risk the costs of world-wide nuclear war in which even the fruits of victory would be ashes in our mouth, but neither will we shrink from that risk at any time it must be faced." Avoiding the use of the word "blockade," Kennedy then described the quarantine that the United States would impose on Soviet warships headed for Cuba.

National Security Action Memorandum No. 196 establishing Excom was written on October 22. All American missile crews were already on "maximum alert." The official status of all commands of the armed forces at this date was Defcon-2—the highest state of readiness next to war. Ninety B-52's carrying multimegaton bombs were flying over the Atlantic. One hundred nuclear warheads were activated on Atlas, Titan, and Minuteman missiles. Some fourteen hundred military aircraft— B-47's, B-52's, and B-58's—were standing by, prepared for takeoff.

October 22, 1962

NATIONAL SECURITY ACTION MEMORANDUM NO. 196

TO: The Vice President
    The Secretary of State
    The Secretary of Defense
    The Secretary of the Treasury
    The Attorney General
    The Chairman, Joint Chiefs of Staff
    The Director of Central Intelligence

SUBJECT: Establishment of an Executive Committee of the
          National Security Council

I hereby establish, for the purpose of effective conduct of the operations of the Executive Branch in the current crisis, an Executive Committee of the National Security Council. This committee will meet, until further notice, daily at 10:00 A.M. in the Cabinet room. I shall act as Chairman of this committee, and its additional regular members will be as follows: the Vice President, the Secretary of State, the Secretary of Defense, the Secretary of the Treasury, the Attorney General, the Director of Central Intelligence, the Under Secretary of State, the Deputy Secretary of Defense, the Chairman of the Joint Chiefs of Staff, the Ambassador-at-Large, the Special Counsel, and the Special Assistant to the President for National Security Affairs.

The first meeting of this committee will be held at the regular hour on Tuesday, October 23rd, at which point further arrangements with respect to its management and operation will be decided.

                      /s/ John F. Kennedy

[180]

* * *

On October 23 and again on October 25, UN Ambassador Stevenson presented the Security Council with evidence that the USSR "has placed and is placing medium—and intermediate—range missiles and sites in Cuba." This resulted in Acting Secretary-General U Thant's drafting a letter of appeal to Premier Khrushchev, which he also sent to President Kennedy. In his letter the secretary-general explained his "grave concern that Soviet ships already on their way to Cuba might challenge the quarantine imposed by the United States and produce a confrontation at sea. . . . what concerns me most is that such a confrontation and consequent aggravation of the situation would destroy any possibility of the discussions I have suggested as a prelude to negotiations on a peaceful settlement."

On October 26 U Thant sent a second message to Kennedy via Ambassador Stevenson urging the President to avoid confrontation. Kennedy replied:

LETTER FROM PRESIDENT KENNEDY
TO SECRETARY GENERAL U THANT
IN REPLY TO HIS LETTER OF OCTOBER 26, 1962

I have your further message of today and I continue to understand and welcome your efforts for a satisfactory solution. I appreciate and share your concern that great caution be exercised pending the inauguration of discussions.

If the Soviet Government accepts and abides by your request "that Soviet ships already on their way to Cuba . . . stay away from the interception area" for the limited time required for preliminary discussions, you may be assured that this Government will accept and abide by your request that our vessels in the Caribbean "do everything possible to avoid direct confrontation with Soviet ships in the next few days in order to minimize the risk of any untoward incident." I must inform you, however, that this is a matter of great urgency in view of the fact that certain Soviet ships are still proceeding toward Cuba and the interception area.

I share your hope that Chairman Khrushchev will also heed your appeal and that we can then proceed urgently to meet the requirement that these offensive military systems in Cuba be withdrawn, in order to end their threat to peace. I must point out to you that at present work on these systems is still continuing.

[181]

On October 26, John Scali, a correspondent for ABC, was contacted by Aleksandr Fomin, a counselor at the Soviet Embassy. The informal discussion between these two men proved to be critical in reaching a solution on the crisis. Fomin suggested that the Soviet Union might be willing to withdraw the Cuban missiles in exchange for a guarantee that the U.S. government would not invade Cuba. Believing that Fomin was speaking with full knowledge and approval of the Soviet government, Scali immediately relayed this critical information to Excom.

Both Fomin and Scali may have misunderstood each other's role. Raymond L. Garthoff, who was special assistant for Soviet bloc affairs during the missile crisis, later wrote in *Foreign Affairs* that "the Fomin meeting with Scali was not a probe by Khrushchev, and it did not even prompt Khrushchev's own probe in the first letter. Yet American leaders were prepared to assume that Fomin was a legitimate channel for communication by the Soviet leadership, despite the absence of any explicit claim on his part." Kennedy assumed, as did other U.S. officials at the time, that a Soviet official like Fomin must have had official authorization. According to Garthoff, this was not the case. Thus, the first "compromise" during the Soviet missile crisis was reached by two men who misunderstood each other's authority—each mistakenly believing that the other was presenting the position of his government.

A number of open letters were subsequently exchanged between Khrushchev and Kennedy. Following is the letter from the President that was released by the Office of the White House Press Secretary:

October 27, 1962

Dear Mr. Chairman:

I have read your letter of October 26th with great care and welcomed the statement of your desire to seek a prompt solution to the problem. The first thing that needs to be done, however, is for work to cease on offensive missile bases in Cuba and for all weapons systems in Cuba capable of offensive use to be rendered inoperable, under effective United Nations arrangements.

Assuming this is done promptly, I have given my representatives in New York instructions that will permit them to work out this weekend—in cooperation with the Acting Secretary General and your representative—an arrangement for a permanent solution to the Cuban problem along the lines suggested in your letter of October 26th. As I read your letter, the key elements of your proposals—which seem generally acceptable as I understand them—are as follows:

1) You would agree to remove those weapons systems from Cuba under appropriate United Nations observation and supervision; and undertake, with suitable safeguards, to halt the further introduction of such weapons systems into Cuba.

2) We, on our part, would agree—upon the establishment of adequate arrangements through the United Nations to ensure the carrying out and continuation of these commitments—(a) to remove promptly the quarantine measures now in effect and (b) to give assurances against an invasion of Cuba. I am confident that other nations of the Western Hemisphere would be prepared to do likewise.

If you will give your representative similar instructions, there is no reason why we should not be able to complete these arrangements and announce them to the world within a couple of days. The effect of such a settlement on easing world tensions would enable us to work toward a more general arrangement regarding "other armaments," as proposed in your second letter which you made public. I would like to say again that the United States is very much interested in reducing tensions and halting the arms race; and if your letter signifies that you are prepared to discuss a détente affecting NATO and the Warsaw Pact, we are quite prepared to consider with our allies any useful proposals.

But the first ingredient, let me emphasize, is the cessation of work on missile sites in Cuba and measures to render such weapons inoperable, under effective international guarantees. The continuation of this threat, or a prolonging of this discussion concerning Cuba by linking these problems to the broader questions of European and world security, would surely lead to an intensification of the Cuban crisis and a grave risk to the peace of the world. For this reason I hope we can quickly agree along the lines outlined in this letter and in your letter of October 26th.

/s/ John F. Kennedy

[182]

In an open letter to the President on October 27 Khrushchev made the additional proposal that the United States would remove its nuclear (Jupiter) missiles from Turkey while the Soviet Union pledged to remove its missiles from Cuba. Khrushchev suggested that "persons enjoying the confidence of the U.N. Security Council" would inspect the bases in Cuba and Turkey to make certain the pledges on each side had been fulfilled.

This suggestion introduced a new element into the negotiations, and in private meetings Kennedy adamantly refused to consider the additional terms. Then, on the twenty-eighth, the President received a further message from Khrushchev providing assurances that Soviet officers would "take appropriate measures to discontinue construction of the aforementioned facilities, to dismantle them, and to return them to the Soviet Union." At the recommendation of Attorney General Robert Kennedy, who was a member of Excom, the President chose to ignore Khrushchev's "Cuba-Turkey proposal" and instead focused on the Soviet premier's October 28 message. In writing to Khrushchev, Kennedy also made efforts to clarify the issue of an air force pilot who had strayed into Soviet airspace, putting Soviet bases on alert.

Dear Mr. Chairman:

I am replying at once to your broadcast message of October twenty-eight even though the official text has not yet reached me because of the great importance I attach to moving forward promptly to the settlement of the Cuban crisis. I think that you and I, with our heavy responsibilities for the maintenance of peace, were aware that developments were approaching a point where events could have become unmanageable. So I welcome this message and consider it an important contribution to peace.

The distinguished efforts of Acting Secretary General U Thant have greatly facilitated both our tasks. I consider my letter to you of October twenty-seventh and your reply of today as firm undertakings on the part of both our governments which should be promptly carried out. I hope that the necessary measures can at once be taken through the United Nations, as your message says, so that the United States in turn will be able to remove the quarantine measures now in effect. I have already made arrangements to report all these matters to the Organization of American States, whose members share a deep interest in a genuine peace in the Caribbean area.

You referred in your letter to a violation of your frontier by an American aircraft in the area of the Chukotsk Peninsula. I have learned that this plane, without arms or photographic equipment, was engaged in an air sampling mission in connection with your nuclear tests. Its course was direct from Eielson Air Force Base in Alaska to the North Pole and return. In turning south, the pilot made a serious navigational error which carried him over Soviet territory. He immediately made an emergency call on open radio for navigational assistance and was guided back to his home base by the most direct route. I regret this incident and will see to it that every precaution is taken to prevent recurrence.

Mr. Chairman, both of our countries have great unfinished tasks and I know that your people as well as those of the United States can ask for nothing better than to pursue them free from the fear of war. Modern science and technology have given us the possibility of making labor fruitful beyond anything that could have been dreamed of a few decades ago.

I agree with you that we must devote urgent attention to the problem of disarmament, as it relates to the whole world and also to critical areas. Perhaps now, as we step back from danger, we can together make real progress in this vital field. I think we should give priority to questions relating to the proliferation of nuclear weapons, on earth and in outer space, and to the great effort for a nuclear test ban. But we should also work hard to see if wider measures of disarmament can be agreed and put into operation at an early date. The United States Government will be prepared to discuss these questions urgently, and in a constructive spirit, at Geneva or elsewhere.

/s/ John F. Kennedy

[183]

Although the exact number of missiles was not known at the time, four out of the six medium-range missile sites were operable by October 23 and forty-two eleven-hundred-mile medium-range missiles were already in Cuba. (Twenty-four twenty-two-hundred-mile-range missiles that Khrushchev had also scheduled for delivery never arrived.) Kennedy was fully aware of the probable consequences of failing to reach a peaceful settlement of the crisis. As he told one adviser, "If anybody is around to write after this, they are going to understand that we made every effort to find peace and every effort to give our adversary room to move."

SECRET

October 28, 1962

NATIONAL SECURITY ACTION MEMORANDUM NO. 200

TO: The Secretary of State

The Secretary of Defense

The Director, Office of Emergency Planning

SUBJECT: Acceleration of Civil Defense Activities

The President has approved the plan for the acceleration of the current civil defense program contained in the memorandum dated October 25, 1962, from the Department of Defense.

The President also gave his qualified approval to plan #2 contained in the memorandum dated October 24, 1962, from the Department of Defense. The plan outlines steps to be taken to prepare for possible nuclear attack in regions which are within MRBM [medium-range ballistic missile] range of Cuba; it will be carried out in conjunction with the plan for the acceleration of the current civil defense program contained in the memorandum dated October 25, 1962, from the Department of Defense. The President's qualifications are (1) that the plan be limited to steps which can be conducted without undue public impact and (2) that any such regional acceleration be limited to the period of the present emergency.

The President also has directed that preparatory steps, including, as necessary, discreet consultation with state and local authorities, be taken to effect plan #1 contained in the memorandum dated October 24, 1962, from the Department of Defense; the plan outlines action to be taken in the vicinity of targets relatively close to Cuba to prepare for attack with conventional weapons. The President wishes to be informed when the preparatory steps have been taken.

/s/ McGeorge Bundy

[184]

*   *   *

Throughout the missile crisis Adlai Stevenson played a crucial role at UN Security Council meetings, communicating with the acting secretary-general and confronting the Security Council's president, Soviet Ambassador Zorin.

October 29, 1962

The Honorable Adlai E. Stevenson
United States Representative
   to the United Nations
799 United Nations Plaza
New York 17, New York

Dear Adlai:

I want to tell you how deeply and personally I appreciate the contribution you have made to the security of the United States and the peace of the world in the last week. Your vindication of American policy before the United Nations was superb; and I know that it accounts in great measure for the understanding and support that policy has received from our friends abroad.

We are not yet out of the woods; and I count on you in the days ahead.

Sincerely,
/s/ John F. Kennedy
[185]

(Several days later, on November 1, after meeting with Stevenson at the UN, Arthur Schlesinger wrote to the President, "Stevenson asked me to tell you how deeply he appreciated your letter to him.")

As chief of naval operations George W. Anderson, Jr., reported to Defense Secretary McNamara during the blockade of Soviet ships. When McNamara questioned the admiral's ability to handle the situation "by the book," Anderson sharply requested that the secretary of defense return to his office and leave naval operations to the Navy. Nonetheless, the President in his November 5 memo asked McNamara to consult with Anderson on the matter of "a secret subterranean base." It is unclear whether Kennedy knew about the serious rift between his chief naval officer and the secretary of defense.

TOP SECRET

November 5, 1962

MEMORANDUM FOR

SECRETARY MCNAMARA

We must operate on the presumption that the Russians may try again. This time they may prepare themselves for action on the sea in the Cuban area. Does Admiral Anderson think they could build up a secret naval base which will put them on a near parity with us if we should once again blockade. If he thinks there is substantial danger of this what suggestions would he now make?

/s/ John F. Kennedy

[186]

As the Cuban missile crisis drew to a close, Kennedy asked for the treasury secretary's opinion on the balance of payments situation.

November 5, 1962

The Honorable Douglas Dillon
Secretary of the Treasury
Washington, D.C.

Dear Doug:

Is it your understanding that our present arrangements in international monetary policy stood up during the last two weeks?

If the crisis had become more pronounced, if there had been a total blockade, and if it had gone on for a longer period of time, would we have had a serious run on gold? What can we do to prevent a disparity in interest rates, such as we have recently seen between ourselves and Great Britain? It should be possible for us to get better coordination with the western governments to limit any causes for concern.

Sincerely,
John F. Kennedy

[187]

As the Soviets began dismantling the missile bases on Cuba, problems remained. Castro, feeling betrayed by Khrushchev, refused to cooperate with the Soviets in allowing observers into Cuba to monitor the withdrawal of Soviet weapons. Surveillance could be conducted only with overflights of high-flying U.S. aircraft. On at least one occasion these flights were harassed by Soviet MiG fighters.

The President was also concerned with removal of Soviet weapons other than the missiles. Kennedy authorized Stevenson to present the Soviet Union's representative at the UN, V. V. Kuznetsov, with a list of weapons considered "offensive" by the U.S. military, including Soviet IL-28 light bombers. Presented with the list, Khrushchev on November 5 wrote to Kennedy, "It is hard for us to understand what aim is being pursued by the introduction of that list, by setting forth such a demand. . . . And it is being done at a moment when we have already agreed with you on the main questions and when we on our part have already fulfilled what we agreed upon—have dismantled rocket weapons, are loading them now on ships and these weapons will be soon shipped from Cuba."

Khrushchev's letter concluded with a plea and a warning:

Let us then bring the achieved understanding to a completion, so that we could consider that each side has fulfilled its pledges and the question has been settled. If, however, additional demands are made, then that means only one thing—the danger that the difficulties on the way to eliminating tension created around Cuba will not be removed. But that may raise then new consequences.

I think that you will understand me correctly. For you and I will evidently have to deal not only with elimination of the remnants of the present tension—there lies ahead for you and me a great, serious talk on other questions. Why then start now complicating the situation by minor things? Maybe there exist some considerations, but they are beyond our comprehension. As for us, we view the introduction of additional demands as a wish to bring our relations back again into a heated state in which they were but several days ago.

*   *   *

President Kennedy's extensive reply was sent the following day:

November 6, 1962

His Excellency
Nikita S. Khrushchev
Chairman of the Council of Ministers
    of the Union of Soviet Socialist Republics
Moscow

Dear Mr. Chairman:

I am surprised that in your letter, which I received yesterday, you suggest that in giving your representative in New York a list of the weapons we consider offensive there was any desire on our part to complicate the situation. Our intention was just the opposite: to stick to a well-known list, and not to introduce any new factors. But there is really only one major item on the list, beyond the missiles and their equipment, and that is the light bombers with their equipment. This item is indeed of great importance to us.

The solution of the Cuban affair was established by my letter to you of October twenty-seventh and your reply of October twenty-eighth. You will recall that in my letter of October twenty-seventh, I referred to "all weapons systems in Cuba capable of offensive use." You will also recall that in my broadcast address of October twenty-second, in addition to medium-range ballistic missiles, I mentioned specifically "jet bombers capable of carrying nuclear weapons" as "an explicit threat to the peace and security of all the Americas." Finally, my proclamation of October twenty-third entitled "Interdiction of the Delivery of Offensive Weapons to Cuba" specifically listed bomber aircraft. These facts were all known at the time of our exchange of letters on Cuba, and so it seems clear to me that our exchange of letters covers the IL-28s, since your undertaking was to remove the weapons we described as offensive.

Your letter says—and I agree—that we should not complicate the situation by minor things. But I assure you that this matter of IL-28s is not a minor matter for us at all. It is true, of course, that these bombers are not the most modern of weapons, but they are distinctly capable of offensive use against the United States and other Western Hemispheric countries, and I am sure your own military men would inform you that the continued existence of such bombers in Cuba would require substantial measures of military defense in response by the United States. Thus, in simple logic these are weapons capable of offensive use. But there is more in it than that, Mr. Chairman. These bombers could carry nuclear weapons for long distances, and they are clearly not needed, any more than missiles, for purely defensive purposes on the island of Cuba. Thus in the present context their continued presence would sustain the grave tension that has been created, and their removal, in my view, is necessary to a good start on ending the recent crisis.

I am not clear as to what items you object to on the list which Ambassador Stevenson handed to Mr. Kuznetsov. I can assure you I have no desire to cause you difficulties by any wide interpretation of the definitions of weapons which we consider offensive and I am instructing my representative in New York to confer promptly with Mr. Kuznetsov and to be as forthcoming as possible in order to meet any legitimate complaints you may have in order to reach a quick solution which would enable our agreement to be carried to completion. I entirely agree with your statement that we should wind up the immediate crisis promptly, and I assure you that on our side we are insisting only on what is immediately essential for progress in this matter. In order to make our position clear, I think I should go on to give you a full sense of the very strong feelings we have about this whole affair here in the United States.

These recent events have given a profound shock to relations between our two countries. It may be said, as Mr. Kuznetsov said the other day to Mr. McCloy, that the Soviet Union was under no obligation to inform us of any activities it was carrying on in a third country. I cannot accept this view; not only did this action threaten the whole safety of this hemisphere, but it was, in a broader sense, a dangerous attempt to change the world-wide *status quo*. Secret action of this kind seems to me both hazardous and unjustified. But however one may judge that argument, what actually happened in this case was not simply that the action of your side was secret. Your Government repeatedly gave us assurances of what it was *not* doing: these assurances were announced as coming from the highest levels, and they proved inaccurate.

I do not refer here only to the TASS article of September, but also to communications which were addressed to the highest levels of our Government through channels which heretofore had been used for confidential messages from the highest levels of your Government. Through these channels we were specifically informed that no missiles would be placed in Cuba which would have a range capable of reaching the United States. In reliance upon these assurances I attempted, as you know, to restrain those who were giving warnings in this country about the trend of events in Cuba. Thus undeniable photographic evidence that offensive weapons were being installed was a deep and dangerous shock, first to this Government and then to our whole people.

In the aftermath of this shock, to which we replied with a measured but necessary response, I believe it is vital that we should re-establish some degree of confidence in communication between the two of us. If the leaders of the two great nuclear powers cannot judge with some accuracy the intentions of each other, we shall find ourselves in a period of gravely increasing danger—not only for our two countries but for the whole world.

I therefore hope that you will promptly recognize that when we speak of the need to remove missiles and bombers, with their immediate supporting equipment, we are not trying to complicate the situation but simply stating what was clearly included in our understanding of October twenty-seventh and twenty-eighth. I shall continue to abide fully by the undertakings in my letter of October twenty-seventh, and specifically, under the conditions stated in that letter I will hold to my undertaking "to give assurances against an invasion of Cuba." This undertaking has already come under attack here and is likely to become increasingly an object of criticism by a great many of my countrymen. And the very minimum that is necessary in regard to these assurances is, as we agreed, the verified removal of the missile and bomber systems, together with real safeguards against their reintroduction.

I should emphasize to you directly, Mr. Chairman, that in this respect there is another problem immediately ahead of us which could become very serious indeed, and that is the problem of continuing verification in Cuba. Your representatives have spoken as if this were entirely a problem for the Castro regime to settle, but the continuing verification of the absence of offensive weapons in Cuba is an essential safeguard for the United States and the other countries of this hemisphere, and is an explicit condition for the undertakings which we in our turn have agreed to. The need for this verification is, I regret to say, convincingly demonstrated by what happened in Cuba in the months of September and October.

For the present we are having to rely on our own methods of surveillance, and this surveillance will surely have to be continued unless, as we much prefer, a better and durable method can be found. We believe that it is a serious responsibility of your Government to insure that weapons which you have provided to Cuba are not employed to interfere with this surveillance which is so important to us all in obtaining reliable information on which improvements in the situation can be based. It was of great importance, for example, for me last week to be able to announce with confidence that dismantling of missiles had begun.

Finally, I would like to say a word about longer range matters. I think we must both recognize that it will be very difficult for any of us in this hemisphere to look forward to any real improvement in our relations with Cuba if it continues to be a military outpost of the Soviet Union. We have limited our action at present to the problem of offensive weapons, but I do think it may be important for you to consider whether a real normalization of the Cuba problem can be envisaged while there remains in Cuba large numbers of Soviet military technicians, and major weapons systems and communications complexes under Soviet control, all with the recurrent possibility that offensive weapons might be secretly and rapidly reintroduced. That is why I think there is much wisdom in the conclusion expressed in your letter of October 26th, that when our undertakings against invasion are effective the need for your military specialists in Cuba will disappear. That is the real path to progress in the Cuban problem. And in this connection in particular, I hope you will understand that we must attach the greatest importance to the personal assurances you have given that submarine bases will not be established in Cuba.

I believe that Cuba can never have normal relations with the other nations of this hemisphere unless it ceases to appear to be a foreign military base and adopts a peaceful course of non-interference in the affairs of its sister nations. These wider considerations may belong to a later phase of the problem, but I hope that you will give them careful thought.

In the immediate situation, however, I repeat that it is the withdrawal of the missiles and bombers, with their supporting equipment, under adequate verification, and with a proper system for continued safeguards in the future, that is essential. This is the first necessary step away from the crisis to open the door through which we can move to restore confidence and give attention to other problems which ought to be resolved in the interest of peace.

Sincerely,

John F. Kennedy

[188]

Throughout the crisis Kennedy and the members of Excom relied on surveillance reports and interpretations of photographs that were provided by the National Photographic Interpretation Center. The director of the center, Arthur C. Lundahl, was a former University of Chicago geology student who had been recruited in 1954 by Richard Bissell and Allen Dulles of the CIA to analyze and interpret U-2 photographs. According to Michael Beschloss, author of *Mayday: The U-2 Affair*, Lundahl's undercover operation was code-named Htautomat.

November 8, 1962

Dear Mr. Lundahl:

While I would like to make public the truly outstanding accomplishments of the National Photographic Interpretation Center, I realize that the anonymity of an organization of your high professional competence in the intelligence field must be maintained.

I do want you and your people to know of my very deep appreciation for the tremendous task you are performing under most trying circumstances. The analysis and interpretation of the Cuban photography and the reporting of your findings promptly and succinctly to me and to my principal policy advisers, most particularly the Secretary of State and the Secretary of Defense, have been exemplary.

You have my thanks and the thanks of your government for a very remarkable performance of duty and my personal commendation goes to all of you.

Sincerely,

John F. Kennedy

[189]

*   *   *

On November 20 the President received a reply from Khrushchev on the question of removing the Soviet light bombers from Cuba. Kennedy's confidential message in reply was declassified in 1979:

November 21, 1962

MESSAGE FOR CHAIRMAN KHRUSHCHEV

Dear Mr. Chairman:

I have been glad to get your letter of November 20, which arrived in good time yesterday. As you will have seen, I was able to announce the lifting of our quarantine promptly at my press conference, on the basis of your welcome assurance that the IL-28 bombers will be removed within a month.

I am now instructing our negotiators in New York to move ahead promptly with proposals for a solution of the remaining elements in the Cuban problem. I do not wish to confuse the discussion by trying to state our present position in detail in this message, but I do want you to know that I continue to believe that it is important to settle this matter promptly and on reasonable terms, so that we may move on to other issues. I regret that you have been unable to persuade Mr. Castro to accept a suitable form of inspection or verification in Cuba, and that in consequence we must continue to rely upon our own means of information. But, as I said yesterday, there need be no fear of any invasion of Cuba while matters take their present favorable course.

[190]

Even though Excom continued to meet daily, some events came to the President's attention through the press rather than through government sources. In his November 21 memo for naval aide Captain Tazewell Shepard, Kennedy suggests that John McCone, head of the CIA, might have information which had not yet been released to the Navy or relayed directly to the President.

November 21, 1962

MEMORANDUM FOR CAPTAIN SHEPARD

Could we get a report on the stories that a Cuban antiaircraft battery fired on a low-flying twin-engine plane over the Havana suburb of Miramar. The stories also state the plane is presumed to be a United States Navy Neptune patrol. In addition, can we get a report on the alleged attack on a merchant ship on the high seas southwest of Bermuda yesterday by an airplane. Could it have been the same plane under the control of the refugees? If the Defense Department has no information about it, it should be referred to John McCone.

[191]

On November 24 the President sent a "personal message" through the State Department to President Charles de Gaulle of France, Germany's Konrad Adenauer, and Britain's Prime Minister Macmillan confirming the lifting of the quarantine of Soviet ships. The text of the message to these leaders was cabled to the foreign embassies:

As you will have seen from the news reports, Khrushchev agreed to remove the IL-28 bombers yesterday morning before my press conference and therefore it has not been necessary to move on at present to further pressure in the Caribbean. We have announced the lifting of the quarantine, and we expect that discussion will go forward in New York on the remaining elements of the understanding of October 27 and 28.

What is almost equally interesting is that Khrushchev's last message indicated that he expected to remove other Soviet military units which have been placed in Cuba for the purpose of defending the missile sites. We shall do our best to assist him in this course. Meanwhile, our own aerial surveillance continues, although we are discussing it as little as possible in public, in order to avoid a question which may complicate Soviet military disengagement. We shall of course continue to do whatever is necessary to keep adequately informed of the situation in Cuba.

So it appears that at this second turning point in the Cuban crisis, Khrushchev has once again chosen the safer course. In a sense, then, my alerting message of the other day has proved unnecessary. I am sure that a major element in Khrushchev's decision was his awareness that we were both serious in our own purpose and confident of the support of our Allies; so let me end by thanking you again for the clarity and firmness of your backing.

[192]

As Kennedy told one of his advisers, he believed that Fowler Hamilton had moved too slowly in helping countries to achieve self-sustaining economic growth that would help them resist communist influence. Hamilton resigned in November, and his place was taken by David Bell, former director of the Bureau of the Budget. Upon Bell's appointment, Kennedy reviewed funding of the military assistance programs (MAP) in South America and chartered a more aggressive course for AID.

SECRET

December 4, 1962

NATIONAL SECURITY ACTION MEMORANDUM NO. 206
TO: The Secretary of State
The Secretary of Defense
The Chairman, Joint Chiefs of Staff
The Director of Central Intelligence
The Administrator, AID
SUBJECT: Military Assistance for Internal Security in Latin
America

The President has signed a determination authorizing the grant of up to $34.9 million of military matefiel for internal security purposes in Latin America. In this connection, the President underscored his concern with the need for the most challenging scrutiny of the justifications advanced for providing items under this determination.

In the complex and rapidly shifting circumstances in Latin America, it is essential that our military aid program be a carefully-tailored and constantly updated part of our overall strategy aimed at development and security in the hemisphere. The program development and review process must assure that the specific items furnished under MAP are appropriate to solving the key internal security problems to which our overall country planning is addressed; and that this program in fact strengthens and supports the other objectives of the U.S. effort in each country, including the development of popularly supported civilian governments and effective civil police authorities.

The President recognizes that considerable effort has already been made to reorient military assistance in Latin America. But because this program is so sensitive in relation to the whole gamut of Latin American problems, he wishes to be assured that you continually stress the need to screen MAP items against the full range of intelligence, political analysis, policy evaluation, and other U.S. programs on a current basis.

Specifically:

Are jet aircraft really justifiable items for the internal security mission, or are they included essentially for political reasons? If so, do we have a clear idea of the full political ramifications, and are they clearly to our advantage?

Does the design of the MAP internal security program reflect our current efforts to strengthen the roles and capabilities of civil police in the same countries?

Is there explicit division of missions between the military and police units we support in each country?

Does the projected level of MAP in Latin America reflect a consciously measured balance between our military and police efforts in the internal security field?

Is an adequate contribution made by the intelligence community in the review of internal security programs?

In this connection, the President desires that careful consideration be given to intensifying civil police programs in lieu of military assistance where such action will yield more fruitful results in terms of our primary internal security objective. Should AID funds be insufficient to meet total requirements, a transfer from military assistance should be seriously considered.

Will you please take whatever steps are necessary to assure that the FY 1963 MAP program for Latin America is appropriate in terms of these criteria. The President wishes to have the Administrator of AID, in his role as coordinator of foreign assistance, submit a report, in cooperation with the Secretary of Defense, on the steps being taken to assure that MAP has the desired effects on our total efforts in Latin America. He also desires a report later in this fiscal year on the scope and character of the program which is finally implemented under the determination which has just been made.

McGeorge Bundy

[193]

Before the Cuban missile crisis the CIA's aerial reconnaissance had succeeded where ground agents had failed. Though CIA agents in and around Cuba had reported the arrival of Soviet troops and noted the delivery of missiles, aircraft, and various arms, they had failed to uncover the missile installation at San Cristóbal. The fact that a U-2 had detected the missile base convinced Kennedy that continued overflights were an essential element in the U.S. surveillance system.

EYES ONLY—TOP SECRET—SENSITIVE

December 4, 1962

NATIONAL SECURITY ACTION MEMORANDUM NO. 208

TO: The Director of Central Intelligence

SUBJECT: Cuban Overflights

The President has approved the attached *Guidelines for the Planning of Cuban Overflights* and would like to have an estimate of the adequacy of such a system of intelligence collection to meet the criteria set forth, on the assumption that it is supplemented by energetic collection of information by all other available means.

McGeorge Bundy

[194]

On September 29, 1961, Khrushchev had initiated correspondence with Kennedy outside the normal diplomatic channels. The first in what was to be a series of letters came from the Black Sea resort where the Soviet premier was vacationing. At the outset Khrushchev suggested that he and Kennedy begin an informal correspondence that would pass directly between the two leaders. Soviet diplomat Georgy Bolshakov was an intermediary.

Two weeks after receiving Khrushchev's first letter, Kennedy drafted a reply from Hyannis Port. The President agreed to an informal exchange of views that, in Sorensen's words, would "be free from the polemics of the 'Cold War' debate."

Thereafter Kennedy continued to receive and send letters that were seen by only a few close associates. The existence of this personal correspondence was not revealed until after the Cuban missile crisis.

Kennedy's letter to Khrushchev on December 14, 1962, was part of this personal correspondence.

SECRET

December 14, 1962

Dear Mr. Chairman:

I was glad to have your message of December 11th and to know that you believe, as we do, that we have come to the final stage of the Cuban affair between us, the settlement of which will have significance for our future relations and for our ability to overcome other difficulties. I wish to thank you for your expression of appreciation of the understanding and flexibility we have tried to display.

I have followed with close attention the negotiations on the final settlement of the Cuban question between your representative, Mr. Kuznetsov, and our representatives, Ambassador Stevenson and Mr. McCloy, in New York. In these negotiations we have tried to understand your position and I am glad to note that Mr. Kuznetsov has also shown efforts to understand our problems. It is clearly in the interest of both sides that we reach agreement on how finally to dispose of the Cuban crisis. To this end, Ambassador Stevenson and Mr. McCloy presented on Wednesday a new draft of a joint statement which by now has certainly reached you. I wish to assure you that it is our purpose to end this affair as simply and clearly as possible.

You refer to the importance of my statements on an invasion of Cuba and of our intention to fulfill them, so that no doubts are sown from the very start. I have already stated my position publicly in my press conference on November 20th, and I am glad that this statement appears to have your understanding; we have never wanted to be driven by the acts of others into war in Cuba. The other side of the coin, however, is that we do need to have adequate assurances that all offensive weapons are removed from Cuba and are not reintroduced, and that Cuba itself commits no aggressive acts against any of the nations of the Western Hemisphere. As I understand you, you feel confident that Cuba will not in fact engage in such aggressive acts, and of course I already have your own assurance about the offensive weapons. So I myself should suppose that you could accept our position—but it is probably better to leave final discussion of these matters to our representatives in New York. I quite agree with you that the larger part of the crisis has now been ended and we should not permit others to stand in the way of promptly settling the rest without further acrimony.

With regard to your reference to the confidential channels set up between us, I can assure you that I value them. I have not concealed from you that it was a serious disappointment to me that dangerously misleading information should have come through these channels before the recent crisis. You may also wish to know that by an accident or misunderstanding one of your diplomats [Aleksandr Fomin] appears to have used a representative of a private television network [John Scali of ABC] as a channel to us. This is always unwise in our country, where the members of the press often insist on printing at some later time what they may learn privately.

Because our systems are so different, you may not be fully familiar with the practices of the American press. The competition for news in this country is fierce. A number of the competitors are not great admirers of my Administration, and perhaps an even larger number are not wholly friendly to yours. Here in Washington we have 1200 reporters accredited to the White House alone, and thousands more in other assignments. Not one of them is accountable to this government for what he reports. It would be a great mistake to think that what appears in newspapers and magazines necessarily has anything to do with the policy and purpose of this government. I am glad to say that I have some friends among newspapermen, but no spokesmen.

But let me emphasize again that we do indeed value these confidential channels. I entirely share your view that some trust is necessary for leading statesmen of our two countries; I believe that it is important to build the area of trust wherever possible. I shall of course continue to hold and to express my convictions about the relative merits of our systems of government, and I will not be surprised if you do the same.

[Seven lines sanitized.]

I appreciate your writing me so frankly, and in return I have tried to be as straightforward, for I agree with you that only through such frank exchanges can we better understand our respective points of view. Partly for this reason I refrained in my last press conference from commenting on certain aspects of your speech before the Supreme Soviet with which you realize, of course, we could not agree.

We also are hopeful that once the Cuban crisis is behind us, we shall be able to tackle the other problems confronting us and to find the path to their solution.

[Twenty lines sanitized.]

I look forward to receiving your confidential letter and proposals on the test ban question, and I think there is every reason to keep working on this problem. I hope that in your message on this subject you will tell me what you think about the position of the people in Peking on this question. It seems to me very important for both of us that in our efforts to secure an end to nuclear testing we should not overlook this area of the world.

Thank you for your expressions of good wishes to me and my family, and let me in turn send you and your wife and family our personal good wishes for the coming year.

[195]

The following day, Kennedy sent a memo to the director of the CIA.

December 15, 1962

MEMORANDUM TO DIRECTOR MCCONE

I am sure that we are watching for any developments by the Soviet Union of a submarine base in Cuba. Will you keep me informed periodically as to whether or not anything of a suspicious nature has turned up in this regard.

/s/ John F. Kennedy

[196]

1963

In early January 1963 the President approved National Security Action Memorandum No. 213, which established a special coordinator to oversee the activities of other departments and agencies in dealing with Cuban affairs. As part of the missile crisis deal between Kennedy and Khrushchev, the President had agreed that in exchange for the withdrawal of Soviet missiles, the United States would make no further attempts to invade Cuba. There was, however, the question of what to do about Cuban refugees—many with military training—who were concentrated in the Miami area.

On December 23, 1962, Castro released from Cuban jails 1,179 veterans from the Bay of Pigs, in exchange for a shipment of fifty-three million dollars worth of U.S. medical equipment, drugs, and baby food. "For the military," wrote Brigadier General C. V. Clifton in a memo to Bundy, "the question was how many of these brigade officers could be used at Fort Jackson, South Carolina, in helping to train the Cuban trainees, how many of the Cuban officers might need a special officers' course for updating and retraining as officers, and finally, how many of the Cuban refugee prisoners would actually go in for a 20-weeks retraining course."

The general also repeated questions that had been raised at a meeting between the Joint Chiefs and the President in Palm Beach. Clifton asked "whether this Cuban brigade would be a focal point for a new political groupment. From all we could learn it looks like they might become such a party. The President pointed out that one of the tough problems in dealing with the 100,000 Cuban refugees in the Miami area is their lack of a formalized party—he stated that there are four major parties and about one hundred splinter groups—and he thinks that the Cuban brigade might become a fifth rallying point, possibly a rather heavily emotionally charged one."

The sixth paragraph of NSAM 213 (declassified in 1979) contains the President's decision that the coordinator for Cuban affairs would have responsibility for covert as well as overt actions relating to the refugee programs. Subsequently Cuban exiles ran "hit-and-run" operations on Cuban targets, and the CIA's Technical Services Division made a number of attempts to assassinate Castro.

SECRET

January 8, 1963

NATIONAL SECURITY ACTION MEMORANDUM NO. 213
TO: The Secretary of State
SUBJECT: Interdepartmental Organization for Cuban Affairs

The President has approved the following organizational arrangements to facilitate the coordinated management of all aspects of our current policy toward Cuba; final policy responsibility of course remains with the President, working with the Executive Committee of the National Security Council when necessary.

1. Day-to-day coordinating responsibility will be vested in a Coordinator of Cuban Affairs in the Department of State, acting as Chairman of an Interdepartmental Committee on Cuba. The Coordinator will be responsible to the Secretary of State for State Department business, and under his guidance to the President and the Executive Committee for interdepartmental coordination.

2. The Interdepartmental Coordinating Committee shall consist of the Coordinator and representatives of the Department of Defense and the Central Intelligence Agency. Representatives of other departments will be associated with the work of this committee as necessary in particular cases. Officers shall also be detailed to the Office of the Coordinator from the Departments of State, Defense, Justice, HEW, CIA, and USIA. Other departments and agencies may be requested to participate in the work of the Interdepartmental

Committee and in the work of the Coordinator's Office as appropriate. A White House office will maintain liaison with the Coordinator and with his Interdepartmental Committee.

[Points 3–5 outline the coordinator's authority.]

6. The Coordinator will assume the same responsibility for covert
operations as he does for overt actions. However, he will report
on covert matters to the Special Group which will be guided by
broader policy established by the President through the Executive
Committee.

McGeorge Bundy

[197]

As he had done after the Berlin crisis, the President asked the
Office of Emergency Planning to review the plans and preparations
for national actions in the event of war.

January 9, 1963

MEMORANDUM FOR

Honorable Edward A. McDermott
Director, Office of Emergency Planning

As we have discussed, I am interested in improving our planning
for the management of our resources and implementing the necessary
steps in the economic stabilization field during periods of national
emergency. Such nonmilitary planning must be based on assumptions which encompass the entire spectrum of possible conflicts,
including the possibility of general nuclear war.

Pursuant to Section 301, Executive Order 11051, I approve the
establishment of an inter-agency committee under your chairmanship, with appropriate level representation from the Departments of
State and Defense and the Central Intelligence Agency, to provide
assumptions on which such plans can be based.

The assumptions developed by this committee should be used by
various Federal Agencies in developing plans in the nonmilitary
preparedness fields. This will permit the departments and agencies
concerned to proceed with their respective nonmilitary preparedness
assignments on a common and consistent basis.

Please coordinate the work of this committee with the staff of the National Security Council.

/s/John F. Kennedy

[198]

Though the flow of dollars into Europe had slowed during the first two years of the Kennedy administration, the President told Sorensen that the deficit "is a club that de Gaulle and all the others hang over my head. Any time there's a crisis or a quarrel, they can cash in all their dollars and where are we?"

January 17, 1963

MEMORANDUM FOR
THE SECRETARY OF THE TREASURY

I would like a breakdown of the make up of the French balance of payments. How much of it is due to American defense expenditures there, to tourists, to American investments in France? What is our trade balance in France?

I would be interested in a similar breakdown for Spain, Italy and Great Britain.

[199]

January 17, 1963

MEMORANDUM FOR THE SECRETARY OF THE TREASURY

I am concerned about the figures that you sent me on the gold drain for 1963. Won't this bring us in January 1964 to a critically low point? What are the prospects that we could bring this under control by 1964? We had thought we could balance it in 1963. Can we do it now in 1964?

[200]

On January 14 De Gaulle put an abrupt end to France's participation in what, up till then, had been called a Grand Design for Europe's future. In a surprise press conference the leader of the Fifth Republic announced that France would insist on an independent nuclear force, veto Britain's entry into the Common Market, and withdraw a number of French forces from NATO. De Gaulle also announced his intention of signing a new treaty of unity with West Germany, and he made it clear that he was opposed to the political unity of the Common Market countries.

January 19, 1963

MEMORANDUM FOR
THE SECRETARY OF THE TREASURY

It is possible that our present difficulty with France may escalate. If things become severe enough it is conceivable that they will take some action against the dollar—to indicate their power to do something if nothing else. I believe we should have a plan for this, including extreme steps if that should prove necessary. I would like to know what two potentials are in this field, theirs and ours.

[201]

January 21, 1963

MEMORANDUM FOR
THE SECRETARY OF STATE

Would you prepare for me an analysis of the methods by which France distributes her assistance to the African countries—is it through balance of payments subsidies, direct budget support or credit for French manufactured merchandise. How much of this is gold drain on France? Are there any lessons to be learned from this as it seems to be quite successful?

[202]

January 21, 1963

MEMORANDUM FOR
SECRETARY OF STATE

Has General de Gaulle ever stated that the French nuclear deterrent would be used for the defense of Europe or has he confined himself to saying that it would be used for the defense of France?

[203]

* * *

As the nations of Western Europe moved toward economic co-operation, the President foresaw opening new markets in Eastern Europe as a possible way to ease trade deficits.

January 22, 1963

MEMORANDUM FOR
THE SECRETARY OF STATE

Would you please send me the figures on the agricultural trade of Western Europe with Eastern Europe, excluding the Soviet Union. Also, will you give me an analysis, if there were no political restrictions, on whether the United States could increase its agricultural trade with Eastern Europe.

/s/ John Kennedy

[204]

In the wake of De Gaulle's anti-British stand in the Common Market, the French leader was criticized by most West European leaders, including Belgian Foreign Minister Paul-Henri Spaak. Kennedy's January 31 memo indicates that the French position prompted far-reaching concerns about U.S. policy in Europe.

In paragraph 6, Kennedy refers to journalist C. L. Sulzberger, who was writing from Paris. Sulzberger's widely read "Foreign Affairs" column, in Kennedy's view, promoted a "pro-de Gaulle" position.

January 31, 1963

Questions to be settled by the United States in the coming months.

1. Trade negotiations with the Common Market. Priority of various goods.

2. Spaak's political stability. Can he continue to sustain anti-de Gaulle position in Belgium? How far can he go in this attack?

3. When will the African countries apply for admission to the Common Market? Can we expect them to be held up by the Belgians and Dutch as a reprisal?

4. What is the multilateral's* future now? Should we proceed ahead? Will de Gaulle top us—the Germans being bilateral?

*Agreement on a multilateral force—i.e., agreement on a combined military force under shared command of NATO nations.

5. Should we wait for the defense minister to come here or should we send a Merchant on the road?

6. How can we improve the American line from the various embassies so that there will not be as [many] pro-de Gaulle stories—i.e., Sulzberger, etc.

7. How can we improve the Washington liaison with foreign correspondents here?

8. How can we improve the technique with those State Department personnel who give out information and talk to members of the press?

9. What kind of a deal can de Gaulle make with the Russians which would be acceptable to the Germans?

10. What are the prospects for a tripartite with de Gaulle?

11. What defense can we build with the dollar to maintain our balance of payments in the next 18 months?

12. What are the prospects for the French nuclear force? When will it be a deterrent even in a limited sense?

13. What should be our proposals for NATO in May? Change in the number of our divisions? Should we bring out the divisions that we have there?

[205]

In the Alliance for Progress, U.S. aid had been used effectively for such Latin American projects as building new houses and new schools, providing food rations, and supplying schoolchildren with textbooks. More difficult were long-range programs such as agricultural development. Richard Goodwin, who by December 1962 was working in the Peace Corps program, had presented the original plan for agricultural development at the InterAmerican Economic and Social Council meeting in Punta del Este, Uruguay, in 1961.

February 7, 1963

MEMORANDUM FOR DAVE BELL

Some time ago Dick Goodwin spoke to me about the idea of having the state of California assume some responsibility for the agricultural development of Chile. This program could be a real breakthrough if it is pushed vigorously and enthusiastically, because if successful here we could follow the same procedure with other states. In addition it would give the Alliance for Progress a new life. I would hope that it would be possible to announce the beginning of the California project at the time Governor [Edmund ("Pat")] Brown visits next week. I have asked Dick Goodwin to keep an eye on this project and I understand Bill Rogers in the Alliance for Progress office has been working on it and knows about it. Would you keep me informed.

/s/ John F. Kennedy

[206]

Romulo Betancourt, the Venezuelan leader, had advocated principles of a "progressive democracy" when U.S. adviser Arthur Schlesinger visited him in 1961. Two years later, Betancourt's government was being harassed by terrorists who, he claimed, were supported by the Communist party and by the Marxist-oriented Movement of the Left.

February 9, 1963

MEMO TO DIRECTOR MCCONE

I would like a memorandum on what hard information we may have on the Cuban connection with the Communist efforts in Venezuela over the past months. It is obvious that the Communists in Venezuela support Castro. Do we have any information that could be presented in a public forum, such as the OAS, that would indicate that the link between the anti-Betancourt terrorists and Castro is direct?

[207]

One of the key issues in the Kennedy presidential campaign was the alleged "missile gap" between the United States and the Soviet Union. In his debates with Nixon, Kennedy had contended that the Eisenhower administration had allowed the USSR to surge ahead of the United States in its long- and medium-range missile delivery systems.

MEMORANDUM FOR MR. BUNDY

The President dictated the following:

"Could you let me know what progress has been made on the history of the missile gap controversy. My recollection was that Gilpatric was going to write a memo on this. I would like to know its genesis, what previous government officials put forth their views and how we came to the judgment that there was a missile gap."

Evelyn Lincoln

[208]

(The request was handed on to Adam Yarmolinsky, special assistant to the secretary of defense. His report to Bundy on March 15 read in part:

. . . The term "missile gap" was an extremely fuzzy one, and it was almost impossible to discuss the subject without saying something which was misleading, or at least sure to be interpreted in a misleading way. In short, there was, and was not, a missile gap in early 1961, depending on whether you included POLARIS or not; whether you were worried that the Air Force estimate might be right or merely a comparison of raw numbers, regardless of the practical significance; and whether you were talking about something *now* or something we feared was coming. It was under these circumstances that reporters came away from Mr. McNamara's background briefing with the impression that he had said there was no gap. . . .

If we are asked, in a political context, what was the difference between Mr. McNamara denying there was a gap and the Eisenhower Administration saying the same thing, the answer is this: Under Eisenhower, the denial that there was [a] gap was accompanied by a belief, at the highest levels, that our defense posture was adequate; under the new Administration, the denial was accompanied by an intense awareness that although we were not in immediate great danger, urgent immediate steps were nevertheless needed to improve our defense position. Thus, although there was little difference in what Defense officials *said* about the missile gap before and after January 1961, there were major differences in what was *done* about the missile gap and the whole range of defense deficiencies which this term had come to symbolize.

Although Kennedy supported U.S. military and economic commitments to Israel, he also hoped to open up U.S.-Egyptian relationships by corresponding with Nasser. With the unexpected and unannounced launch of new Israeli missiles, the President was concerned about a drastic change in the balance of power in the Middle East.

February 11, 1963

MEMORANDUM FOR MR. BUNDY

The President dictated the following:

"In my weekend reading I found the following quote. 'The firing on 5 July 1961 of the meterological rocket, Shavit 2, of Israeli construction and design lends credibility to reports of Israeli efforts to develop an independent missile capability. Our last inspection was perfunctory.' What arrangements are we making this spring to ascertain whether or not the Israelis are developing this capacity?"

Signed,
Evelyn Lincoln
[209]

Thomas Dodd, a Democratic senator from Connecticut, was a vocal anti-communist who issued frequent warnings about international Soviet aggression.

February 12, 1963

MEMORANDUM FOR
SECRETARY MCNAMARA
DIRECTOR MCCONE

I have received a copy of a letter which Senator Dodd has sent to you both making various allegations in regard to the Soviet build up.

Could the intelligence community go through the allegations and indicate which may be accurate and which inaccurate. I would like to see a copy of any communication to Senator Dodd on the matter before it goes out.

[210]

Preparing to meet Central American presidents in Costa Rica, Kennedy knew that he would be speaking to students at the University of Costa Rica. The forum gave him an opportunity to express the ideals of the Alliance for Progress. But he was concerned about reports that Latin American students were visiting Cuba with increasing frequency.

February 15, 1963

MEMORANDUM FOR
SECRETARY OF STATE
SECRETARY OF DEFENSE
DIRECTOR OF CIA

I think, as I said at my press conference yesterday, the United States should make a maximum effort now to lessen, and possibly eliminate, the flow of students, labor leaders, etc., who go to Cuba for training and indoctrination and then go back to their own country as possible Communist organizers. I understand that "over 1200 such students" were trained in Cuba last year.

I would appreciate it if CIA would assign a leading official to this effort to work with Ed Martin and Ralph Dungan at the White House. I would like to get weekly reports on what progress we are making with the members of the OAS on this matter.

This certainly should be a matter for discussion at the Costa Rican meeting.

[211]

Despite the President's insistence that aides in State and Defense should have a knowledge of languages, both departments were slow to comply.

MEMO FOR THE SECRETARY OF DEFENSE
February 15, 1963

One of our military social aides to the White House is about to go to Laos as an Assistant Military Attaché. I do not want to interfere with his assignment, but I find this morning that he has only a very limited knowledge of French. I do not see how he can be effective in Laos without knowledge of the language. I would think that the Army must have many officers who have language facility. I would like to receive a report on whether attachés are expected to have a language facility in French or Spanish before they are sent to countries where these languages are spoken. I do not think we should expect an attaché to pick up the language upon his arrival there. Would you let me have your thoughts on this.

[212]

The presence of U.S. Jupiter missiles in Turkey had seriously hampered the U.S. bargaining position in the negotiations with Khrushchev during the Cuban crisis. Subsequently the President examined closely any proposals for new missile sites near the Soviet Union.

February 15, 1963
MEMORANDUM FOR BILL BUNDY

I would appreciate a report on the proposed Nike Hawk site on the island of Crete. I do not understand the justification for it at this time.

[213]

As a senator Kennedy had endorsed independence for Algeria as early as 1957. That position earned him criticism from some Foreign Service officials, from the French ambassador, and from De Gaulle. On July 3, 1962, eighteen months into the Kennedy presidency, Algeria declared its independence. Despite Kennedy's outspoken earlier support of the independence movement, the President was dismayed at Algerian leader Ben Bella's decidedly pro-Castro stance.

In the winter of 1962–63 there was widespread famine in Algeria. Kennedy saw a way to bring American aid to the Algerians without directly supporting the Ben Bella government.

February 20, 1963

NATIONAL SECURITY ACTION MEMORANDUM NO. 221

MEMORANDUM TO

The Secretary of State

The Secretary of Defense

The Director of Central Intelligence

The Administrator, Agency for International Development

The Director, United States Information Agency

The Director, Peace Corps

SUBJECT: U.S. Policy Toward Algeria

I generally approve the Plan of Action for Algeria in the Secretary of State's memorandum to me of 2 February 1963, responding to NSAM 211.

All concerned should bear in mind the need for a program commensurate with our policy interests in this key North African country. While we want France to shoulder the lion's share of the burden, we also want to increase our own influence. For example, I should like to be advised if it should appear highly desirable to exceed somewhat the $15 million FY 1964 AID level currently projected.

Since Prime Minister Ben Bella has requested assistance from the Peace Corps and the Algerians need just the sort of help the Peace Corps is peculiarly suited to give, I hope it will be able to respond if other commitments permit.

John F. Kennedy

[214]

(The President, as well as representatives of AID and the State Department, tried to convince Peace Corps Director Shriver to send volunteers to Algeria. In a confidential memo on January 19, McGeorge Bundy asked Shriver to give serious consideration to State Department requests. "As an entirely accidental benefit," wrote Bundy, "I note that entry by the Peace Corps in Algeria might be mildly irritating to some of those in Europe who are giving us most trouble at the moment—but fooling aside, the real point is that Ben Bella is impressed with the Peace Corps, with you, and with the President. And a little help here might butter a lot of parsnips.'')

A front-page article in *The New York Times* on February 19 contained a report on De Gaulle's position on nuclear arms. According to the *Times*, De Gaulle hoped that the United States would offer Polaris missiles ''for use in an exclusively French nuclear force.'' The article concluded: ''Sources here believe therefore that, if the United States does not make an offer, France will canvass her European allies, particularly West Germany, for assistance in further development of her nuclear armaments.''

February 20, 1963

MEMORANDUM FOR
THE SECRETARY OF STATE

The two articles which I sent you yesterday struck me forcibly as representing plausible accounts of French nuclear intentions. The immediate question they raise is whether we have done all that is necessary and desirable to insure that the Germans do not join with the French, openly or secretly, in any joint arrangements for the development of nuclear warheads or associated weapons systems. I do not want the Germans to be in any doubt whatever that such cooperation would be inconsistent with their current reliance on us in this field.

I would like to have a report from the State Department as to what we have done to make this point clear in the past, and what is now recommended that we might do to emphasize it.

/s/ John F. Kennedy

[215]

Although India needed direct help from Washington, Prime Minister Nehru was in failing health, and decisions of how much military aid to provide India—and in what form—were left largely in the hands of the White House.

February 26, 1963

NATIONAL SECURITY ACTION MEMORANDUM NO. 223

TO: The Secretary of State
    The Secretary of Defense
    The Director of Central Intelligence
SUBJECT: Appraisal of Sino-Indian Situation

The President would like an analysis of the possibility that the Chinese might return to the attack on India any time this spring. Obviously, the intelligence requirements are essential, but he would like a political and military appraisal as well, and I suggest that an informal and prompt report be coordinated by the Department of State. If there is a prospect of the Chinese resuming the offensive, are we doing enough to help India? If we are doing enough, are we doing it soon enough?

McGeorge Bundy

[216]

Yemen occupies a strategically important position at the mouth of the Red Sea. On September 26, 1962, the imam Ahmad, who had ruled Yemen in traditional royalist style since 1948, was assassinated, and the government was ousted by a military revolutionary group led by Brigadier General Adallah al-Salal.

Egyptian President Nasser immediately declared his support for Salal, but the new ruler was opposed by Saudi Arabia, Yemen's giant oil-rich neighbor. When Nasser sent a contingent to support the new revolutionary government in Yemen, the Saudis took the Egyptian action as a sign of aggression. Unless the United States or United Nations effectively intervened, Kennedy feared there would be all-out war between Egypt and Saudi Arabia, which would halt the flow of Saudi oil to the West.

SECRET

February 27, 1963

NATIONAL SECURITY ACTION MEMORANDUM NO. 227

TO: The Secretary of State

    The Secretary of Defense

SUBJECT: Decision Taken at President's Meeting on

           Yemen Crisis, 25 February 1963

After hearing a presentation by the State Department of proposed new steps to damp down the Yemen crisis, the President approved the following actions:

1. We will send a special emissary to [Saudi Arabian Crown Prince] Faysal as soon as possible with a letter from the President to Faysal.

2. His mission will be to: (a) reassure Faysal of U.S. interest in Saudi Arabia; (b) convince him of the importance of his disengaging from Yemen; (c) explain to him how we think this can be done without loss of face.

3. To this end, our emissary is authorized to tell Faysal that the U.S. will consider temporary stationing of a token air defense squadron with associated ground environment in western Saudi Arabia to deter UAR air operations.

4. This offer will be subject to the following expressed conditions: (a) it will be wholly contingent on a firm Saudi undertaking to suspend aid simultaneously to the Yemeni royalists and not to use Saudi soil for air operations against the YAR/UAR; (b) it will be a tentative offer so that the U.S. will have a chance to consider it further before final agreement; (c) the offer will be for a brief period of two months or so, but with the understanding that we will be prepared to keep the squadron there longer if the situation required; (d) the squadron will be withdrawn if Saudi Arabia resumes aid to the royalists without U.S. concurrence.

5. Our emissary should also offer U.S. assistance in expediting the buildup of Saudi Arabia's own air defense capabilities at Saudi expense.

6. Our emissary should try to convince Faysal to use the visit of a UN mediator as a means of promoting simultaneous UAR and Saudi disengagement with honor.

7. If the Saudis accept our offer, we will inform Nasser of the

planned U.S. deployment and present it to him as an essential gesture to get Faysal to disengage. We will press Nasser to withdraw an initial contingent from Yemen simultaneously with Saudi suspension of aid, as an earnest of UAR good faith, and to restate UAR determination to withdraw.

McGeorge Bundy

[217]

To prevent continued balance of payments deficits, Walter Heller and James Tobin of the Council of Economic Advisers proposed international monetary reforms that would change the terms of settlement among nations. Instead of embracing such reforms, Kennedy looked to Treasury Secretary Dillon to encourage trade expansion and foreign investments in U.S. securities. Although Kennedy could not control the Federal Reserve Board, he also looked to its chairman, William McChesney Martin, to raise short-term interest rates, which would make foreign investment in the United States more attractive.

February 27, 1963

NATIONAL SECURITY ACTION MEMORANDUM NO. 225

TO: The Secretary of State
    The Secretary of Defense
    The Secretary of the Treasury
    The Administrator, Agency for International Development
    The Director of Central Intelligence

1. The deficit in our balance of payments and the problems associated with it continue to be major problems which influence national security policy along a broad front. The prospects that they will cease to do so in the immediate future are not bright. I think we must, therefore, make sure that financial elements in our relations with other countries are given a proper weight in any transactions we have with them. Conversely, we must be sure that any financial transactions and arrangements we make with other countries tie in with our broader foreign policy needs.

2. I therefore request that the Secretary of State, in exercising his coordinating responsibilities for all our dealings with other coun-

tries, give special attention to this point. He should see that the Secretary of the Treasury is informed in a timely way of significant forthcoming negotiations or renegotiations on any topic involving those foreign countries with which our financial relations are particularly important. I request the Secretary of Defense, the Administrator of AID and, in those cases in which he is concerned, the Director of Central Intelligence, to review the arrangements for keeping the Secretary of State informed on those negotiations on which they have the primary action responsibility so that he can perform this task effectively. The Secretary of the Treasury, in turn, will provide the Secretary of State, and others concerned, his estimate of our financial interests and financial possibilities in any such negotiations.

3. In the same way, I request the Secretary of the Treasury to notify the Secretary of State and, where appropriate, the Secretary of Defense and the Director of AID in advance of any financial negotiations involving other countries which might have an impact on our general relations with them.

4. I direct particular attention at this time to any negotiations involving the following countries because of the importance of their gold and dollar holdings or of their commercial transactions with us: Austria, Canada, France, Germany, Italy, Japan, Spain, Switzerland and the United Kingdom.

/s/ John F. Kennedy

[218]

During the OAS conference in 1961, using Alliance for Progress aid for leverage, the United States had backed trade sanctions against Castro. Although Argentina, Brazil, and Mexico were originally opposed to sanctions, they finally caved in to pressure from the United States, and the OAS countries agreed to halt all further trade with Cuba. Nonetheless, students and labor leaders still traveled freely to and from Cuba.

March 2, 1963

MEMORANDUM FOR
SECRETARY OF STATE
DIRECTOR, CIA

While there has been a good deal of conversation about devices for stopping the flow of students, etc. in and out of Cuba it does not seem to me that we have made much progress in developing our proposals. In part this may be due to lack of precise information as to their travel techniques. I understand President [Adolfo] López Mateos [of Mexico] told Betancourt that the travel from Mexico did not amount to much.

I think the government in the next two weeks should develop precise proposals based on accurate information, which can be placed before the OAS, the Costa Rican conference and bilateral negotiations to eliminate this traffic.

/s/ John Kennedy

[219]

The passage of the Trade Expansion Act by Congress in October 1962 had been viewed as a major legislative victory for the administration. Under the terms of the act, which easily passed both houses, tariffs would be lowered on certain goods. The President would have authority to reduce tariffs by 50 percent on selected categories of products, and he could completely eliminate duties "on those trade items where the United States and the Common Market controlled eighty percent of the market."

The Act would expand trade with Western Europe, which was about to be united by the Common Market. In his address to Congress the President had presented the alternatives to an "Atlantic partnership" in stark terms: "The two great Atlantic markets will either grow together or they will grow apart. . . . That decision will either mark the beginning of a new chapter in the alliance of free nations—or a threat to the growth of Western unity."

March 4, 1963

NATIONAL SECURITY ACTION MEMORANDUM NO. 224

MEMORANDUM FOR

The Secretary of Defense

The Secretary of the Treasury

The Secretary of Agriculture

The Secretary of the Interior

The Secretary of Commerce

The Secretary of Labor

Governor [Christian] Herter (for information)

The Secretary of State (for information)

SUBJECT: Coordination of U.S. Efforts Under the Trade
          Relations Act

1. We are engaged in major activities of a military, financial, trade and diplomatic nature centering on the European countries, in addition to carrying on a large volume of more routine discussions and negotiations with them. In particular, and of high importance, we are already preparing for our first round of negotiations under the Trade Expansion Act.

While the Secretary of State has the primary responsibility for the conduct of foreign policy, all of you are involved in one way or another in aspects of our relations with Europe. I think it is necessary that all our relations with Europe be conducted in a unified way and related to a central strategy aimed at the advancement of U.S. interests.

Governor Herter is charged with conducting the trade negotiations and related trade matters. The success of these negotiations, given their scope and implications for the future, is of the highest importance. Since many aspects of policy for which each of you has some responsibility bear on our trade relations and hence the trade negotiations, it is particularly important that these activities be coordinated with those for which Governor Herter has responsibility.

2. In accordance with the responsibilities of the Secretary of State, he should be the point of coordination for all important statements and actions bearing on relations with Europe. I have asked the Under Secretary to assume responsibility for this function in behalf of the Secretary of State, and I should like you to make suitable arrangements to keep him informed of your activities in this area, and for

getting his views as to how they fit into our total foreign policy efforts. I have asked Carl Kaysen of my staff to be in touch with the Under Secretary to keep me informed on these matters. In this way I hope to assure that the many issues of policy involved in the totality of our relations with Europe will be properly coordinated in order to insure that the trade negotiations will proceed, with the best prospect for their success.

/s/ John F. Kennedy

[220]

In January 1962 Iranian leader Shah Mohammed Reza Pahlavi had signed a land reform law that affected more than ten thousand villages. Under the law landowners were forced to surrender all but one of their villages to the government, which redistributed land to the peasants on a payback basis. Despite the land reforms and some moves toward decentralization, left-wing parties demanded new elections.

By early 1963 Kennedy viewed Iran as potentially another Cuba, where a popular movement might eventually overthrow a U.S.-backed regime. Whether or not such a popular movement was in itially communist-inspired, in Kennedy's view, any revolution of this kind was likely to play into communist hands.

The "Third Plan" referred to in point 3 was a third five-year program announced by the new prime minister Assadollah Alam. The plan stressed industrial and agricultural development.

March 14, 1963

NATIONAL SECURITY ACTION MEMORANDUM NO. 228

MEMORANDUM FOR

Secretary of State
Secretary of Defense
Administrator, Agency for International Development
Director, Central Intelligence Agency

SUBJECT: Review of Iranian Situation

While I have approved the recent 1550 determination concerning five year military assistance to Iran, I am concerned over the fulfillment of other aspects of the basic strategy which underlay my earlier approval of this military commitment, i.e., that it was intimately linked to an overall strategy for moving Iran toward more effective solutions to its crucial internal problems.

Therefore, I wish a review of our policy and programs in Iran. It should include: (a) analysis of the results achieved to date under our current policy, including the status of local development efforts and military force reductions; (b) our estimate of the likely course of events in Iran; and (c) recommendations, if any, for adaptation or revision of current strategy and programs in this key country. The following questions suggest the problems which I would like covered:

1. Is the thrust of existing U.S. policy toward Iran still basically valid? Is the strategy which it implied feasible under present circumstances?

2. Since the Shah has apparently committed himself to a politically motivated reform program, should we be doing anything to guide it, if possible, into constructive channels? Would active U.S. assistance to this program further our interests? If not, what should be the U.S. attitude?

3. What progress has been achieved during the past year in development of the Third Plan? What is the outlook for its use as the basis of effective development assistance by the U.S. and other donors?

4. What progress has been achieved in strengthening the public and private institutional framework for development in Iran? Are we getting satisfactory movement on integrated planning, establishment of priorities, budgetary controls, tax reforms, and other measures to mobilize Iranian resources for sound development?

5. What is the current and projected pattern of resource allocation among various elements of consumption and investment? Is there a satisfactory relationship between the ordinary budget, including military expenditures, and the development budget? Is the outlook encouraging in this respect?

6. How effectively is the combined use of all our instruments of foreign policy influencing the course of events in Iran? What results can reasonably be predicted from our present effort over the next two to five years?

7. If our existing policy and programs are no longer satisfactory, what changes should be made to produce better results?

I would appreciate a report by the Department of State, in consultation with other appropriate agencies, by 15 April 1963.

/s/ John F. Kennedy

[221]

In his speeches, books, and articles, J. William Fulbright, chairman of the Senate Foreign Relations Committee, maintained that the best way to oppose communism was to bolster growth in "free-society" nations. To support growth in developing nations, he advocated foreign aid in the form of economic assistance rather than direct military aid.

March 25, 1963

MEMORANDUM FOR ED MARTIN

Senator Fulbright the other day made a suggestion that perhaps we could arrange with the Panamanians to have an additional sum paid to them for the Panama canal. The sum might be paid under a joint American-Panamanian education economic development, etc. plan or perhaps under the control of the international bank. The idea would be that we would satisfy the Panamanians who feel that $1,900,000 is insufficient for rent. On the other hand, the additional funds would not be wasted by the government. I feel this idea should be pursued. What are your thoughts?

[222]

During debates in the Canadian Parliament in early spring 1963, Prime Minister John Diefenbaker had misrepresented discussions he had held with U.S. officials regarding the deployment of nuclear "Bomarc" missiles in Canada. The Department of State aggravated the problem by quoting remarks made by McNamara that were cleared by White House advisers but not by the President.

April 2, 1963

MEMORANDUM FOR THE SECRETARY OF DEFENSE

It might be worthwhile to bring to the attention of those who read your testimony re: the Bomarcs in Canada, that their failure to catch the political significance has strengthened Diefenbaker's hand considerably and increased our difficulties. It would seem to me that every word in those sentences flashed a red light. They should be on the alert for political, as well as military, security.

[223]

(As a result of Diefenbaker's actions in Parliament, his party fell, to be replaced by that of Lester Pearson. On August 16 Canada signed an agreement with the U.S. government to acquire nuclear warheads for Bomarc ground-to-air missiles, fighter aircraft, and artillery rockets. According to the agreement reached between the two countries, the stockpiles of nuclear warheads were under U.S. custody but could not be used without authorization from the Canadian government.)

President Eisenhower had been alarmed by the growth of what he labeled the "military-industrial complex," yet the launch of Sputnik and ICBMs by the Soviet Union in 1957 had led to increased demands for military spending. After Eisenhower left office, he continued to warn against the dangers of the United States becoming a military-based economy.

April 3, 1963

MEMORANDUM FOR
THE SECRETARY OF DEFENSE

It would be helpful if we could get an analysis of what our military strength was in 1961 if there had been a call for military action at that time, what is available to us today, and what will be available next summer.

I am thinking particularly of President Eisenhower's statement that the defense budget could be cut back to the levels which were maintained in his last defense budget without in any way weakening the security of the United States.

I think we should have a positive response to that thesis.

/s/ John F. Kennedy

[224]

*   *   *

In 1962, the same year John Glenn became the first American to orbit the earth, the United States had launched a Telstar satellite to relay TV programs and telephone signals. Although its launch was a NASA project, the satellite was used by private companies for telecommunications.

April 5, 1963

MEMORANDUM FOR
THE ATTORNEY GENERAL

I am concerned about the situation on the Telstar matter. It could develop that there would either be too great a profit, which would result in a scandal, or the profit would be too little, which would cause a stock loss and the blame [would be] placed on the administration.

I wonder if you could have [U.S. Deputy Attorney General Nicholas] Katzenbach make a review of this situation and give me a report on it. He should call upon other experts in this field to help him in this review. He and Mike Feldman should follow through on this.

[225]

President João Goulart of Brazil was considered pro-leftist. Kennedy was concerned that if the Soviets supported a Brazilian for president of the General Assembly of the UN, pro-Castro Latin American countries might rally behind that nation.

April 9, 1963

MEMORANDUM FOR
ED MARTIN

It is my understanding that a Latin American may be considered for President of the General Assembly in the next session and the Soviets may support a Brazilian. What is our strategy on that?

[226]

*   *   *

The President consistently argued against rising prices of steel and other commodities. At his press conference the year before, when he announced that the big steel companies were raising prices, he stated that "the American people have a right to expect . . . a higher sense of business responsibility for the welfare of their country. . . ."

April 22, 1963

MEMO FOR CHAIRMAN HELLER

I shall be having a press conference on Wednesday. I think we should be prepared to discuss the prospects of inflation and should be considering if a warning statement should be made. I am also interested in finding out about price increases during the past few weeks in industries other than steel, particularly General Electric, whose profit rate is high.

[227]

In late April preparations began for the President's Harvard alumni dinner which was to be held on May 13 in the White House. White House Social Secretary Letitia Baldrige handled the arrangements. Kennedy responded to her memorandum by writing "yes" and "no" in the margin.

April 26, 1963

MEMORANDUM FOR THE PRESIDENT

For your Harvard dinner, would you let me know your thoughts about the attached ideas?

1. Would you like to have all Harvard chairs used? We could have enough of them flown down, in that there are several flights between Boston and here, and when there is no hurry, a flight can easily be arranged. [NO]

2. Would you like all Harvard crimson and white carnations to be used as flowers for the table? [YES]

3. Would you like a big cake with an "H.U." monogram on the icing (served with a light dessert?) [YES]

4. Would you like the Strolling Strings to come in at dessert time and the Marine Band to play in the hall? [YES]

5. Would you like the menus to have printed at the top: "Harvard Overseers Dinner" [YES]

6. Would you like a comedian to come in during coffee and liqueurs? [NO]

7. Do you want candids taken of the whole table as you first sit down? (Photographers could shoot everybody quickly—then each one would have a photograph of himself at the table.) [YES]

8. Would you like to give each man a small silver matchbox as a souvenir of the occasion ($5 retail) engraved thus: The White House, 5-13-63." (Not Presidential Seal—that is too expensive.) [YES]

Tish B.

[228]

Anthony J. Celebrezze, Secretary of HEW, took over the department from Abraham A. Ribicoff in July 1962. In the Kennedy administration Celebrezze was an advocate of medical care for the elderly. Later, when he served in Congress, he warned that failure to pass a health care bill for the elderly represented a "major threat to the financial security and peace of mind of our older citizens."

May 6, 1963

MEMORANDUM FOR SECRETARY CELEBREZZE

There seems to be some speculation that we have abandoned health insurance for this year. While it may be that events will not permit legislative action in 1963, I believe we should proceed on the assumption that we are attempting to secure it. The failure then will not be ours.

/s/ John F. Kennedy

[229]

Early in 1961 Kennedy's appointee John McCloy established the U.S. Arms Control and Disarmament Agency for full-time research on disarmament alternatives. In early planning for Soviet negotiations, McCloy tried to get the Soviet Union to agree to principles governing formal negotiations in East-West disarmament talks. When the first round of talks failed to produce results at the UN,

McCloy resigned, leaving the U.S. ACDA in the hands of William C. Foster.

Throughout 1962 and early 1963 Foster worked on a limited treaty to ban atmospheric testing and permit on-site inspection of Soviet and U.S. bases. The Soviet Union rejected the treaty in this form when it was presented in Geneva in August 1962. Foster continued to campaign for his proposals, meeting with Soviet officials in New York and Geneva. In February 1963 he became head of the Eighteen-Nation Disarmament Conference.

SECRET

May 6, 1963

NATIONAL SECURITY ACTION MEMORANDUM NO. 239

TO: The Director, U.S. Arms Control and Disarmament Agency
    The Committee of Principals

SUBJECT: U.S. Disarmament Proposals

1. Discussions in the 18 Nation Disarmament Conference at Geneva on both general and complete disarmament and a nuclear test ban treaty have unfortunately resulted in almost no progress. There has been no serious discussion of general and complete disarmament for some time. While discussions of a test ban treaty have shown important developments since the beginning of the 18 Nation Conference, they are now stalled.

2. I have in no way changed my views of the desirability of a test ban treaty or the value of our proposals on general and complete disarmament. Further, the events of the last two years have increased my concern for the consequences of an unchecked continuation of the arms race between ourselves and the Soviet Bloc.

3. We now expect the 18 Nation Disarmament Committee in Geneva to recess shortly for six weeks to two months. I should like the interval to be used for an urgent re-examination of the possibilities of new approaches to significant measures short of general and complete disarmament which it would be in the interest of the United States to propose in the resumed session of the Geneva Conference. ACDA will, in accordance with its statutory responsibilities, take the leadership in this effort and coordinate with the other agencies concerned through the usual procedures of the Com-

mittee of Principals. I should like to review the results at an appropriate time in the process.

/s/ John F. Kennedy

[230]

(In June the deadlock was broken when Kennedy suggested that negotiations continue in Moscow. Khrushchev accepted the proposal, and the President sent Averell Harriman as State Department emissary. Agreement on a limited test ban treaty was reached on July 25, 1963.)

In early May Dean Rusk returned to Washington from a visit to India and the Far East.

May 8, 1963

The Honorable Dean Rusk
Secretary of State
Washington, DC

Dear Mr. Secretary,

I would hope that you would take a few days off. You and Secretary McNamara work much too hard and it gives me a guilty feeling. I did prevail upon Secretary McNamara to stop off for a couple of days in Hawaii. It seems to me that after a long trip like you have had, that it really would be wise for you to take three or four days in the sun. I would be delighted if you would use Camp David.

[231]

In 1962 conservative Senator Bourke B. Hickenlooper of Iowa, chairman of the Republican Policy Committee, proposed a controversial amendment placing contingencies on foreign aid. According to the Hickenlooper Amendment, the United States would automatically deny aid after a six-month grace period to any country that seized U.S. property without providing compensation. The amendment applied to Ceylon (now Sri Lanka), whose government in 1962 took over U.S. plants owned by Esso Standard Eastern, Inc. and Caltex Ceylon Ltd. On February 8 the U.S. Agency for International Development suspended about $3.5 million in economic aid.

May 8, 1963

MEMORANDUM FOR
SECRETARY OF STATE

It would be interesting to make a case study of relations with Ceylon in recent months and whether the Hickenlooper amendment has affected them. In retrospect, should we have waited until after the February 6th meeting before applying the amendment? Also, what effect has the amendment had on our friends or opponents in Ceylon and elsewhere?

[232]

In May 1963, when riots broke out in Birmingham, Alabama, Secretary of the Army Cyrus R. Vance advised President Kennedy to intercede with federal troops.

May 13, 1963

MEMORANDUM FOR
THE SECRETARY OF DEFENSE

In our conversation last evening it was indicated that the planes from North Carolina would arrive in the vicinity of Birmingham around 7:30 our time. I understand now that they did not begin to arrive at Maxwell [Air Force Base] until sometime after 11:00 our time. Would you ask Secretary Vance to look into this because it is vital that we have precise timing on troop movements if we are to act effectively.

[233]

During the fifteen-nation NATO ministers' meeting that was to open on May 22, the chief matter for discussion was the alliance's military structure. On the question of nuclear weapons, the United

States, Britain, and West Germany wanted to use existing nuclear forces under a new allied command.

May 13, 1963

MEMORANDUM FOR
THE SECRETARY OF DEFENSE

1. Would you examine the report of the House Committee on NATO defense released for yesterday morning's papers and give me your judgment on it.

2. Would it be worthwhile for us, prior to the Ottawa meeting, to get an up-to-date report from General Lemnitzer, speaking as NATO Commander, on the relative preparedness of the various national units in Europe, their supplies, their ability to sustain long combat, etc. We could also ask General Lemnitzer the prospects of improving our position. We could then determine whether we should make a presentation on persuading them to up their standards or to reduce ours.

[234]

Alan S. Boyd was chairman of the Civil Aeronautics Board (CAB). After a reorganization of the agency in July 1961, Boyd and other CAB members exercised a great deal of control over routing, airline mergers, and subsidies. However, under the Federal Aviation Act of 1958, the board was not specifically authorized to exercise control over international rates.

At a September 1962 meeting of the ninety-member International Air Transport Association, a majority of world airlines, including U.S.-based Pan American and TWA, agreed to raise their trans-oceanic round-trip economy fare by 5 percent. Subsequently, the CAB nullified the 5 percent increase for the American carriers.

In late April, after discussion among European carriers, Britain and Switzerland threatened to suspend Pan American and TWA landing rights unless the U.S. carriers raised their fares to parity with European airlines. After U.S. and foreign aviation officials failed to reach an accord, the State Department intervened with the CAB. The board capitulated, allowing the fare increases to go through. It was estimated that increased transatlantic fares would cost travelers $25 to $30 million in 1963.

On Capitol Hill the fare increase drew fire from both Democrats and Republicans who accused the CAB and State Department of "bungling" and "[surrendering] the interests of United States flag airlines, their stockholders and the American traveling public."

May 15, 1963

MEMORANDUM FOR

CHAIRMAN, CIVIL AERONAUTICS BOARD

I would like to have an accounting of the strategy of the CAB in the recent international dispute. As the press made clear this morning this matter not only involves the CAB, but also the reputation of this administration and government at home and abroad.

1. Did the CAB expect the British Government to conform to the American position in this dispute?

2. What action did the CAB intend to take if the British Government did not conform? What weapons would be used in order to compel a compromise?

3. What countries were prepared to support our position and what countries the British Government?

4. What effort did we make to persuade the American lines to oppose the unanimous decision of the international lines?

5. What are our future plans in this matter?

In the future I wish you would keep the White House informed in advance of actions which may later involve it.

[235]

Egypt's President Nasser had many close ties to the Soviet Union, which had funded the Aswan Dam and provided military aid. Nasser was at first wary of close U.S. relations with Israel, but his position softened during the Kennedy administration partially as a result of correspondence with the President. By 1963 the time seemed ripe for a change in U.S. military relations with Egypt.

May 15, 1963

MEMORANDUM FOR THE SECRETARY OF DEFENSE

I would like to have the department consider what the effect would be of our permitting the sale of arms to any country in the Middle East which might be able to purchase [them]. I do not think we would want to go the whole way, but inasmuch as we are financing the purchase of a good deal of military equipment for Israel through France, I would not want the other countries to charge that Egypt is able to obtain equipment from the Soviet Union while the United States makes it available to Israel.

/s/ John F. Kennedy

[236]

Inevitably U.S. efforts to expand exports raised the question of which goods, at what price, would be traded with the Soviet Union. This was of vital concern to Secretary of Commerce Hodges, who had to arrive at a policy that would respect the restrictions imposed by the Defense and State departments.

May 16, 1963

Honorable Luther H. Hodges
Secretary of Commerce
Washington, D.C.

Dear Luther:

Thank you for your thoughtful letter of May 8 on the problems of administering the Export Control Act. The questions you raise about Soviet purposes in purchasing American items of advanced technology are important ones which deserve attention.

In the past we have operated under the assumption that only that technology which had a direct military bearing needed to be denied the Soviets through the export control machinery. In other transactions, we have left the question of whether the Soviets are paying a fair price for our technology to the workings of the market. If individual businessmen, fully conscious of Soviet practices in respect to copying and aware of the unlikelihood of re-orders on many of the items which they sell, have been content to strike bargains with the Soviets, we have seen no reason to conclude that the prices involved did not adequately compensate for the transfer of advanced technology. You ask whether this mechanism does the job it should; I agree that the question is worth examination.

Accordingly, I am sending a memorandum to you, the Secretary of State and the Secretary of Defense requesting that the Export Control Review Board examine whether there are other arrangements which would give us a more reasonable *quid pro quo*. I will look forward with interest to the recommendations of this group.

In the meantime, it is my desire that we follow the third alternative suggested in your letter and construe the "economic potential" provision of the Act as narrowly as possible. There are so many major issues between ourselves and the Soviets, that I think it unwise to engage in actions which are likely to cause irritation out of proportion to their real significance. I am willing to do anything which can reasonably be expected to enable us to strike better bargains with the Soviets in these commercial matters, but when it comes to the question of a complete denial, the statute itself speaks only in terms of a "significant contribution to . . . economic potential . . . which would prove detrimental to the national security and welfare of the United States." It is not my judgment that the gains to our national security which can be achieved by denying the Soviets access to American machines and factories of the kind we are discussing, many of which they can get in Europe in any event, balance the cost to our national security of making it more difficult to deal with the Soviets on vital military and political issues.

Sincerely,

/s/ John F. Kennedy

[237]

Accompanying the President's letter to Hodges was a memorandum addressed to the Export Control Review Board. (Both documents were declassified in September 1985.)

SECRET

May 16, 1963

MEMORANDUM FOR THE EXPORT CONTROL REVIEW BOARD:

The Secretary of Commerce
The Secretary of State
The Secretary of Defense

The Secretary of Commerce has raised two important questions about our present trade with the Soviet Union which I think worth serious high-level examination.

1. Do we now deal with the Soviet Union on the export of technically advanced machinery and equipment in a manner which adequately protects U.S. interests? Where a national security issue is presented, we of course deny an export license. There are, however, many cases in which no clear security issue arises and yet we know that the Soviets are using American machinery and equipment as a basis for copying our technology. Are we being adequately compensated in these sales?

Is there any method of organizing these transactions which would secure a better *quid pro quo* than the present method of leaving it to the individual seller to secure the best price he can in the transaction, in the light of the fact the Soviet Union does not ordinarily respect the patent and copyright arrangements on which we rely in our commercial transactions with other nations?

2. Should we reconsider the whole of our trade with the Soviet Union in the light of trade between Western Europe and the Soviet Union and its European satellites? Considering the character and volume of that trade, would a generally less restrictive policy be more in keeping with the interests of the United States? How much possibility is there for a significant broadening of trade that is consistent with our security interests? Would this possibility be such as to justify a general negotiation on trade and commercial matters with the Soviet Union?

3. I would like the Export Control Review Board to examine these questions and report its findings to me in ninety days.

/s/ John F. Kennedy

[238]

*   *   *

In April Haitian police under François Duvalier stormed the embassy of the Dominican Republic in Port-au-Prince and seized political refugees who had sought asylum. When U.S. Ambassador Raymond Thurston protested, U.S. Embassy personnel were harassed. Thurston threatened to bring in the Marines. On May 17, five days before the President issued NSAM 246, the United States suspended diplomatic relations and embassy personnel were evacuated. Thurston remained in Port-au-Prince.

(NSAM 246 was released in 1987, with portions sanitized.)

TOP SECRET

May 23, 1963

NATIONAL SECURITY ACTION MEMORANDUM NO. 246
TO: The Secretary of State
    The Secretary of Defense
    The Director of Central Intelligence
SUBJECT: Future Policy Toward Haiti

The following conclusions were reached during a meeting with the President on Haiti on May 20, 1963.

1. Ambassador Thurston should be recalled for consultation and a final decision on his return to Haiti will be held in abeyance until the Ambassador can give his views on this matter. (Action: Department of State)

2. Fleet units now positioned off the island of Gonaive [Gonâve] may be withdrawn after May 23 if there have been no untoward developments before then indicating reconsideration of this decision. There will continue to be an increased patrol of the Windward Passage to insure against illicit traffic between Cuba and Haiti. (Action: Department of Defense)

3. [Sanitized.]

4. [Sanitized.]

5. It is extremely important that there be no discussion with the press about our plans for handling the Haitian problem.

McGeorge Bundy

[239]

Although Agriculture Secretary Orville Freeman received support from both the National Farmers Union and the National Grange, many of his farm policies were opposed by wheat farmers throughout the Midwest. To prevent a glut in the annual wheat crop, Freeman hoped to impose strict mandatory controls—a move that was opposed by many farmers.

May 24, 1963

MEMO FOR THE SECRETARY OF AGRICULTURE

What would you think of the idea of taking a tour by automobile among the farmers this summer or fall for about ten days? You could stress that you wanted to talk to the farmers about the farm problem. I think you would be well received and also would inspire the members of the Agriculture Department to get as close to the farmers as possible.

[240]

CIA Director McCone was asked to appear before the Senate Armed Services Preparedness Subcommittee headed by Senator John C. Stennis. Stennis, a powerful Democrat, was behind an increased bomber program and an enlarged military role in the space program. The senator was wary of concessions the United States might make to the Soviets during upcoming test ban negotiations. The following correspondence from the President indicates that McCone conferred with Kennedy before giving testimony.

May 24, 1963

Dear Mr. John McCone,

I want you to know that I have heard glowing reports of your testimony before the Stennis Committee on Wednesday about the test ban problem. As I hear it, the committee was deeply impressed by the firmness and clarity with which you discussed the parts of the problem which are within your responsibility and the equal firmness and clarity with which you explained why you did not wish to complicate your professional task by discussing your personal opinion on policy issues outside your official responsibility. I knew when you and I discussed this matter that this was the right stand to take, but what I know now is that it was effective too. Many thanks.

Sincerely,
John Kennedy

[241]

*   *   *

(In August, after the treaty was initialed in Moscow, Stennis joined Senator Barry Goldwater and Armed Services Committee Chairman Richard B. Russell in opposing Senate ratification.)

Cuban Premier Castro's visit to the USSR began on April 27 and was not to end until June 3. On May 24 Khrushchev and Castro issued a joint communiqué that stated, in part, that tension still existed in the Caribbean but that "Cuba and the USSR would tirelessly struggle for the triumph of the Leninist policy of peaceful coexistence."

May 31, 1963

MEMORANDUM FOR THE SECRETARY OF STATE

Would you have an analysis made of the Khrushchev and Castro statements during the latter's visit to the Soviet Union to determine whether significant policies were developed for action in Latin America. Do we have any reason to feel according to hard intelligence through the CIA that there is at present an accelerated use of Cuba as a base for subversion, sabotage, etc. in Latin America?

/s/ John F. Kennedy

[242]

At an OAS meeting in Santo Domingo on May 3, Juan Bosch, the newly elected president of the Dominican Republic, threatened to invade Haiti unless the Duvalier regime gave safe-conduct passes to twenty-two refugees at the Dominican Embassy.

June 4, 1963

MEMORANDUM FOR
THE SECRETARY OF STATE

I note several references, most recently in the Washington Post this morning, about the United States stopping Bosch from invading Haiti. Is this correct? What instructions did we send to our Ambassador to the Dominican Republic? Did we in short "intervene at least twice against positive steps to remove Duvalier from office with force of arms''?

[243]

(Subsequently Haiti promised the five-member OAS investigating commission that fifteen of the refugees would be allowed safe-conduct and seven would be allowed to take refuge in the Colombian Embassy.)

While Averell Harriman from the United States and Lord Hailsham in Great Britain prepared for a test ban summit in Moscow, the President braced for opposition at home. Kennedy knew that opponents to the treaty would be quick to note that the Soviets had resumed atmospheric testing and were continuing to authorize new tests of nuclear weapons. The President saw the Harriman-Hailsham mission as a vital chance to reach agreement with the Soviets, and he feared that the mission would be sabotaged by congressional opposition if news of Soviet low-yield tests was not properly managed. NSAM 250 is the detailed contingency plan that was approved by the President for controlling a possible security leak about Soviet testing.

TOP SECRET—RESTRICTED DATA

June 22, 1963

NATIONAL SECURITY ACTION MEMORANDUM NO. 250

TO: The Director of Central Intelligence
    The Secretary of State
    The Secretary of Defense
    The Chairman, U.S. Atomic Energy Commission

SUBJECT: *Contingency Plan for Dealing with Possible Low-Yield*
       Soviet
       Atmospheric Tests

The President has approved the following procedures for dealing with the current evidence of low-yield Soviet tests.

1. At present there should be no announcement and every effort should be made to prevent leaks with respect to the current evidence.

2. In the event of a leak, the Atomic Energy Commission would promptly issue the following statement, with any amendment made necessary by the specific circumstances of the situation at the time:

"The Commission's attention has been called to press reports of Soviet nuclear testing. The Commission reports that in recent weeks there has been evidence of events in the Soviet Union which may be nuclear tests of very low yield. The evidence remains inconclusive, and it is expected that more definite conclusions must wait further evidence and analysis."

At the same time, the Department of State would announce that there is no change in the plans for the Harriman-Hailsham mission.

Throughout the Government senior officials would be authorized to inform the press on a background basis of the following relevant facts:

a. The phrase "very low yield" means what it says and refers to evidence in the range of 1 KT.

b. The U.S., in its underground series, is currently conducting tests much more numerous than anything of which we have any signal from the Soviet Union and the yields of some of the U.S. tests are substantially higher than those of which there is a question now in the Soviet Union.

c. The President is of course fully informed and does not consider that this inconclusive evidence of very low-yield tests should be regarded as invalidating his American University position against resumption of atmospheric tests until others do the same.

d. Even if the U.S. atmospheric testing were approved, the forward planning of AEC and DOD would not call for a major series of tests until 1964.

e. The reason for avoiding any earlier public announcement was the fact that there was still genuine uncertainty as to whether the evidence justifies a final conclusion as to just what the Soviet Government is doing. For example, evidence to date is consistent with very large non-nuclear explosions.

3. In the event that there is more conclusive evidence on the nature of these or later events, the AEC would issue the following statement, adjusted to fit the exact situation:

"The AEC announces that analysis of evidence recently received shows that the Soviet Government has resumed nuclear testing in the atmosphere, with explosions of (very low) (low) yield.''

The State Department would then announce that these events did not change the plans for the Harriman-Hailsham mission, but merely made that mission more urgent and its prospects more uncertain.

Officials of the U.S. Government would inform the press on a background basis of the following position:

a. We are disappointed that the Soviets are resuming atmospheric testing. Of course, the tests in question are very small and are more nearly comparable, both in technical purpose and in fallout effects, to our underground tests and certain cratering tests we have conducted in Nevada than to the large atmospheric test series that the Soviets and we conducted last year. Nonetheless, we may wish to review the President's American University position. Even if the President were to decide to resume atmospheric testing on technical grounds, it is unlikely that we would wish to test before 1964.

b. Some information on the current level of U.S. underground tests, in terms of numbers and size, should be offered as a comparison for interpreting the Soviet level of testing.

4. If we receive evidence of Soviet testing in the atmosphere on a larger scale, we will need to reconsider our position urgently. A large scale will mean tests of 100 KT or over or several tests of 20 KT or over.

/s/ McGeorge Bundy

[244]

The U.S. Army's Special Forces (Green Berets) numbered about eighteen hundred when Kennedy took office. The President advocated a much larger force trained in antiguerrilla fighting, jungle warfare, and counterinsurgency tactics. By 1963 the Special Forces units trained at Fort Bragg included more than nine thousand men. When Kennedy visited West Germany in late June, he reviewed one of the units stationed there.

July 15, 1963

MEMORANDUM FOR
SECRETARY MCNAMARA

I was tremendously impressed with the Special Forces Unit in West Germany. However, I am wondering if we are making the best use of this Unit? Wouldn't it be a good idea to send them on training missions through the Latin American countries, Africa, Asia or the Middle East? They could go in groups of various sizes. It seems to me a wasted effort to keep them as a single unit in West Germany where the prospects of guerrilla action are very slight. Should we tie up approximately 1,000 of our best men on what amounts to garrison duty when they could be demonstrating and training all over the underdeveloped world where the guerrilla actions are rising in intensity?

[245]

In mid July, as negotiators in Moscow began to resolve the terms of a limited test ban treaty, the President raised the question of whether the United States could detect violations of the treaty provisions. The secondary question was whether the United States would conduct tests in outer space if such testing were permitted.

July 17, 1963

MEMORANDUM FOR
THE SECRETARY OF DEFENSE

Negotiations in Moscow make it clear that the only test ban agreement which is likely in the near future is one limited to the atmosphere, outer space, and under water. In these circumstances, the President would like a fresh review of the technical possibilities of clandestine violation of such an agreement. In the light of the special responsibilities falling to the Department of Defense for military security, he would like this study conducted under the leadership of your Department.

The President has a general concern for accurate assessment of the possible technical effect of undetected violations in the atmosphere and under water. He has a more particular concern, in the light of questions which have been raised by some observers, for the problem of the significance of possible violations in outer space.

The President would like this study to be conducted on the assumption of an agreement in which underground testing is permitted, and he would also wish an estimate of such factors as the cost of cheating, and whether it would lead to results of such value as to justify the expense. One relevant question here is whether the U.S. would be likely to test extensively in the undetectable ranges of outer space if, in fact, such an area were exempted from a treaty.

The President assumes that you will coordinate this study within the Pentagon and with other interested Departments. What he wishes to have is a clear statement of the technical situation on these matters as it is now understood.

/s/ McGeorge Bundy

[246]

In late July Kennedy endorsed a proposed $1.025 billion power project that would harness energy in the tides of Passamaquoddy Bay on the border of Maine and Canada. According to the plan, all power plants would be built on the U.S. side, with some dams on the Canadian side. The cost would be borne by the United States, and power from the plants would be supplied to Canada "at cost."

In Canada there was mounting opposition to the project, amid claims that Passamaquoddy power would ultimately cost about twice as much as the power that came from thermal sources in the Maritime Provinces. Secretary of the Interior Stewart Udall remained a proponent of the plan, which would add an estimated 1.25 million kilowatts per day to U.S. energy resources.

August 20, 1963

NATIONAL SECURITY ACTION MEMORANDUM NO. 260
MEMORANDUM FOR THE SECRETARY OF STATE
SUBJECT: Restudy of the International Passamaquoddy Tidal Power Project and the Hydroelectric Potential of the Saint John River, Maine

Secretary Udall, in cooperation with the Corps of Engineers, has completed a restudy of the International Passamaquoddy Tidal

Power Project and the hydroelectric potential of the Saint John River, Maine, and has concluded that these developments are desirable and economically feasible.

The plans of the Secretary of the Interior are outlined in his report of July 1, 1963. The basic project requires the attainment of satisfactory agreements with the Canadian Government with regard to the construction of this project, the sharing of benefits, both in Canada and in the United States, and such other arrangements as may be desirable for both parties.

I request that you undertake the necessary negotiations with the Canadian Government looking toward these objectives so that we may be in a position to seek authorization for the Passamaquoddy-Saint John River Project from the Congress in the spring of 1964. These negotiations should be conducted in consultation with the Secretary of the Interior and the Secretary of Defense.

/s/ John F. Kennedy

[247]

In the "Nassau Pact" between Kennedy and Macmillan in December 1963, the two leaders came to an understanding about a multilateral force (MLF) in NATO that would be, in part, owned by member governments and operated by a combination of NATO officers and commanders. Theodore Sorensen, writing in *Kennedy*, described the diplomatic problems of this hastily conceived pact: "The MLF idea envisioned an all-NATO force; but the British began to back away from it, the Greeks and Turks couldn't afford it, the Italian elections avoided it. . . ."

August 23, 1963

MEMORANDUM FOR
SECRETARY OF STATE
SECRETARY OF DEFENSE

I think we should have a discussion of the status of the multilateral force in the next few days, particularly the proposal to put a ship with a multilateral crew in European waters in the next few months. Is this feasible, and if not, how can we keep the multilateral concept alive? Our difficulties with the Germans seem to me to make this most desirable.

[248]

To improve the U.S. balance of payments position, Treasury Secretary Dillon, with the backing of Undersecretary for Monetary Affairs Robert V. Roosa, advanced an "interest equalization tax" to be imposed on foreign securities sold in the United States. The tax would act as a disincentive for Americans investing in high-interest-bearing foreign securities—and thereby stem the flow of investment dollars that were going abroad.

August 29, 1963

MEMORANDUM FOR
THE SECRETARY OF THE TREASURY

I am concerned that the proposed tax on foreign investment may not be sufficient, making it possible for them [United States investors] to absorb [the tax loss] and still do business. If that is true [it] would make us look rather foolish.

Are you satisfied that 1% is enough or do you believe it would be possible for us to ask for an extra ½% which we could put on at our discretion if the situation should warrant?

[249]

As the question of test ban treaty ratification dragged on in Congress, Kennedy considered various moves toward U.S.-Soviet cooperation. The following memo contemplating changes in trade policy was drafted but not sent by the President:

September 16, 1963

MEMORANDUM FOR
SECRETARY OF COMMERCE
SECRETARY OF STATE
SECRETARY OF DEFENSE

I have read the report of the Export Control Review Board. It is possible it is somewhat dated by the course of events during the last two months, most particularly the test ban agreement and the evidence of greater increase in trade by our European Allies with the Soviet and Eastern bloc. We must not be left behind. I would appreciate the Board meeting again and considering how we could move ahead to improve our trade with the bloc. I believe Secretary Freeman should be included in this meeting. I think one person in government should bear the responsibility of setting this program into action. Would you give me your recommendations on this?

[250]

Frederick E. Nolting, ambassador to South Vietnam, maintained throughout 1962 and 1963 that U.S. military support for the Diem regime was effective in holding off the North Vietnamese. When U.S. relations with Diem cooled, Nolting was replaced by Henry Cabot Lodge.

Nolting returned to Washington on August 15 but continued to attend meetings on Vietnam policy.

October 11, 1963

MEMORANDUM FOR
THE SECRETARY OF STATE

What do you propose to do with Fritz Nolting? I think he was a very faithful service officer in Saigon and I know you would agree with me that he should not in any way be penalized because of the course of events in Vietnam. What would you think of his being assigned to assist Governor Herter in the trade negotiations? Would this be of interest to him?

[251]

Fred Korth, who assumed the position of secretary of the navy in January 1962, was an advocate of nuclear power for naval vessels. In this he was opposed by Secretary of Defense McNamara, who believed that nuclear propulsion would never be cost-effective. When Korth resigned in October 1963, the press reported that his resignation stemmed from differences with the defense secretary. It was later reported that Kennedy himself requested Korth's resignation when he learned that the secretary of the navy had used his position to solicit business for a bank in which he had a personal investment.

October 12, 1963

The Honorable Fred Korth
The Secretary of the Navy
Washington, D.C.

Dear Fred:

As Secretary of the Navy you have made a real contribution to the advancement of U.S. national security interests, and the nation is in your debt for your many years of public service, including this last period of almost two years when you have worked so devotedly to strengthen the U.S. Navy.

You deserve particular credit for the manner in which you conducted the comprehensive review of the organization of the Navy Department, which resulted in far reaching improvements in Navy readiness and management; for the new accounting system that you established for expendable ammunition stores, saving many millions of dollars; for the steps you have taken to improve the quality of education in the Naval Academy; and for your untiring efforts in behalf of the recently enacted Military Pay Bill.

I thank you for all you have done to advance our national defense.

Sincerely,

[252]

In a March 14 memorandum from the Office of the Attorney General, Robert Kennedy questioned what had happened to the estimated fifteen hundred "guerrillas and terrorists being trained in Cuba and being returned to their countries for purposes of subversion."

The attorney general said he was surprised to discover that "no one, not even John McCone or Ed Martin, seemed to know what had happened to the 1500."

October 21, 1963

MEMORANDUM FOR
ED MARTIN

I would like to get a report on what progress has been made on limiting the movement of students from Latin America who will train for guerrilla activities in Cuba. What is being done on it and what recommendations do you make.

[253]

In 1962 Representative Wright Patman of Texas, chairman of the Select Small Business Committee, launched a study of the abuses of tax-exempt status by foundations. Among the 534 foundations that the committee examined, Patman found evidence of many abuses, including the financing of stock purchases for friends of foundation managers. In its report released on October 19, the committee stated that the three Baird foundations had purchased more than $6.5 million worth of securities for Serge Semeneko, a Boston financier who held "an influential position" in Warner Brothers Pictures, Inc.

October 23, 1963

MEMORANDUM FOR
THE SECRETARY OF THE TREASURY

I understand that the Patman Committee in its report this week mentioned that the David G. Baird Foundation had put up money to finance Semeneko to purchase stock in the movie industry.

I know the Treasury has been analyzing the foundation situation, but I think we should either consider new legislation or change administrative regulations to prevent foundations from functioning as a racket.

[254]

The Trust Territories were former German colonies that came under the administration of Allied governments after World War II. Territories administered by the United States were the Marshall, Carolina, and Marianas Islands in the Pacific. On May 7, 1962,

President Kennedy had issued an executive order placing these islands under the jurisdiction of the Interior Department.

November 4, 1963

MEMORANDUM FOR THE SECRETARY OF THE INTERIOR

I am shocked at the report on the spread of polio in the Trust Territories. It seems to me that this is inexcusable. I would like to have an investigation made into why there were inadequate funds in 1958 for administering preventive medicine and why no action was undertaken between 1958 and 1963 when the spread of the disease again became acute. How much would it have cost to have taken precautionary steps? Is there a difference in treatment for United States citizens in this country and the people for whom the United States is responsible in the Trust territory?

Whose responsibility was it to initiate an appropriate program? In short, I would like a complete investigation into the reason why the United States Government did not meet its responsibility in this area.

Would you expedite this matter.

/s/ John F. Kennedy

[255]

In November 1963, after Paul Nitze took over as secretary of the navy, Kennedy sent a detailed memo describing what he viewed as the military and political responsibilities of the chiefs of the armed forces, the importance of education and language training, and the role of Special Forces units. The memo was also addressed to Admiral David L. McDonald, chief of naval operations.

7 November 1963

MEMORANDUM FOR:
Secretary Nitze
Admiral McDonald

I recently sent to the Senate the nomination of [Rear] Admiral [Charles C.] Kirkpatrick [Superintendent of the United States Naval Academy] as Chief of Naval Personnel. When I did so I was reminded that I have transmitted to the Secretary of Defense, the

Secretary of the Navy, and the Chief of Naval Operations a number of thoughts during the last two and one-half years, many relating to personnel matters. It might be well to summarize them for your information.

I believe that military and political factors are so interwoven that they cannot be separated into clear, well-defined categories, and that both must be mastered as a prerequisite to sound military and naval concepts. High ranking officers who hold positions of responsibility in the military departments must be thoroughly aware of the delicate sensitivities involved throughout the broad spectrum of international policy. The education, outside reading, duty patterns, and promotion processes of the officer corps must be designed to achieve this result.

It seems to me that service as an attaché is extremely valuable for preparing officers for high command positions. It gives them much of the political breadth so necessary in senior officers if our military and political policies are to form an integrated national policy. Furthermore, attachés can make both short- and long-term contributions of major significance. In the short term, a valuable assessment of the political and military situation in a country can be made by attachés because of their access to information resulting from respect held by most foreigners for our military power. This will be particularly true where the military of the country have a prominent role.

To exploit this advantage they must be bilingual to verify what they hear. Otherwise they will be merely an information channel for what the government to which they are accredited wants us to believe. In the long term, the admiration attachés earn for the United States and the bonds of friendship they forge with the coming leaders of these countries can be of inestimable value to this country. For these reasons, I believe that only our best officers should be assigned as attachés, that they and their staffs must be language qualified, and that their creditable performance in this billet must carry added weight in the promotion process.

In August and September of 1961 I had an exchange of correspondence with the Secretary of the Navy concerning an officer whom the Secretary called "the finest scientist in uniform"; yet this officer had been passed over by the selection board for the grade of Rear Admiral. At that time I inquired if there were not values other than technical achievement which carried greater weight with selection boards. I was advised that there was in process a reorientation of thought throughout the Navy relative to the demands of the times for greater education and specialization in science, technology, and other fields. I said then that I would be glad to write a letter to selection boards, or take any other course of action you deem necessary, to emphasize this need. I still stand ready to do so. I would like to assure that officers who devote the time and energy to improving their capabilities through study do not lose promotion opportunity. Not only would such losses waste the resources that such trained officers represent, but they would discourage our bright young officers from so applying themselves.

One of the best ways for one to expand his horizons is through a regular reading program. That is why I have been so interested in the Service programs. The books proposed, and provided, must cover the full range of national security policy—not just professional military subjects.

I know that much weight is placed on command assignments for developing the decision-making processes and sense of responsibility of our officers. Equally important is the need to serve in a staff capacity—particularly joint staffs—where the officer will be required to analyze, study, and prepare position papers on acute problems. I, therefore, support the present requirement that an officer must have served on a joint staff or an equivalent billet to be eligible for flag rank.

When I was in Norfolk in 1962 I noted particularly the members of the Seal Teams. I was impressed by them as individuals and with the capability they possess as a group. As missiles assume more and more of the nuclear deterrent role and as your limited war mission grows, the need for special forces in the Navy and Marine Corps will increase.

I could summarize my thoughts by saying that an officer's career must not consist of four years' education and thirty years of experience. Throughout his career he must continue to study and to grow mentally if he is to provide the base upon which balanced decisions can be made. Personnel policies must be specifically pointed and administered to this end.

Since many of these points were raised with your predecessors as much as two years ago, I would appreciate your views on the following:

1. Has the quality of our attachés increased during this time? As a group how would you compare them with their contemporaries?

2. What percent of naval personnel assigned to attaché staffs are bilingual?

3. To what degree has there been a reorientation of thought on the need for special training for officers? Is this reflected in their promotion success?

4. Do you have any quantitative measure of the success of the reading program?

5. What is the status of your Special Forces?

John F. Kennedy

[256]

On September 20, 1963, in his address to the UN General Assembly, President Kennedy said, "Surely we should explore whether the scientists and astronauts of our two countries—indeed of all the world—cannot work together in the conquest of space, sending someday in this decade to the moon not the representatives of a single nation, but the representatives of all of our countries."

On November 12 Kennedy sent National Security Action Memorandum No. 271 to the director of the space program, James Webb:

November 12, 1963

NATIONAL SECURITY ACTION MEMORANDUM NO. 271

MEMORANDUM FOR

The Administrator, National Aeronautics and Space
Administration

SUBJECT: Cooperation with the USSR on Outer Space Matters

I would like you to assume personally the initiative and central responsibility within the Government for the development of a program of substantive cooperation with the Soviet Union in the field of outer space, including the development of specific technical proposals. I assume that you will work closely with the Department of State and other agencies as appropriate.

These proposals should be developed with a view to their possible discussion with the Soviet Union as a direct outcome of my September 20 proposal for broader cooperation between the United States and the USSR in outer space, including cooperation in lunar landing programs. All proposals or suggestions originating within the Government relating to this general subject will be referred to you for your consideration and evaluation.

In addition to developing substantive proposals, I expect that you will assist the Secretary of State in exploring problems of procedure and timing connected with holding discussions with the Soviet Union and in proposing for my consideration the channels which would be most desirable from our point of view. In this connection the channel of contact developed by Dr. [Warren A.] Dryden between NASA and the Soviet Academy of Sciences has been quite effective, and I believe that we should continue to utilize it as appropriate as a means of continuing the dialogue between the scientists of both countries.

I would like an interim report on the progress of our planning by December 15.

/s/ John F. Kennedy

[257]

Among the final papers in the presidential folders is an inquiry from Thomas J. Walsh in the Kennedy family's New York office and a personal reply from Evelyn Lincoln. Clark Clifford, who was mentioned in Mrs. Lincoln's letter of December 22, was the attorney whom Kennedy had appointed to his Foreign Intelligence Board in May 1961.

Office of Joseph P. Kennedy
200 Park Avenue
New York 17, NY

December 23, 1963

PERSONAL AND CONFIDENTIAL
Mrs. Evelyn Lincoln
The White House
Washington, DC

Dear Evelyn:
  Have you seen the last salary check of the late President?
  Kindest personal regards.

Most sincerely,
Tom

Thomas J. Walsh

[258]

THE WHITE HOUSE
WASHINGTON
December 27, 1963

Dear Tom:
  I have your letter concerning the President's last salary check. I
checked into it, and I learned that Mrs. Kennedy has to put in a
claim for the amount that was owing to him for the amount of his
service during the month of November.
  I further understand that all of these papers have been turned over
to Clark Clifford for handling.
  My warmest regards to you.

Sincerely,
Evelyn Lincoln

[259]

Sources

The John Fitzgerald Kennedy Library at Columbia Point in Boston is a presidential library administered by the National Archives and Records Administration.

In the following source list, the papers on file in the Kennedy Library are indicated by key initials followed by numbers. Initials indicate:

POF = Presidential Office Files
NSF = National Security Files

Papers from the National Security Archives in Washington, D.C., are listed by document number.

KEY	DATE	SOURCE
1961		
[1]	Undated	POF 62
[2]	1/28/61	NSF 283A
[3]	2/3/61	NSF 328–30
[4]	2/3/61	NSF 328–30
[5]	2/3/61	NSF 275–83
[6]	2/3/61	POF BOX 65
[7]	2/4/61	POF BOX 62

KEY	DATE	SOURCE
1961		
[8]	2/6/61	NSF 328–30
[9]	2/6/61	NSF 328–30
[10]	2/6/61	NSF 328–30
[11]	2/6/61	NSF 328–30
[12]	2/6/61	NSF 328–30
[13]	2/6/61	NSF 328–30
[14]	2/6/61	NSF 328–30
[15]	2/8/61	POF 62
[16]	2/8/61	POF 62
[17]	2/14/61	POF 65
[18]	2/15/61	NSF 328–30
[19]	2/15/61	NSF 328–30
[20]	2/15/61	POF 62
[21]	2/16/61	POF 62
[22]	2/17/61	POF 68
[23]	2/20/61	NSF 328–30
[24]	2/22/61	NSF 183
[25]	2/24/61	NSF 345–373
[26]	3/5/61	POF 62
[27]	3/6/61	NSF 328–30
[28]	3/11/61	NSF 328–30
[29]	3/21/61	NSF 328–30
[30]	3/28/61	NSF 285–283
[31]	4/10/61	POF 62
[32]	4/12/61	NSF 270A–273
[33]	4/14/61	POF 62
[34]	4/18/61	NSF 183
[35]	4/25/61	NSF 328–30
[36]	4/25/61	NSF 328–30
[37]	4/25/61	NSF 328–30
[38]	4/25/61	NSF 328–30
[39]	4/25/61	NSF 328–30
[40]	4/25/61	NSF 328–30
[41]	4/25/61	NSF 328–30

KEY	DATE	SOURCE
1961		
[42]	6/28/61	POF 68
[43]	6/28/61	NSF 328–30
[44]	6/28/61	NSF 328–30
[45]	6/30/61	NSF 283A
[46]	7/5/61	POF 68
[47]	7/5/61	POF 62
[48]	Undated	POF 62
[49]	7/5/61	POF 62
[50]	7/10/61	NSF 319
[51]	7/10/61	POF 68
[52]	7/10/61	POF 62
[53]	7/10/61	POF 62
[54]	7/10/61	POF 62
[55]	7/10/61	POF 62
[56]	7/10/61	POF 62
[57]	7/14/61	NSF 328–30
[58]	7/14/61	NSF 328–30
[59]	7/24/61	NSF 328–30
[60]	7/26/61	NSF 284–85
[61]	7/28/61	NSF 328–30
[62]	8/2/61	NSF 284–5
[63]	8/7/61	POF 62
[64]	8/7/61	POF 62
[65]	8/7/61	POF 62
[66]	8/7/61	POF 62
[67]	8/8/61	POF 31
[68]	8/8/61	NSF 328–30
[69]	8/11/61	NSF 328–30
[70]	8/14/61	POF 62
[71]	8/14/61	POF 62
[72]	8/14/61	POF 68
[73]	8/14/61	POF 68
[74]	8/14/61	POF 62
[75]	8/14/61	POF 62

KEY	DATE	SOURCE
1961		
[76]	8/14/61	POF 62
[77]	8/15/61	NSF 328–30
[78]	8/16/61	POF 68
[79]	8/19/61	NSF 283A
[80]	8/21/61	POF 88
[81]	8/21/61	POF 62
[82]	8/21/61	POF 68
[83]	8/21/61	POF 68
[84]	8/21/61	NSF 273
[85]	8/21/61	POF 62
[86]	8/21/61	NSF 284–5
[87]	8/21/61	NSF 331–32
[88]	8/21/61	POF 62
[89]	8/21/61	POF 68
[90]	8/21/61	POF 68
[91]	8/23/61	NSF 284–5
[92]	8/28/61	POF 62
[93]	8/28/61	POF 62
[94]	8/28/61	NSF 331–32
[95]	8/28/61	NSF 331–32
[96]	8/28/61	POF 88
[97]	8/29/61	NSF 331–32
[98]	8/30/61	NSF 273A–274
[99]	9/5/61	NSF 331–32
[100]	9/5/61	POF 68
[101]	9/5/61	POF 62
[102]	9/5/61	POF 62
[103]	9/5/61	NSF 331–32
[104]	9/5/61	POF 62
[105]	9/6/61	NSF 331–32
[106]	9/8/61	POF 62
[107]	9/8/61	NSF 284–5
[108]	9/11/61	POF 68
[109]	9/14/61	POF 68

KEY	DATE	SOURCE
1961		
[110]	9/15/61	POF 68
[111]	9/18/61	POF 68
[112]	9/19/61	NSF 331–32
[113]	9/29/61	NSF 326–327
[114]	10/2/61	POF 68
[115]	10/13/61	NSF 331–32
[116]	Undated	NSF 331–32
[117]	11/8/61	NSF 284–5
[118]	11/16/61	NSF 183
[119]	11/16/61	POF 68
[120]	11/22/61	NSF 331–32
[121]	11/24/61	POF 68
[122]	11/30/61	NSF 331–32
[123]	12/31/61	NSF 183
1962		
[124]	1/5/62	POF 68
[125]	2/7/62	NSF 333
[126]	2/13/62	NSF 183
[127]	2/14/62	NSF 320–321
[128]	2/19/62	NSF 335A–338
[129]	2/20/62	NSF 320–321
[130]	3/2/62	NSF 334–335
[131]	3/7/62	NSF 183
[132]	3/7/62	NSF 296–7
[133]	3/13/62	NSF 334–335
[134]	3/8/62	NSF 335A–338
[135]	3/15/62	NSF 335A–338
[136]	3/20/62	NSF 335A–338
[137]	4/11/62	NSF 335A–338
[138]	4/16/62	POF 68
[139]	4/17/62	POF 68
[140]	4/19/62	NSF 335A–338
[141]	4/30/62	NSF 335A–338

KEY	DATE	SOURCE
1962		
[142]	5/2/62	NSF 320–321
[143]	5/21/62	POF 68
[144]	5/26/62	NSF 335A–338
[145]	5/29/62	NSF 335A–338
[146]	6/9/62	NSF 335A–338
[147]	6/12/62	NSF 335A–338
[148]	6/14/62	NSF 335A–338
[149]	6/15/62	NSF 335A–338
[150]	6/19/62	POF 68
[151]	6/20/62	POF 68
[152]	6/20/62	POF 68
[153]	6/22/62	POF 68
[154]	6/23/62	POF 68
[155]	6/25/62	POF 68
[156]	6/25/62	POF 68
[157]	7/9/62	POF 68
[158]	7/13/62	NSF 285–86
[159]	7/16/62	NSF 335A–338
[160]	7/23/62	NSF 335A–338
[161]	7/25/62	NSF 283A
[162]	7/25/62	POF 68
[163]	8/7/62	NSF BOX 335A–338
[164]	8/7/62	NSF 265–270
[165]	8/15/62	NSF 183
[166]	8/15/62	POF 68
[167]	8/16/62	NSF 335A–338
[168]	8/21/62	POF 68
[169]	8/23/62	POF 68
[170]	8/23/62	NSF 335A–338
[171]	8/24/62	NSF 335A–338
[172]	8/27/62	POF 68
[173]	8/27/62	NSF 335A–338
[174]	8/29/62	POF 68
[175]	9/7/62	POF 68

KEY	DATE	SOURCE
1962		
[176]	9/15/62	NSF 183
[177]	9/28/62	NSF 338–342
[178]	10/2/62	POF 68
[179]	10/22/62	NSF 183
[180]	10/22/62	NSF 338–342
[181]	10/26/62	National Security Archives, #21961
[182]	10/27/62	National Security Archives, #2709
[183]	10/28/62	National Security Archives, #4099
[184]	10/28/62	NSF 338–342
[185]	10/29/62	National Security Archives, #4869
[186]	11/5/62	National Security Archives, #3800
[187]	11/5/62	POF 68
[188]	11/6/62	NSF 184
[189]	11/8/62	National Security Archives, #3976
[190]	11/21/62	NSF 184
[191]	11/21/62	POF 68
[192]	11/24/62	National Security Archives, #4991
[193]	12/4/62	NSF 338–342
[194]	12/4/62	NSF 338–342
[195]	12/14/62	NSF 184
[196]	12/15/62	POF 68
1963		
[197]	1/8/63	NSF 338–342
[198]	1/9/63	NSF 283A
[199]	1/17/63	POF 68
[200]	1/17/63	POF 68
[201]	1/19/63	POF 68

KEY	DATE	SOURCE
1963		
[202]	1/21/63	POF 68
[203]	1/21/63	POF 68
[204]	1/22/63	NSF 285–286
[205]	1/31/63	POF 62
[206]	2/7/63	POF 68
[207]	2/9/63	POF 68
[208]	2/11/63	POF 62
[209]	2/11/63	POF 62
[210]	2/12/63	POF 68
[211]	2/15/63	POF 68
[212]	2/15/63	POF 68
[213]	2/15/63	POF 68
[214]	2/20/63	NSF 338–342
[215]	2/20/63	NSF 285–286
[216]	2/26/63	NSF 338–342
[217]	2/27/63	NSF 338–342
[218]	2/27/63	NSF 338–342
[219]	3/2/63	POF 68
[220]	3/4/63	NSF 338–342
[221]	3/14/63	NSF 338–342
[222]	3/25/63	POF 68
[223]	4/2/63	POF 68
[224]	4/3/63	National Security Archives (unnumbered doc.)
[225]	4/5/63	POF 68
[226]	4/9/63	POF 68
[227]	4/22/63	POF 68
[228]	4/26/63	POF 62
[229]	5/6/63	POF 68
[230]	5/6/63	NSF 338–342
[231]	5/8/63	POF 68
[232]	5/8/63	POF 68
[233]	5/13/63	POF 68

KEY	DATE	SOURCE
1963		
[234]	5/13/63	POF 68
[235]	5/15/63	POF 68
[236]	5/15/63	POF 68
[237]	5/16/63	NSF 296–297
[238]	5/16/63	NSF 296–297
[239]	5/23/63	NSF 338–342
[240]	5/24/63	POF 68
[241]	5/24/63	POF 68
[242]	5/31/63	POF 68
[243]	6/4/63	POF 68
[244]	6/22/63	NSF 338–342
[245]	7/15/63	POF 68
[246]	7/17/63	NSF 338–342
[247]	8/20/63	NSF 338–342
[248]	8/23/63	POF 68
[249]	8/29/63	POF 68
[250]	9/16/63	POF 68
[251]	10/11/63	POF 68
[252]	10/12/63	POF 68
[253]	10/21/63	POF 68
[254]	10/23/63	POF 68
[255]	11/4/63	POF 68
[256]	11/7/63	NSF 283A
[257]	11/12/63	NSF 338–342
[258]	12/23/63	POF 130
[259]	12/27/63	POF 130

Index

295